全国高等院校法律英语统编教材
法律英语证书（LEC）全国统一考试推荐用书

大学
法律英语

College
Legal English

张法连　姜　芳　主编

北京大学出版社
PEKING UNIVERSITY PRESS

图书在版编目(CIP)数据

大学法律英语 / 张法连，姜芳主编. —北京：北京大学出版社，2018.6
ISBN 978-7-301-29446-8

Ⅰ.①大…　Ⅱ.①张…②姜…　Ⅲ.①法律－英语－高等学校－教材　Ⅳ.①D9

中国版本图书馆CIP数据核字(2018)第061064号

书　　名	大学法律英语 DAXUE FALÜ YINGYU
著作责任者	张法连　姜　芳　主编
责任编辑	郝妮娜
标准书号	ISBN 978-7-301-29446-8
出版发行	北京大学出版社
地　　址	北京市海淀区成府路205号　100871
网　　址	http://www.pup.cn　新浪微博：@北京大学出版社
电子邮箱	编辑部 pupwaiwen@pup.cn　总编室 zpup@pup.cn
电　　话	邮购部 62752015　发行部 62750672　编辑部 62759634
印刷者	北京飞达印刷有限责任公司
经销者	新华书店
	787毫米×1092毫米　16开本　23.25印张　610千字 2018年6月第1版　2024年5月第4次印刷
定　　价	59.00元

未经许可，不得以任何方式复制或抄袭本书之部分或全部内容。
版权所有，侵权必究
举报电话：010-62752024　电子邮箱：fd@pup.cn
图书如有印装质量问题，请与出版部联系，电话：010-62756370

前 言

随着经济全球化进程的不断加快，尤其是"一带一路"倡议的提出与快速推进，中国与世界各国的合作与交流日益加强，各种涉外活动日益增多，涉外法务活动空前频繁。为适应世界多极化、经济全球化深入发展和国家对外开放的需要，我国急需大批具有国际视野、通晓国际规则、能够参与国际法律事务和国际竞争的国际化人才。党的十八届四中全会对发展涉外法律服务业做出了重要部署，提出了明确要求，要为"一带一路"等沿线国家重大发展战略提供高质量法律服务。为更好地引领经济全球化，司法部、教育部、外交部、中央政法委等部委对开展涉外法律工作进行了全面部署，凸显涉外法律人才的重要性和紧迫性。

涉外法律人才是需要具备两方面能力的复合型人才：一方面，具有国际视野，能熟练运用外语，能在国际事务中进行有效的交流与谈判，即精通外语（尤其是英语）的涉外人才；另一方面，通晓国际规则，善于国际谈判，能够参与国际法律事务，维护国家利益，即明晰国际规则的法律人才。而现实情况是，中国的高端外语人才稀缺。全国范围内，精通法律外语，熟知国际法、国际贸易法和WTO规则，能直接从事胜任涉外法律业务的涉外律师寥寥无几。

作为法律科学与英语语言学的交叉学科，法律英语理应承担起培养"精英明法"复合型人才的重任。法律英语是以普通英语为基础，在立法、司法及其他与法律相关的活动中形成和使用的具有法律专业特点的语言，是表述法律科学概念以及从事诉讼或非诉讼法律事务时所使用的英语。法律英语学科的目标是要适应国家社会发展的需要，培养具有国际视野、通晓国际规则、能够参与国际事务的精通外语、通晓涉外法律知识、具有涉外法律技能的"精英明法"复合型国际化人才。

"一带一路"建设凸显了涉外法律的重要性，而法律英语是涉外法律人才培养的关键。法律语言与经济发展关系密切，经济全球化背景下法律英语与涉外经济的联系越发紧密。"一带一路"沿线65国，官方语言61种，且大多数是非通用语种，因此，在一定程度上可以说，"一带一路"建设面临的首当其冲的挑战就是语言。推动"一带一路"建设，分别使用沿线65个国家的母语，既无条件，也不现实，更不经济。英语作为国际通用语，是涉外法律工作必需的工具语言。法律英语成为

"一带一路"建设中的主要工作语言是必然选择。法律英语语言价值更高，必将有效助推"一带一路"建设进程。

涉外法律人才的培养有赖于法律英语教学的落实与推进。具备条件的高等学校、科研院所要按照涉外法律服务业发展需求，创新涉外法律人才培养机制和教育方法，与相关涉外政府部门和企业密切合作，系统培养"精英明法"复合型涉外法律人才。有条件的高校要重视法律英语学科内涵发展研究，系统开设法律英语课程，包括法律英语视听说、法律英语阅读、法律英语写作、法律英语翻译、英美法律文化、法律语言、中西法律语言与文化比较等知识型课程，以及涉外法务谈判、涉外律师实务、审判实务与庭辩技巧、涉外诉辩文书应用、WTO法律制度与中国、ADR实务、双语模拟法庭等实务性课程，也包括到涉外律所、涉外政府部门或企业的社会实践和涉外法务专业实习。

北京大学出版社已率先出版了法律英语专业套编教材，包括《法律英语精读教程》（上、下）《法律英语泛读教程》（上、下）《法律英语写作教程》《法律英语翻译教程》《英美法律文化教程》《法律英语视听说》以及配套学习使用的《英美法律术语双解》。本书既是通向法律英语专业的桥梁课程，也是面向法学院、经济学院等专业本科生、研究生的法律英语通识课程。

为了力求实现教材内容的权威性和丰富性，编者参考了大量的英美原版法学书籍资料。在此谨对原作者表示谢忱。教材在编写上遵循由总述到具体、由浅入深的原则，基本上达到《大学法律英语教学大纲》《法律英语专业教学大纲》提出的目标要求。本书共由四部分组成：第一部分是英美法律基础知识简介；第二部分主要介绍美国法律体系中主要部门法；第三部分介绍法律翻译及法律文书写作的基础知识；第四部分为选择阅读，主要介绍美国法体系中的海商法、娱乐法等专业知识。这四部分内容浑然一体，又相互独立。学习本教材不一定要严格按前后编写顺序进行，教师完全可以根据学生的具体情况挑选合适的内容安排教学。

参加本书编写工作的还有甘肃政法学院赵永平副教授、马彦峰副教授，河南财经政法大学朱洁副教授，河南工程学院李跃凯副教授，河北师范大学顾维忱教授，中国政法大学曲欣博士以及山东政法学院刘艳老师等。感谢法律英语证书（LEC）全国统一考试指导委员会将该套教材推荐为复习应考LEC的参考用书。

编著者
2018年4月于中国政法大学

Contents

Part I Basics of Anglo-American Law **1**

    Chapter 1   Surviving Law School 3

    Chapter 2   Legal Systems of the World 14

    Chapter 3   Precedent 38

    Chapter 4   Law of the United States 61

    Chapter 5   Reading Legal Cases 73

    Chapter 6   The Civil Litigation Process 89

Part II An Introduction to American Laws **97**

    Chapter 7   Constitutional Law 99

    Chapter 8   Contract Law 121

    Chapter 9   Tort Law 139

    Chapter 10 Property Law 160

    Chapter 11 Criminal Law 196

    Chapter 12 Criminal Procedure 215

    Chapter 13 Criminal Evidence 235

Part III WTO Law & Legal Translation and Writing **255**

    Chapter 14 Understanding the WTO: Basics 257

    Chapter 15 Legal Translation 277

    Chapter 16 Legal Writing 290

Selected Readings ········ 314
   1. Entertainment & Sports Law ········ 314
   2. Admiralty ········ 321
   3. Intellectual Property ········ 327
   4. Introduction to International Law ········ 344

Glossary of 101 Key Legal Terms ········ 357

Part I
Basics of Anglo-American Law

Chapter 1
Surviving Law School

Law school is not a walk in the park. It's a jungle out there, and you've got to be savvy to survive. There's a lot to know, and if you're not feeling a little nervous when you show up for Orientation, you're probably not human. Apprehension is to be expected. But don't despair. You can do this, and I can help. I've put together some of my very best tips below, so get to it!

Four Strategies to Think like a Lawyer

Law school is not about learning a set of rules. Law school is designed to teach you how to "think like a lawyer." Professors have long ago settled that lawyers can always look the law up in a book, but designing an argument and analyzing a legal problem is a matter of reshaping the way a person thinks. Four key strategies will aid you in thinking like a lawyer.

Strategy 1: Accept Ambiguity.

Consider the following rule of law:

There is *always* an exception for *every* rule of law, except for the rules in which there are no exceptions.

At first glance this statement seems circular and contradictory. It states a general proposition that every rule has an exception. Then it goes onto say that there's an exception to this rule for rules that have no exceptions. It's like the childhood riddle, where someone states, *"I am a liar."* If that person is a liar, how do you know that they are telling the truth in the statement that they are a liar?

The law is full of conundrums and ambiguities like this one. If you can accept the interplay between those two statements without being distressed at the inherent fuzziness, then you will do well in studying the law. The law is inherently fuzzy in order to be flexible. Although judges attempt to interpret laws that are clear, there is almost always a set of circumstances where applying the rule would be unjust. Consequently, some latitude exists in the law in order to reach a just result.

This can drive you mad as a first year law student. You want as clear of an answer as you would get in mathematics or physics. The law is seldom black and white. Everything is a shade of gray. The right answer is almost always couched in terms of probabilities. "Maybe he's liable for damages." "He'll probably go to jail for murder."

There is no way around this, and the best method is to embrace and accept the inherent ambiguity of the law as a strength. Instead of thinking of the law as ambiguous, consider it flexible. Your skill as a lawyer will be in how you can use this flexibility to achieve the correct result for your client.

Strategy 2: Don't be Emotionally Tied to a Position.

One of the biggest traps that professors use on unwary first year law students is playing on the emotions. The professor poses a hypothetical situation in which it's easy to hate one of the parties and sympathize with the other. The trick is to apply the law neutrally in response to the parties' legal rights and not your personal feelings.

The classic example is a situation in which a group of Neo-Nazis attempts to assert their First Amendment rights for free speech by holding demonstrations in a city largely populated with Jewish people who are concentration camp survivors.

Naturally, almost everyone feels sympathy for the concentration camp survivors. These people shouldn't have to be subjected to a Neo-Nazi's political belief in their own home. However, professors purposefully set up situations that create internal emotional conflict in order to illustrate that you should judge a situation according to the law and not let your individual biases get in the way. The correct legal result here is that the Neo-Nazi possesses a free speech right even in these circumstances so long as they are not inciting a riot.

This does not mean that you have to check your ethics at the door of law school. People complain that lawyers have no morals but these critics don't see the higher principles that are at stake. Those higher principles might be constitutional rights such as free speech or the right to be represented by counsel. This is the higher ethical ground that you need to take as an attorney rather than siding with one party or another merely because of your own political beliefs.

Finally, be aware that the professor's hypothetical situations are not the real world. While you may not like the result of the hypothetical, you need to demonstrate to the professor that you know how to apply the law. If you really feel that the result is unjust, then state the law with the correct legal result followed by your reasons on why you don't think the result is just. Just remember that it's a hypothetical. Don't be tied emotionally to things that don't matter.

Strategy 3: Argue Both Sides.

In order to avoid being emotionally tied to a position, you should always try to argue both sides of an issue. Luckily, the same ambiguity of the law that drives you crazy in Strategy 1 allows you the flexibility to be on either side of a question in Strategy 3. Adopting this attitude will better prepare you for the exam and the practice of law. You want to be able to take on either a defendant's or plaintiff's position for any given legal issue because you don't know whether the facts on the exam will lean towards one side or the other.

One of the biggest traps that first year law students fall into is studying only from their own point of view. For instance, some people are naturally plaintiff's attorneys—fighting for the underdog against the big corporate giant. Others tend towards representing defendants — protecting shareholder interests from people out to make a quick buck on a fraudulent claim. Each side is sometimes right and sometimes wrong. Your immediate goal on the exam is not to figure out what kind of lawyer you are. Your immediate goal is to do well on the exam. This means that you need to be able to argue the side that seems to be correct given the facts. This may, in fact, be a party that you wouldn't normally side with.

One major upside to this sort of training is that it will make you a better lawyer to be able to argue both sides of a case. Once you do adopt a plaintiff's or defendant's posture in real life, you will benefit from knowing what arguments the other side will bring forth. If you can understand the intricacies of another side's case, then you can better attack that argument.

Strategy 4: Question Everything.

Around the age of two years old, a child often starts asking his or her parents "Why?" You should be like a two-year-old. Every rule of law, judicial decision, statute and legal construct has a reason for its existence. It may not be a very good reason, but you will be a better lawyer for behaving like a two year old and repeatedly asking "Why?"

This act of questioning focuses you on policy as a basis for the law. Understanding policy will carry you far in successfully writing exams. Arguing policy is one of the four key methods of analysis.

Four Strategies to Excel as a Student

Law school is as much a psychological game as it is an intellectual game. Students defeat themselves ahead of time by stressing out on the workload. You can put yourself in a better position as a student by adopting these simple attitudes.

Strategy 1: Keep Your Cool.

Law professors use fear as a tool to motivate students to (1) work hard and (2) be cautious lawyers. Many professors feel that a little anxiety is a good thing for students. The very structure of the case method and Socratic dialogue used in most classrooms helps foster this fear since nothing is laid out on the table.

However, fear also takes you away from learning. It's a waste of valuable energy. Instead of focusing on the learning, you focus on the fear of not "getting it." To counteract the fear that is inherent in law school, consider three ideas:

First, everyone in your class is in the same state of ignorance. No one knows what's coming next.

Second, if you make a mistake in the classroom, it doesn't count. The only grade that counts in most law school classes is the final. Relax and make mistakes. It will help you in the exam to know your weak points.

Third, hundreds of thousands of students have sat where you're sitting now and have survived and thrived.

Some people purposefully create stress as a motivator for themselves. They freak out at the workload and use it as a way to bond with other students. Stay away from the people who are stressing out. Stress creates stress, and you want to focus your energies on studying, not stressing out.

Strategy 2: Compete Only with Yourself.

Although grades are important, it's also important to put them in perspective. One key factor in getting good grades is to forget about them and concentrate on the learning. Focusing on the competition — i.e. your fellow students — takes your eye off the ball, which is to learn the law. If you are constantly sizing up the competition and comparing yourself then you are taking yourself away from valuable study time.

Consider the following truism:

While grades are the only thing that counts, grades also count as only one thing. The idea here is to recognize the importance of grades in determining certain things, such as law review, summer jobs and so on. At the same time, you realize that the learning and relationships are far more important keys to happiness than grades.

The stress of getting good grades often creates competition, which leads to bad feelings between students. There are true stories of people hiding books in the library or ripping pages out of case books that are necessary to complete an assignment. This sort of competition can be very destructive.

The best strategy to deal with the stress of grades is to compete only with yourself and not others. The people in your class are your future colleagues. Building trust and relationships with these people will take you much further than any marginal increase in grades you might get from cut-throat competitive tactics for grades. The most successful people in the world are not those who are most competitive with others. Rather, the most successful are those who compete with themselves to learn the most.

Strategy 3: Play with Concepts Like a New Toy.

Whenever you learn a new legal concept, play with as if you were a kid and the concept was the coolest, neatest, newest toy that you own.

Make the concept your own by restating the principle in your own words. Turn the idea over in your head as you're walking to class or taking a shower. Whenever you learn a new rule, restate it a dozen times until you don't need notes to say it by heart. Once you really understand that concept by putting it in your own words, move on to other principles.

Apply the rule to your everyday situations. For instance, you might begin to apply the principles you learn in Contract law to your everyday dealings with grocers and retailers. As you drive down the highway, consider what you would have to prove to bring a negligence suit in Tort if there were an accident. If the car crash was caused by a faulty part in a foreign car you were driving, how could you use Civil Procedure to haul the manufacturer into Federal Court.

Closely related to this concept is the idea of making up hypothetical fact patterns in which the rule of law will or will not apply. Try this make-believe technique in order to better learn how to apply the rule. You'll be surprised at how closely you might come to guessing what fact pattern is on the exam.

A lot of the difficulty in learning comes from fighting it. We put ourselves into a non-receptive state by saying, "This is difficult. I don't understand." We also make it harder to learn by not focusing on the learning but by focusing on where we are on the general curve of learning — i.e. what's our class rank. By wasting energy on these areas we don't focus on the area where the true energy should flow — the actual learning of the law. Playing with the concepts like they were toys will defuse that difficulty.

Strategy 4: Strive for Balance in Your Life.

A lot of law students end up studying 12–14 hours a days in order to get through all of the reading and work of law school. This can easily lead to burn out. Putting in more hours doesn't necessarily lead to more knowledge. The law of diminishing returns suggests that 80 hours a week may lead to less advancement in the study of law than a focused 40-hour week.

It is essential to have a balance in your life with exercise, eating right and fun time with your friends and family. You will get more out of the classroom if you are alert, well fed and otherwise on top of your game physically and emotionally than you will if you have read yet another treatise about the law.

You need to give law school a break in order to give it your maximum attention later on. You need time when you're not thinking like a lawyer in order to better achieve becoming a lawyer. In the words of the Alan Watts, a professor of Eastern religions, "By going out of your mind, you come to your senses."

Two Strategies to Bolster Self Confidence

Many law students suffer academically because they lack self confidence in their ability to handle the material. By deciding ahead of time that they don't have the ability, they fulfill that prophesy before even trying. In order to succeed academically in law school you have to adopt a belief in your ability. Belief alone won't carry you through to your goals. You also have to put in the work. But without a belief in your ability, you defeat yourself before you begin.

Strategy 1: Reprogramming for Success

If you've gotten as far as being accepted into law school, then you have the native intelligence to understand legal reasoning. Hundreds of thousands of people have learned to analyze issues like a lawyer, and you can do it too. If that isn't proof enough, then consider adopting a few techniques to foster self-confidence in studying the law.

One method is through affirmations. Affirmations are a tool you can use to counteract the negative self-image that is ingrained in the subconscious mind. Through the negative messages we receive in childhood, the subconscious mind develops limitations as to what we can achieve. The subconscious tells us that we aren't an "A student," so we never put forth the effort to counteract that negative message.

Affirmations are a powerful tool to reprogram the subconscious. Affirmations are said in front of the mirror in the morning immediately when you get up and in the evening right before you go to sleep. It could be something as simple as:

"I, (your name), am an intelligent, confident, and articulate student who will become an outstanding advocate and attorney for my clients."

Affirmations generally get a bad rap. It's easy to dismiss affirmations as hokey, and, in a way, they are. But affirmations are also incredibly empowering. Affirmations illustrate just how powerful language can be. I challenge you to use affirmations for a week and see if they make a difference in your underlying attitude.

Another method to improve self-confidence is through visualization. High-performance athletes visualize winning a race before running it. During the actual race, they merely put into action what they have already visualized. You can use visualization to be successful in law school before you crack a book. Take a moment to visualize your first year in law school. Close your eyes and imagine a classroom where you and your fellow students engage in a lively debate. See in your mind a situation where you convince your peers to adopt a different viewpoint. Imagine taking your first test, having fun with it and knowing that you aced the exam. Fast-forward to your third year when you graduate. See yourself successfully taking the bar exam in your state. Visualizing doesn't mean that you don't have to do the work, but it will foster the belief in your ability to accomplish the task.

Strategy 2: The Myth of Mistakes

Fostering a belief in your ability is difficult when you are constantly faced with making mistakes. Mistakes are a fact of life in law school. The number of mistakes that a law school student makes is enormous. Everything about law school is new. The language of lawyering is new. The process of learning is different than most academic fields. The analytical thought process is a skill that doesn't come easily. You should expect to make

Chapter 1
Surviving Law School

mistakes.

Success is determined by what you do with those mistakes. Are mistakes a learning experience or do those mistakes reinforce a belief that you can't do the material? If you can look at each mistake you make in law school as an opportunity to get it right for the exam, I guarantee you that you'll excel.

You're not alone in making mistakes. Did you realize that the best baseball players in the world strike out two thirds of the time they are at bat? Do they let that huge failure ratio deter them? No. Each time they step up to the plate, they have an unwavering belief that this is the ball they are going to hit out of the park. They don't let their failures get in the way of believing in their ultimate ability to succeed.

Recognize to yourself that you are only a beginner. As a beginner, you have to start out with simple concepts and take small steps in learning the material. Sometimes you won't succeed, but that's part of being a beginner. In fact, you want to make mistakes in order to see where you got it wrong the first time through. You must never let your mistakes fool you into believing that you are not capable.

Summing up, there is a two-step approach to putting yourself in the right state of mind. Adopt this phrase as your guiding principle:

> Think like a *winner* by knowing that you will ultimately succeed, but act like a *beginner* by learning from your mistakes.

Exercises

I. Please match the terms on the left with the definitions on the right. Write the term number in the blank.

Terms
1. Matter of law
2. Appellate cases
3. Appeal

Definitions
A. ____ Reference to legal authorities.
B. ____ Person who brings the lawsuit.
C. ____ Seeking compensation in the form of money.

4. Treatises	D.	____	The court of original jurisdiction where all evidence is first received and considered.
5. Pass	E.	____	A test question that forces a student to select the best of several answers.
6. Prima facie case	F.	____	Issues which can be sustained by substantial evidence and creates the slightest doubts as to the facts.
7. Monetary damages	G.	____	Lawsuit that have been appealed.
8. Plaintiff	H.	____	Resort to a superior court to review the decision of an inferior court or administrative agency.
9. Defendant	I.	____	Instructing the professor that you do not wish to speak in class.
10. Interrogatories	J.	____	Whatever is to be ascertained or decided by the application of statutory rules or the principles and determinations of the law.
11. Genuine issue	K.	____	Facts which constitute a legal defense or affect the result of the action.
12. Statue	L.	____	A methodical explanation of law.
13. Material fact	M.	____	Person against whom a lawsuit is brought.
14. Cite	N.	____	A formal written enactment of a legislative body.
15. Intermediate courts	O.	____	The deceased.
16. Assigned seats	P.	____	Written questions used during discovery.
17. Decedent	Q.	____	A case that has sufficient evidence so that the case can go to the jury.
18. U.S. Supreme Court	R.	____	Appellate courts; courts of appeal
19. Multiple-choice question	S.	____	Court of last resorts.
20. Seating chart	T.	____	Listing of where people sit usually in alphabetical order.
21. Trial courts	U.	____	Seat the registrar selects for each individual student.

II. Please fill in the blank with the appropriate article ("a", "an", or "the") or leave it blank to indicate that no article is necessary.

"George Pavlicic is not asking for _____ damages because of _____ broken

Chapter 1
Surviving Law School

heart or _____ mortified spirit. He is asking for _____ return of _____ things which he bestowed with _____ attached condition precedent, _____ condition which was never met. In demanding _____ return of his gifts, George cannot be charged with _____ Indian giving. Although he has reached _____ Indian summer of his life and now at _____ 80 years of age might, in _____ usual course of human affairs, be regarded as beyond _____ marrying age, everyone has _____ inalienable right under his own constitution as well as that of _____ United States to marry when he pleases, if and when he finds _____ woman who will marry him. George Pavlicic believed that he had found that woman in Sara Jane. He testified that he asked her at least 30 times if she would marry him and on each occasion she answered in _____ affirmative. There is nothing in _____ law which required him to ask _____ 31 times. But even so, he probably would have continued asking her had she not taken his last $5,000 and decamped to another city. Moreover he had to accept _____ 30 offers of marriage as _____ limit since she now had married someone else. Of course, mere multiplicity of _____ proposals does not make for _____ certainty of acceptance. _____ testimony, however, is to _____ effect that on _____ occasion of each proposal by George, Sara Jane accepted not only _____ proposal but _____ gift which invariably accompanied it.

_____ Act of 1935 in no way alters or modifies _____ law on _____ antenuptial conditional gifts as expounded in _____ 28 C.J. 651, and quoted by us with approval in _____ case of Stranger v. Elper, 382 Pa. 411, 415, 115 A.2d 197, 199, namely:

> "_____ gift to _____ person to whom _____ donor is engaged to be married, made in _____ contemplation of _____ marriage, although absolute in _____ form, is conditional; and upon breach of _____ marriage engagement by _____ done _____ property may be recovered by _____ donor.'"

Excerpt from Pavlicic v. Vogtsberger, 136 A.2d 127, 131(Pa. 1957).

Chapter 2
Legal Systems of the World

The contemporary legal systems of the world are generally based on one of four basic systems: civil law, common law, statutory law, religious law or combinations of these. However, the legal system of each country is shaped by its unique history and so incorporates individual variations.

Both Civil (also known as *Roman*) and Common law systems can be considered the most widespread in the world, Civil law because it is the most widespread by landmass, and Common law because it is employed by the greatest number of people.

Common Law

Common law and equity are systems of law whose sources are the decisions in cases by judges. Alongside, every system will have a legislature that passes new laws and statutes. The relationships between statutes and judicial decisions can be complex. In some jurisdictions, such statutes may overrule judicial decisions or codify the topic covered by several contradictory or ambiguous decisions. In some jurisdictions, judicial decisions may decide whether the jurisdiction's constitution allowed a particular statute or statutory provision to be made or what meaning is contained within the statutory provisions. Statutes were allowed to be made by the government. Common law developed in England, influenced by Anglo-Saxon law and to a much lesser extent by the Norman conquest of England, which introduced legal concepts from Norman law, which, in turn, had its origins in Salic law. Common law was later inherited by the Commonwealth of Nations, and almost every former colony of the British Empire has adopted it (Malta being an exception). The doctrine of *stare decisis*, also known as *case law* or *precedent by courts*, is

Chapter 2
Legal Systems of the World

the major difference to codified civil law systems.

Common law is currently in practice in Ireland, most of the United Kingdom (England and Wales and Northern Ireland), Australia, New Zealand, Bangladesh, India (excluding Goa), Pakistan, South Africa, Canada (excluding Quebec), Hong Kong, the United States (on a state level excluding Louisiana), and many other places. In addition to these countries, several others have adapted the common law system into a mixed system. For example, Nigeria operates largely on a common law system, but incorporates religious law.

In the European Union, the Court of Justice takes an approach mixing civil law (based on the treaties) with an attachment to the importance of case law. One of the most fundamental documents to shape common law is the English Magna Carta, which placed limits on the power of the English Kings. It served as a kind of medieval bill of rights for the aristocracy and the judiciary who developed the law.

Country	Description
American Samoa	Based on law of the United States
Antigua and Barbuda	Based on English common law
Australia	Based on English common law. Some Indigenous Aboriginal laws are partially recognised in the system.
Bahamas	Based on English common law
Bangladesh	Based on English common law
Barbados	Based on English common law
Belize	Based on English common law
Bhutan	Based on English common law, with Indian influence. Religious law influences personal law.
British Virgin Islands	Based on English common law
Canada	Based on English common law, except in Quebec, where a civil law system based on French law prevails in most matters of a civil nature, such as obligations (contract and delict), property law, family law and private matters. Federal statutes take into account the bijuridical nature of Canada and use both common law and civil law terms where appropriate.

(Continued)

Country	Description
Cayman Islands	Based on English common law
Cyprus	Based on English common law as inherited from British colonisation, with civil law influences, particularly in criminal law.
Dominica	Based on English common law
England and Wales (UK)	Primarily common law, with early Roman and some modern continental European influences
Fiji	Based on English common law
Gibraltar	Based on English common law
Ghana	
Grenada	Based on English common law
India	Based on English common law, except in Goa, Daman and Diu and Dadra and Nagar Haveli which follow a Civil law system based on the Portuguese Civil Law
Ireland	Based on Irish law before 1922, which was itself based on English common law
Israel	Based on English common law from the period of the British Mandate (that includes laws from Ottoman Empire time), also incorporating civil law and fragments of Halakha and Sharia for family law cases
Jamaica	Based on English common law
Kiribati	Based on English common law
Liberia	Based on Anglo-American and customary law
Marshall Islands	Based on law of the United States
Myanmar	Based on English common law
Nauru	Based on English common law
Nepal	Based on English common law
New Zealand	Based on English common law
Northern Ireland (UK)	Based on Irish law before 1921, in turn based on English common law
Palau	Based on law of the United States

Chapter 2
Legal Systems of the World

(Continued)

Country	Description
Pakistan	Based on English common law with some provisions of Islamic law
Saint Kitts and Nevis	Based on English common law
Saint Vincent and the Grenadines	Based on English common law
Singapore	Based on English common law, but Muslims are subject to the Administration of Muslim Law Act, which gives the Sharia Court jurisdiction over Muslim personal law, *e.g.*, marriage, inheritance and divorce.
Tonga	Based on English common law
Trinidad and Tobago	Based on English common law
Tuvalu	Based on English common law
Uganda	Based on English common law
United States	Federal courts and 49 states use the legal system based on English common law, which has diverged somewhat since the mid-nineteenth century in that they look to each other's cases for guidance on issues of first impression and rarely, if ever, look at contemporary cases on the same issue in the UK or the Commonwealth. State law in the U.S. state of Louisiana is based on French and Spanish civil law (see above)

Civil Law

The central source of law that is recognized as authoritative is codifications in a constitution or statute passed by legislature, to amend a code. While the concept of codification dates back to the Code of Hammurabi in Babylon ca. 1790 BC, civil law systems derive from the Roman Empire and, more particularly, the *Corpus Juris Civilis* issued by the Emperor Justinian ca. AD 529. This was an extensive reform of the law in the Byzantine Empire, bringing it together into codified documents. Civil law was also partly influenced by religious laws such as Canon law and Islamic law. Civil law today, in theory, is interpreted rather than developed or made by judges. Only legislative enactments (rather than legal precedents, as in common law) are considered legally binding.

Scholars of comparative law and economists promoting the legal origins theory usually subdivide civil law into four distinct groups:

- French civil law: in France, the Benelux countries, Italy, Romania, Spain and former colonies of those countries;
- German civil law: in Germany, Austria, Russia, Switzerland, Estonia, Latvia, Bosnia and Herzegovina, Croatia, Kosovo, Macedonia, Montenegro, Slovenia, Serbia, Greece, Portugal and its former colonies, Turkey, Japan;
- Scandinavian civil law: in Denmark, Norway and Sweden. As historically integrated in the Scandinavian cultural sphere, Finland and Iceland also inherited the system.
- Chinese law: a mixture of civil law and socialist law in use in the People's Republic of China.

However, some of these legal systems are often and more correctly said to be of hybrid nature:

- Napoleonic to Germanistic influence (Italian civil law)

The Italian civil code of 1942 replaced the original one of 1865, introducing germanistic elements due to the geopolitical alliances of the time. The Italian approach has been imitated by other countries including the Netherlands (1992), Argentina (2014), Brazil (2002) and Portugal (1966). Most of them have innovations introduced by the Italian legislation, including the unification of the civil and commercial codes.

- Germanistic to Napoleonic influence (Swiss civil law)

The Swiss civil code is considered mainly influenced by the German civil code and partly influenced by the French civil code. The civil code of the Republic of Turkey is a slightly modified version of the Swiss code, adopted in 1926 during Mustafa Kemal Atatürk's presidency as part of the government's progressive reforms and secularization.

Chapter 2
Legal Systems of the World

A comprehensive list of countries that base their legal system on a codified civil law follows:

Country	Description
Albania	Based on Napoleonic Civil law. The Civil Code of the Republic of Albania, 1991
Angola	Based on Portuguese civil law
Argentina	The Spanish legal tradition had a great influence on the Civil Code of Argentina, basically a work of the Argentine jurist Dalmacio Vélez Sársfield, who dedicated five years of his life on this task. The Civil Code came into effect on 1 January 1871. Beyond the influence of the Spanish legal tradition, the Argentinian Civil Code was also inspired by the Draft of the Brazilian Civil Code, the Draft of the Spanish Civil Code of 1851, the Napoleonic code and the Chilean Civil Code. The sources of this Civil Code also include various theoretical legal works, mainly of the great French jurists of the 19th century. It was the first Civil Law that consciously adopted as its cornerstone the distinction between i. rights from obligations and ii. real property rights, thus distancing itself from the French model. The Argentinian Civil Code was also in effect in Paraguay, as per a Paraguayan law of 1880, until the new Civil Code went in force in 1987. In Argentina, this 1871 Civil Code remained in force until August 2015, when it was replaced by the new *Código Civil y Comercial de la Nación*. During the second half of the 20th century, the German legal theory became increasingly influential in Argentina.
Andorra	Courts apply the customary laws of Andorra, supplemented with Roman law and customary Catalan law.
Armenia	Based on Napoleonic Civil law. The Legal System of Armenia
Aruba	Based on Dutch civil law

(Continued)

Country	Description
Austria	Based on Germanic Civil law. The Allgemeines bürgerliches Gesetzbuch (ABGB) of 1811
Azerbaijan	Based on German, French, Russian and traditional Azerbaijani Law
Belarus	Based on Germanic Civil law
Belgium	The Napoleonic Code is still in use, although it is heavily modified (especially concerning family law)
Benin	Based on Napoleonic Civil law.
Bolivia	Influenced by the Napoleonic Code
Bosnia and Herzegovina	Influenced by Austrian law. The Swiss civil law (Zivilgesetzbuch) was a model for the Law on Obligations of 1978.
Brazil	Based on Portuguese civil law
Bulgaria	Civil Law system influenced by Germanic and Roman law systems
Burkina Faso	
Burundi	
Chad	
People's Republic of China	Based on Germanic Civil law with influences from the Soviet Socialist from Soviet Union
Republic of the Congo	Based on the Napoleonic Civil law.
Democratic Republic of the Congo	Based on Belgian civil law
Cote d'Ivoire	
Cambodia	
Cape Verde	Based on Portuguese civil law
Central African Republic	

(Continued)

Country	Description
Chile	Based on the Chilean Civil Law inspired by the Napoleonic Civil Law. The Spanish legal tradition exercised an especially great influence on the civil code of Chile. On its turn, the Chilean civil code influenced to a large degree the drafting of the civil codes of other Latin-American states. For instance, the codes of Ecuador (1861) and Colombia (1873) constituted faithful reproductions of the Chilean code, but for very few exceptions. The compiler of the Civil Code of Chile, Venezuelan Andrés Bello, worked for its completion for almost 30 years, using elements, of the Spanish law on the one hand, and of other Western laws, especially of the French one, on the other. Indeed, it is noted that he consulted and used all of the codes that had been issued till then, starting from the era of Justinian. The Civil Code came into effect on 1 January 1857. The influence of the Napoleonic code and the Law of Castile of the Spanish colonial period (especially the Siete Partidas), is great; it is observed however that *e.g.* in many provisions of property or contract law, the solutions of the French *code civil* were put aside in favor of pure Roman law or Castilian law.
Colombia	Based on the Chilean Civil Law. Civil code introduced in 1873. Nearly faithful reproduction of the Chilean civil code.
Costa Rica	Based on the Napoleonic Civil Law. First Civil Code (a part of the General Code or Carrillo Code) came into effect in 1841; its text was inspired by the South Peruvian Civil Code of Marshal Andres de Santa Cruz. The present Civil Code went into effect 1 January 1888, and was influenced by the Napoleonic Code and the Spanish Civil Code of 1889 (from its 1851 draft version).

(Continued)

Country	Description
Croatia	Based on the Germanic Civil Law. Croatian Law system is largely influenced by German and Austrian law systems. It is significantly influenced by the Civil Code of the Austrian Empire from 1811, known in Croatia as "*General Civil Law*"("*Opći građanski zakon*"). OGZ was in force from 1853 to 1946. The Independent State of Croatia, a Nazi-controlled puppet state that was established in 1941 during World War II, used the OGZ as a basis for the 1943 "*Base of the Civil Code for the Independent State of Croatia*" ("*Osnova građanskoga zakona za Nezavisnu Državu Hrvatsku*"). After the War, Croatia become a member of the Yugoslav Federation which enacted in 1946 the "*Law on immediate voiding of regulations passed before April 6, 1941 and during the enemy occupation*" ("*Zakon o nevaženju pravnih propisa donesenih prije 6. travnja 1941. i za vrijeme neprijateljske okupacije*"). By this law OGZ was declared invalid as a whole, but implementation of some of its legal rules was approved. During the post-war era, the Croatian legal system became influenced by elements of the socialist law. Croatian civil law was pushed aside, and it took norms of public law and legal regulation of the social ownership. After Croatia declared independence from Yugoslavia on June 25, 1991, the previous legal system was used as a base for writing new laws. "*The Law on Obligations*" ("*Zakon o obveznim odnosima*") was enacted in 2005. Today, Croatia as a European union member state implements elements of the EU acquis into its legal system.
Cuba	Influenced by Spanish and American law with large elements of Communist legal theory.
Curaçao	Based on Dutch Civil Law.

(Continued)

Country	Description
Czech Republic	Based on Germanic civil law. Descended from the Civil Code of the Austrian Empire (1811), influenced by German (1939–1945) and Soviet (1947/68–1989) legal codes during occupation periods, substantially reformed to remove Soviet influence and elements of socialist law after the Velvet Revolution (1989). The new Civil Code of the Czech Republic was introduced in 2014.
Denmark	Based on Nordic law. Scandinavian-German civil law
Dominican Republic	Based by the Napoleonic Code
Ecuador	Based on the Chilean civil law. Civil code introduced in 1861.
El Salvador	
Estonia	Based on German civil law.
Finland	Based on Nordic law.
France	Based on Napoleonic code (*code civil* of 1804)
Egypt	Based on Napoleonic civil law and Islamic law.
Equatorial Guinea	
Ethiopia	
Gabon	
Guinea	Based on French civil law system, customary law, and decree.
Guinea–Bissau	Based on Portuguese civil law.
Georgia	
Germany	Based on Germanic civil law. The Bürgerliches Gesetzbuch of 1900 ("BGB"). The BGB is influenced both by Roman and German law traditions.

(Continued)

Country	Description
Greece	Based on Germanic civil law. The Greek civil code of 1946, highly influenced by traditional Roman law and the German civil code of 1900 (Bürgerliches Gesetzbuch); the Greek civil code replaced the Byzantine-Roman civil law in effect in Greece since its independence (Νομική Διάταξη της Ανατολικής Χέρσου Ελλάδος, Legal Provision of Eastern Mainland Greece, November 1821: 'Οι Κοινωνικοί Νόμοι των Αειμνήστων Χριστιανών Αυτοκρατόρων της Ελλάδος μόνοι ισχύουσι κατά το παρόν εις την Ανατολικήν Χέρσον Ελλάδα', 'The Social [i.e. Civil] Laws of the Dear Departed Christian Emperors of Greece [referring to the Byzantine Emperors] alone are in effect at present in Eastern Mainland Greece')
Guatemala	Based on Napoleonic civil law. Guatemala has had three Civil Codes: the first one from 1877, a new one introduced in 1933, and the one currently in force, which was passed in 1963. This Civil Code has suffered some reforms throughout the years, as well as a few derogations relating to areas which have subsequently been regulated by newer laws, such as the Code of Commerce and the Law of the National Registry of Persons. In general, it follows the tradition of the Roman-French system of civil codification. Regarding the theory of 'sources of law' in the Guatemalan legal system, the 'Ley del Organismo Judicial' recognizes 'the law' as the main legal source (in the sense of legislative texts), although it also establishes 'jurisprudence' as a complementary source. Although jurisprudence technically refers to judicial decisions in general, in practice it tends to be confused and identified with the concept of 'legal doctrine', which is a qualified series of identical resolutions in similar cases pronounced by higher courts (the Constitutional Court acting as a 'Tribunal de Amparo', and the Supreme Court acting as a 'Tribunal de Casación') whose theses become binding for lower courts.

(Continued)

Country	Description
Haiti	Based on Napoleonic civil law.
Honduras	
Hungary	Based on Germanic, codified Roman law with elements from Napoleonic civil law.
Iceland	Based on Nordic law. Germanic traditional laws and influenced by Medieval Norwegian and Danish laws.
India (only Goa, Daman and Diu and Dadra and Nagar Haveli)	Based on Portuguese civil law.
Italy	Based on Germanic civil law, with elements of the Napoleonic civil code; civil code of 1942 replaced the original one of 1865.
Japan	Based on Germanic civil law. Japanese civil code of 1895.
Latvia	Based on Napoleonic and German civil law, as it was historically before the Soviet occupation. While general principles of law are prerequisites in making and interpreting the law, case law is also regularly applied to present legal arguments in courts and explain application of law in similar cases. Civil law largely modeled after Napoleonic code mixed with strong elements of German civil law. Criminal law retains Russian and German legal traditions, while criminal procedure law has been fully modeled after practice accepted in Western Europe. Civil law of Latvia enacted on 1937.
Lebanon	Based on Napoleonic civil law.
Lithuania	Modeled after Dutch civil law
Luxembourg	Based on Napoleonic civil law.
Libya	Based on Napoleonic civil law, with Ottoman, Italian, and Egyptian sources.
Macau	Based on the Portuguese civil law; also influenced by the law of the PRC.
Mauritius	

(Continued)

Country	Description
Mexico	Based on Napolenoic civil law. "The origins of Mexico's legal system are both ancient and classical, based on the Roman and French legal systems, and the Mexican system shares more in common with other legal systems throughout the world (especially those in Latin America and most of continental Europe) …"
Mongolia	Based on Germanic civil law.
Montenegro	Based on Napoleonic and German civil law. First: the General Property Code for the Principality of Montenegro of 1888, written by Valtazar Bogišić. Present: the Law on Obligations of 2008.
Mozambique	Based on Portuguese civil law.
Netherlands	Based on Napoleonic.
Nepal	Based on Civil Code.
Norway	Scandinavian-German civil law. King Magnus VI the Lawmender unified the regional laws into a single code of law for the whole kingdom in 1274. This was replaced by Christian V's *Norwegian Code* of 1687.
Panama	
Paraguay	The Paraguayan Civil Code in force since 1987 is largely influenced by the Napoleonic Code and the Argentinian Code.
Peru	Based on civil law system; accepts compulsory International Court of Justice (ICJ) jurisdiction with despotic and corrupting reservations.
Poland	The Polish Civil Code in force since 1965.
Portugal	Influenced by the Napoleonic Code and later by the German Civil Law.
Romania	Civil Code came into force in 2011. Based on the Civil Code of Quebec, but also influenced by the Napoleonic Code and other French-inspired codes (such as those of Italy, Spain and Switzerland)

(Continued)

Country	Description
Russia	Civil Law system descendant from Roman Law through Byzantine tradition. Heavily influenced by German and Dutch norms in 1700–1800s. Socialist-style modification in 1900s, and Continental European Law influences since 1990s.
Rwanda	Mixture of Belgian civil law and English common law
São Tomé e Príncipe	Based on Portuguese civil law.
Serbia	First: the Civil Code of Principality of Serbia of 1844, written by Jovan Hadžić, was influenced by the Austrian Civil Code (Allgemeines bürgerliches Gesetzbuch). Present: The Swiss civil law (Zivilgesetzbuch) was a model for the Law on Obligations of 1978.
Slovakia	Descended from the Civil Code of the Austrian Empire (1811), influenced by German (1939–1945) and Soviet (1947/68–1989) legal codes during occupation periods, substantially reformed to remove Soviet influence and elements of socialist law after the Velvet Revolution (1989).
Slovenia	A Civil Law system influenced mostly by Germanic and Austro-Hungarian law systems.
Spain	Influenced by the Napoleonic Code, it also has some elements of Spain's legal tradition, starting with the Siete Partidas, a major legislative achievement from the Middle Ages. That body of law remained more or less unchanged until the 19th century, when the first civil codes were drafted, merging both the Napoleonic style with the Castilian traditions.

(Continued)

Country	Description
Sweden	Scandinavian-German civil law. Like all Scandinavian legal systems, it is distinguished by its traditional character and for the fact that it did not adopt elements of Roman law. It is indeed worth mentioning that it assimilated very few elements of foreign laws whatsoever. It is also interesting that the Napoleonic Code had no influence in codification of law in Scandinavia. The historical basis of the law of Sweden, just as for all Nordic countries, is Old German law. Codification of the law started in Sweden during the 18th century, preceding the codifications of most other European countries. However, neither Sweden, nor any other Nordic state created a civil code of the kind of the *Code Civil* or the BGB.
Switzerland	The Swiss Civil Code of 1908 and 1912 (obligations; fifth book)
Timor-Leste	Based on Portuguese civil law.
Turkey	Modeled after the Swiss civil law (Zivilgesetzbuch) of 1907.
Ukraine	Civil Code of Ukraine of 2004
Uruguay	
Uzbekistan	Represents an evolution of Soviet civil law. Overwhelmingly strong impact of the Communist legal theory is traceable.
Vietnam	Communist legal theory and French civil law
Venezuela	Civil law

Religious Law

Religious law refers to the notion of a religious system or document being used as a legal source, though the methodology used varies. For example, the use of Jewish and Halakha for public law has a static and unalterable quality, precluding amendment through legislative acts of government or development through judicial precedent; Christian

Chapter 2
Legal Systems of the World

Canon law is more similar to civil law in its use of codes; and Islamic Sharia law (and Fiqh jurisprudence) is based on legal precedent and reasoning by analogy (*Qiyas*), and is thus considered similar to common law.

The main kinds of religious law are Sharia in Islam, Halakha in Judaism, and canon law in some Christian groups. In some cases these are intended purely as individual moral guidance, whereas in other cases they are intended and may be used as the basis for a country's legal system. The latter was particularly common during the Middle Ages.

The Halakha is followed by orthodox and conservative Jews in both ecclesiastical and civil relations. No country is fully governed by Halakha, but two Jewish people may decide, because of personal belief, to have a dispute heard by a Jewish court, and be bound by its rulings.

The Islamic legal system of Sharia (Islamic law) and Fiqh (Islamic jurisprudence) is the most widely used religious law, and one of the three most common legal systems in the world alongside common law and civil law. It is based on both divine law, derived from the Qur'an and Sunnah, and the rulings of Ulema (jurists), who used the methods of *Ijma* (consensus), *Qiyas* (analogical deduction), *Ijtihad* (research) and *Urf* (common practice) to derive *Fatwā* (legal opinions). An Ulema was required to qualify for an *Ijazah* (legal doctorate) at a *Madrasa* (law school/college) before they could issue *Fatwā*. During the Islamic Golden Age, classical Islamic law may have had an influence on the development of common law and several civil law institutions. Sharia law governs a number of Islamic countries, including Saudi Arabia and Iran, though most countries use Sharia law only as a supplement to national law. It can relate to all aspects of civil law, including property rights, contracts or public law.

Country	Description
Afghanistan	Islamic law & American/British law after invasion
Egypt	Islamic law is ensured in Article 2 of the Egyptian constitution.
The Gambia	English common law, Islamic law and customary law

(Continued)

Country	Description
Ghana	Based on English common law
Iran	Shia Islamic law
Libya	Islamic law
Mauritania	mix of Islamic law and French Civil Codes, Islamic law largely applicable to family law.
Morocco	mix of Islamic law and French Civil Codes, Islamic law largely applicable to family law. Halakha recognized to family law cases for Jewish citizens.
Nigeria	Sharia in the northern states, common law in the south and at the federal level.
Oman	Sharia and tribal custom laws
Saudi Arabia	Islamic law
Sudan	Based on Islamic law
Yemen	Islamic law

Pluralistic Systems

Civil Law and Canon Law

Canon law is not divine law, properly speaking, because it is not found in revelation. Instead, it is seen as human law inspired by the word of God and applying the demands of that revelation to the actual situation of the church. Canon law regulates the internal ordering of the Catholic Church, the Eastern Orthodox Church and the Anglican Communion. Canon law is amended and adapted by the legislative authority of the church, such as councils of bishops, single bishops for their respective sees, the Pope for the entire Catholic Church, and the British Parliament for the Church of England.

Chapter 2
Legal Systems of the World

Civil Law and Common Law

Country	Description
Vatican City/Holy See	Based on Roman, Italian, and Catholic canon law
Botswana	Based on South African law. An 1891 proclamation by the High Commissioner for Southern Africa applied the law of the Cape Colony (now part of South Africa) to the Bechuanaland Protectorate (now Botswana).
Cameroon	
Cyprus	Based on English common law (Cyprus was a British colony 1878–1960), with admixtures of French and Greek civil and public law, Italian civil law, Indian contract law, Greek Orthodox canon law, Muslim religious law, and Ottoman civil law.
Guyana	
Jersey	The Bailiwick of Jersey's legal system draws on local legislation enacted by the States of Jersey, Norman customary law, English common law and modern French civil law.
Lesotho	Based on South African law. An 1884 proclamation by the High Commissioner for Southern Africa applied the law of the Cape Colony (now part of South Africa) to Basutoland (now Lesotho).
Louisiana (U.S.)	Based on French and Spanish civil law, but federal laws (based on common law) are also in effect in Louisiana because of federal Supremacy Clause.
Malta	Initially based on Roman Law and eventually progressed to the Code de Rohan, the Napoleonic Code with influences from Italian Civil Law. English common law however is also a source of Maltese Law, most notably in Public Law.
Mauritius	
Namibia	Based on South African law. South Africa conquered South-West Africa (now Namibia) in 1915, and a 1919 proclamation by the Governor-General applied the law of the Cape Province of South Africa to the territory.
Philippines	Based on Spanish law; influenced by U.S. common law after 1898 Spanish- and Philippine-American Wars, personal law based on sharia law applies to Muslims.

31

(Continued)

Country	Description
Puerto Rico (U.S.)	Based on Spanish law; influenced by U.S. common law after 1898 (victory of the U.S. over Spain in the Spanish-American War of 1898 and cession of Puerto Rico to the U.S.); federal laws (based on common law) are in effect because of federal Supremacy Clause.
Quebec (Canada)	After the 1763 Treaty of Paris awarded French Canada to Great Britain, the British initially attempted to impose English Common Law, but in response to the deteriorating political situation in the nearby Thirteen Colonies, the Quebec Act was passed in 1774, which allowed a mix of English Common Law and customary civil law, based on the Coutume de Paris. Codification occurred in 1866 with the enactment of the Civil Code of Lower Canada, which continued in force when the modern Province of Quebec was created at Confederation in 1867. Canadian federal law in force in Quebec is based on common law, but federal statutes also take into account the bijuridical nature of Canada and use both common law and civil law terms where appropriate.
Saint Lucia	
Scotland (UK)	Based on Roman and continental law, with common law elements dating back to the High Middle Ages.
Seychelles	The substantive civil law is based on the French Civil Code. Otherwise the criminal law and court procedure are based on the English common law. See Seychelles Legal Environment.
South Africa	An amalgam of Roman-Dutch civil law and English common law, as well as Customary Law.
Sri Lanka	An amalgam of English common law, Roman-Dutch civil law and Customary Law
Swaziland	Based on South African law. A 1907 proclamation by the High Commissioner for Southern Africa applied the Roman-Dutch common law of the Transvaal Colony (now part of South Africa) to Swaziland.
Thailand	The Thai legal system became an amalgam of German, Swiss, French, English, Japanese, Italian, and Indian laws and practices. Even today, Islamic laws and practices exist in four southern provinces. Over the years, Thai law has naturally taken on its own Thai identity.

Chapter 2
Legal Systems of the World

(Continued)

Country	Description
Vanuatu	Consists of a mixed system combining the legacy of English common law, French civil law and indigenous customary law.
Zimbabwe	Based on South African law. An 1891 proclamation by the High Commissioner for Southern Africa applied the law of the Cape Colony (now part of South Africa) to Southern Rhodesia (now Zimbabwe).

Civil Law and Sharia Law

Country	Description
Afghanistan	
Algeria	
Bahrain	
Comoros	
Djibouti	
Egypt	Family Law (personal Statute) for Muslims based on Islamic Jurisprudence, Separate Personal Statute for non Muslims, and all other branches of Law are based on French civil law system
Eritrea	
Indonesia	Based on civil law of Holland and adat (cultural law of Indonesia) [citation needed]
Jordan	Mainly based on French Civil Code and Ottoman Majalla, Islamic law applicable to family law.
Morocco	Based on Islamic law and French and Spanish civil law system
Oman	
Qatar	Based on Islamic law and Egyptian civil law system (after the French civil law system)
Syria	Based on Islamic law and French civil law system
United Arab Emirates	Based on Islamic law and Egyptian civil law system (after the French civil law system)

Common Law and Sharia Law

Country	Description
Bangladesh	Common law, personal law based on sharia law applies to Muslims
Brunei	
Gambia	
Malaysia	Based on English common law, personal law based on sharia law applies to Muslims.
Nigeria	Sharia is applied in some northern states.
Pakistan	Based on English Common Law, some Islamic law applications in inheritance. Tribal Law in FATA
United Arab Emirates	Based on Common law system in the Dubai International Financial Center (DIFC Courts) and Abu Dhabi Global Market (ADGM) Courts (after the English Common law system).

Hybrid Law

Country	Description
India	The most prominent example of a hybrid legal system is the Indian legal system. India follows a mixture of civil, common law and customary or religious law. Separate personal law codes apply to Muslims, Christians, and Hindus. Decisions by the Supreme Court of India and High Courts are binding on the lower courts. Further, most of the laws are statutory and it also has a constitution which signifies the Civil nature of law in India. Ethiopia also follow this system.

Chapter 2
Legal Systems of the World

Exercises

I. Collocations are word combinations, or words that occur next to or near each other, often in a particular sequence. When becoming familiar with legal English, students may not always know which word combinations are permitted and which are not. Take, for example, the noun phrase *common law*. We know that in English prepositions can precede noun phrases, but what specific prepositions can precede *common law*?

Consider this sentence:

_____ common law, the possessor of land owes a duty of ordinary care to his invitees, who are persons whom he invites onto his land for some purpose beneficial to him.

You may not know the answer and therefore may only be able to make some guesses, such as *in*, *under*, or *at*. Look at these example containing instances of *common law*. What preposition precedes *common law* in these cases?

1. There is no physician-patient privilege at common law, but a majority of states have enacted statutes.

2. Article I, Section 16 of the Alaska Constitution provides in relevant part: "In civil cases where the amount in controversy exceeds two hundred fifty dollars, the right of trial by a jury of twelve is preserved to the same extent as it existed at common law."

Based on what you know so far, what preposition would you use to fill in the blanks in these three excerpts?

1. Civil fraud, as with suits _____ common law, involves lower evidentiary standards — e.g., a preponderance of the evidence, not guilt beyond a reasonable doubt.

2. _____ the common law, an insurance agent whose principal is the insurance company owes on duty to advise a potential insured about any coverage.

3. _____ the common law, "one who suffers from deficient mental capacity is not

35

immune from tort liability solely for that reason..."

Is the preposition *at* the only preposition that can occur with common law? Does it make a difference if common law is preceded by *the*, as in Excerpts 2 and 3?

Since the answers are not likely to be found in your dictionary, you would normally have to conduct more inquiries. If you have access to a corpus of legal documents via Westlaw or Lexis Nexis, you can find the answers to these questions on your own by choosing a database (such as state cases) and then typing in key terms or word combinations, such as "common law". Hint: Avoid beginning your entry with a high-frequency word like *the*. You will be able to find examples of prepositions that occur with *common law*. Alternatively, you can go to *scholar. google. com* and type in some possibilities, such as "at the common law"(law), to see if they exist.

II. Please fill in the blank with the appropriate article ("a", "an", or "the") or leave it blank to indicate that no article is necessary.

"Dennis has only pled that _____ police responded to _____ call for assistance. _____ mere response to _____ call for assistance or aid does not create _____ special relationship between _____ police and _____ person in need of _____ aid..., In Yates, _____ Yates family called _____ police to break up _____ gang fight behind their home. _____ police arrived, but instead of stopping _____ fight, they remained in their car. After _____ car departed, _____ shot was fired at _____ rear of _____ Yates' house which struck and killed their daughter. This court refused to find _____ special relationship where _____ police 'did not assure _____ Yates family that they would protect them from _____ dangers caused by _____ gang fight. _____ focus of Melendez is on _____ individual and any danger unique to _____ individual from which _____ police specifically promise protection.'...

In Rankin, _____ plaintiff was stabbed on _____ local Philadelphia train. _____ plaintiff alleged that _____ police officer witnessed _____ stabbing and failed to prevent it. He further alleged that _____ officer escorted him from _____ train, told him to sit down on _____ bench, and told him he would be 'alright.' _____ plaintiff subsequently passed out and was left on _____ without _____ medical attention for some four hours...

This court concluded that _____ special relationship existed because _____ three elements of _____ Thomas test were met. We inferred that _____ third element was met by _____ allegation that _____ police escorted _____ plaintiff from _____ train, seated him, and reassured him. In _____ case now before us, there are simply no facts pled from which we can make such _____ inference. Without _____ third element of _____ voluntary assumption by _____ officer in this case to protect _____ decedent, there can be no special relationship, no duty, and hence no liability."

Excerpt from City of Philadelphia v. Estate of Dennis, 636 A. 2d 240 (Pa. Commw. Ct. 1993).

Chapter 3
Precedent

In legal systems based on common law, a precedent, or authority, is a principle or rule established in a previous legal case that is either binding on or persuasive for a court or other tribunal when deciding subsequent cases with similar issues or facts. Common law legal systems place great value on deciding cases according to consistent principled rules so that similar facts will yield similar and predictable outcomes, and observance of precedent is the mechanism by which that goal is attained. The principle by which judges are bound to precedents is known as stare decisis. Black's Law Dictionary defines "precedent" as a "rule of law established for the first time by a court for a particular type of case and thereafter referred to in deciding similar cases." Common law precedent is a third kind of law, on equal footing with statutory law (statutes and codes enacted by legislative bodies), and delegated legislation (in U.K. parlance) or regulatory law (in U.S. parlance) (regulations promulgated by executive branch agencies).

Case law, in common law jurisdictions, is the set of decisions of adjudicatory tribunals or other rulings that can be cited as precedent. In most countries, including most European countries, the term is applied to any set of rulings on law which is guided by previous rulings, for example, previous decisions of a government agency.

Essential to the development of case law is the publication and indexing of decisions for use by lawyers, courts and the general public, in the form of law reports. While all decisions are precedent (though at varying levels of authority as discussed throughout this article), some become "leading cases" or "landmark decisions" that are cited especially often.

Chapter 3
Precedent

Principle

Stare decisis (Anglo-Latin) is a legal principle by which judges are obligated to respect the precedent established by prior decisions. The words originate from the phrasing of the principle in the Latin maxim Stare decisis et non quieta movere: "to stand by decisions and not disturb the undisturbed." In a legal context, this is understood to mean that courts should generally abide by precedent and not disturb settled matters. The principle of stare decisis can be divided into two components.

The first is the rule that a decision made by a superior court, or by the same court in an earlier decision, is binding precedent that the court itself and all its inferior courts are obligated to follow. The second is the principle that a court should not overturn its own precedent unless there is a strong reason to do so and should be guided by principles from lateral and inferior courts. The second principle, regarding persuasive precedent, is an advisory one that courts can and do ignore occasionally.

Case Law in Common Law Systems

In the common law tradition, courts decide the law applicable to a case by interpreting statutes and applying precedent which record how and why prior cases have been decided. Unlike most civil law systems, common law systems follow the doctrine of stare decisis, by which most courts are bound by their own previous decisions in similar cases, and all lower courts should make decisions consistent with previous decisions of higher courts. For example, in England, the High Court and the Court of Appeal are each bound by their own previous decisions, but the Supreme Court of the United Kingdom is able to deviate from its earlier decisions, although in practice it rarely does so.

Generally speaking, higher courts do not have direct oversight over day-to-day proceedings in lower courts, in that they cannot reach out on their own initiative (sua sponte) at any time to reverse or overrule judgments of the lower courts. Normally, the burden rests with litigants to appeal rulings (including those in clear violation of established case law) to the higher courts. If a judge acts against precedent and the case is not appealed, the decision will stand.

A lower court may not rule against a binding precedent, even if the lower court feels that the precedent is unjust; the lower court may only express the hope that a higher court or the legislature will reform the rule in question. If the court believes that developments or trends in legal reasoning render the precedent unhelpful, and wishes to evade it and help the law evolve, the court may either hold that the precedent is inconsistent with subsequent authority, or that the precedent should be distinguished by some material difference between the facts of the cases. If that judgment goes to appeal, the appellate court will have the opportunity to review both the precedent and the case under appeal, perhaps overruling the previous case law by setting a new precedent of higher authority. This may happen several times as the case works its way through successive appeals. Lord Denning, first of the High Court of Justice, later of the Court of Appeal, provided a famous example of this evolutionary process in his development of the concept of estoppel starting in the High Trees case: Central London Property Trust Ltd v. High Trees House Ltd [1947] K.B. 130.

Judges may refer to various types of persuasive authority to reach a decision in a case. Widely cited non-binding sources include legal encyclopedias such as Corpus Juris Secundum and Halsbury's Laws of England, or the published work of the Law Commission or the American Law Institute. Some bodies are given statutory powers to issue Guidance with persuasive authority or similar statutory effect, such as the Highway Code.

In federal or multi-jurisdictional law systems there may exist conflicts between the various lower appellate courts. Sometimes these differences may not be resolved and it may be necessary to distinguish how the law is applied in one district, province, division or appellate department. Usually only an appeal accepted by the court of last resort will resolve such differences and, for many reasons, such appeals are often not granted.

Any court may seek to distinguish its present case from that of a binding precedent, in order to reach a different conclusion. The validity of such a distinction may or may not be accepted on appeal. An appellate court may also propound an entirely new and different analysis from that of junior courts, and may or may not be bound by its own previous decisions, or in any case may distinguish the decisions based on significant differences in the facts applicable to each case. Or, a court may view the matter before it as one of "first impression", not governed by any controlling precedent.

Where there are several members of a court, there may be one or more judgments given; only the ratio decidendi of the majority can constitute a binding precedent, but all may be cited as persuasive, or their reasoning may be adopted in argument. Quite apart from the rules of precedent, the weight actually given to any reported judgment may depend on the reputation of both the court and the judges.

Categories and Classifications of Precedent, and Effect of Classification

Verticality

Generally, a common law court system has trial courts, intermediate appellate courts and a supreme court. The inferior courts conduct almost all trial proceedings. The inferior courts are bound to obey precedent established by the appellate court for their jurisdiction, and all supreme court precedent.

Under the doctrine of stare decisis, all tribunals exercising inferior jurisdiction are required to follow decisions of courts exercising superior jurisdiction. Otherwise, the doctrine of stare decisis makes no sense. The decisions of this court are binding upon and must be followed by all the state courts of California. Decisions of every division of the District Courts of Appeal are binding upon all the justice and municipal courts and upon all the superior courts of this state, and this is so whether or not the superior court is acting as a trial or appellate court. Courts exercising inferior jurisdiction must accept the law declared by courts of superior jurisdiction. It is not their function to attempt to overrule decisions of a higher court.

An Intermediate state appellate court is generally bound to follow the decisions of the highest court of that state.

The application of the doctrine of stare decisis from a superior court to an inferior court is sometimes called vertical stare decisis.

Horizontality

The idea that a judge is bound by (or at least should respect) decisions of earlier judges of similar or coordinate level is called horizontal stare decisis.

In the United States federal court system, the intermediate appellate courts are divided into thirteen "circuits", each covering some range of territory ranging in size from the District of Columbia alone up to seven states. Each panel of judges on the court of appeals for a circuit is bound to obey the prior appellate decisions of the same circuit. Precedent of a United States court of appeals may be overruled only by the court en banc, that is, a session of all the active appellate judges of the circuit, or by the United States Supreme Court, not simply by a different three-judge panel.

When a court binds itself, this application of the doctrine of precedent is sometimes called horizontal stare decisis. The state of New York has a similar appellate structure as it is divided into four appellate departments supervised by the final New York Court of Appeals. Decisions of one appellate department are not binding upon another, and in some cases the departments differ considerably on interpretations of law.

Federalism and Parallel State and Federal Courts

In federal systems the division between federal and state law may result in complex interactions. In the United States, state courts are not considered inferior to federal courts but rather constitute a parallel court system.

- When a federal court rules on an issue of state law, the federal court must follow the precedent of the state courts, under the Erie doctrine. If an issue of state law arises during a case in federal court, and there is no decision on point from the highest court of the state, the federal court must either attempt to predict how the state courts would resolve the issue by looking at decisions from state appellate courts, or, if allowed by the constitution of the relevant state, submit the question to the state's courts.

- On the other hand, when a state court rules on an issue of federal law, the state court is bound only by rulings of the Supreme Court, but not by decisions of federal district or circuit courts of appeals. However, some states have adopted a practice of considering themselves bound by rulings of the court of appeals embracing their states, as a matter of comity rather than constitutional obligation.

In practice, however, judges in one system will almost always choose to follow relevant case law in the other system to prevent divergent results and to minimize forum shopping.

Binding Precedent

Precedent that must be applied or followed is known as binding precedent (alternately metaphorically precedent, mandatory or binding authority, etc.). Under the doctrine of stare decisis, a lower court must honor findings of law made by a higher court that is within the appeals path of cases the court hears. In state and federal courts in the United States of America, jurisdiction is often divided geographically among local trial courts, several of which fall under the territory of a regional appeals court. All appellate courts fall under a highest court (sometimes but not always called a "supreme court"). By definition, decisions of lower courts are not binding on courts higher in the system, nor are appeals court decisions binding on local courts that fall under a different appeals court. Further, courts must follow their own proclamations of law made earlier on other cases, and honor rulings made by other courts in disputes among the parties before them pertaining to the same pattern of facts or events, unless they have a strong reason to change these rulings (see Law of the case re: a court's previous holding being binding precedent for that court).

In law, a binding precedent (also known as a mandatory precedent or binding authority) is a precedent which must be followed by all lower courts under common law legal systems. In English law it is usually created by the decision of a higher court, such as the Supreme Court of the United Kingdom, which took over the judicial functions of the House of Lords in 2009. In Civil law and pluralist systems precedent is not binding but case law is taken into account by the courts.

Binding precedent relies on the legal principle of stare decisis. Stare decisis means to stand by things decided. It ensures certainty and consistency in the application of law.

Existing binding precedent from past cases are applied in principle to new situations by analogy.

One law professor has described mandatory precedent as follows:

Given a determination as to the governing jurisdiction, a court is "bound" to follow a precedent of that jurisdiction only if it is directly in point. In the strongest sense, "directly in point" means that: (1) the question resolved in the precedent case is the same as the question to be resolved in the pending case, (2) resolution of that question was necessary to the disposition of the precedent case; (3) the significant facts of the precedent case are also presented in the pending case, and (4) no additional facts appear in the pending case that might be treated as significant.

In extraordinary circumstances a higher court may overturn or overrule mandatory precedent, but will often attempt to distinguish the precedent before overturning it, thereby limiting the scope of the precedent.

Under the U.S. legal system, courts are set up in a hierarchy. At the top of the federal or national system is the Supreme Court, and underneath are lower federal courts. The state court systems have hierarchy structures similar to that of the federal system.

The U.S. Supreme Court has final authority on questions about the meaning of federal law, including the U.S. Constitution. For example, when the Supreme Court says that the First Amendment applies in a specific way to suits for slander, then every court is bound by that precedent in its interpretation of the First Amendment as it applies to suits for slander. If a lower court judge disagrees with a higher court precedent on what the First Amendment should mean, the lower court judge must rule according to the binding precedent. Until the higher court changes the ruling (or the law itself is changed), the binding precedent is authoritative on the meaning of the law.

Lower courts are bound by the precedent set by higher courts within their region. Thus, a federal district court that falls within the geographic boundaries of the Third Circuit Court of Appeals (the mid-level appeals court that hears appeals from district court decisions from Delaware, New Jersey, Pennsylvania, and the Virgin Islands) is bound

Chapter 3
Precedent

by rulings of the Third Circuit Court, but not by rulings in the Ninth Circuit (Alaska, Arizona, California, Guam, Hawaii, Idaho, Montana, Nevada, Northern Mariana Islands, Oregon, and Washington), since the Circuit Courts of Appeals have jurisdiction defined by geography. The Circuit Courts of Appeals can interpret the law how they want, so long as there is no binding Supreme Court precedent. One of the common reasons the Supreme Court grants certiorari (that is, they agree to hear a case) is if there is a conflict among the circuit courts as to the meaning of a federal law.

There are three elements needed for a precedent to work. Firstly, the hierarchy of the courts needs to be accepted, and an efficient system of law reporting. "A balance must be struck between the need on one side for the legal certainty resulting from the binding effect of previous decisions, and on the other side the avoidance of undue restriction on the proper development of the law (1966 Practice Statement (Judicial Precedent) by Lord Gardiner L.C.)".

Binding Precedent in English Law

Judges are bound by the law of binding precedent in England and Wales and other common law jurisdictions. This is a distinctive feature of the English legal system. In Scotland and many countries throughout the world, particularly in mainland Europe, civil law means that judges take case law into account in a similar way, but are not obliged to do so and are required to consider the precedent in terms of principle. Their fellow judges' decisions may be persuasive but are not binding. Under the English legal system, judges are not necessarily entitled to make their own decisions about the development or interpretations of the law. They may be bound by a decision reached in a previous case. Two facts are crucial to determining whether a precedent is binding:

1. The position in the court hierarchy of the court which decided the precedent, relative to the position in the court trying the current case.

2. Whether the facts of the current case come within the scope of the principle of law in previous decisions.

Super Stare Decisis

"Super stare decisis" is a term used for important precedent that is resistant or immune from being overturned, without regard to whether correctly decided in the first place. It may be viewed as one extreme in a range of precedential power, or alternatively, to express a belief, or a critique of that belief, that some decisions should not be overturned.

In 1976, Richard Posner and William Landes coined the term "super-precedent", in an article they wrote about testing theories of precedent by counting citations. Posner and Landes used this term to describe the influential effect of a cited decision. The term "super-precedent" later became associated with different issue: the difficulty of overturning a decision. In 1992, Rutgers professor Earl Maltz criticized the Supreme Court's decision in Planned Parenthood v. Casey for endorsing the idea that if one side can take control of the Court on an issue of major national importance (as in Roe v. Wade), that side can protect its position from being reversed "by a kind of super-stare decisis." The controversial idea that some decisions are virtually immune from being overturned, regardless of whether they were decided correctly in the first place, is the idea to which the term "super stare decisis" now usually refers.

The concept of super-stare decisis (or "super-precedent") was mentioned during the interrogations of Chief Justice John Roberts and Justice Samuel Alito before the Senate Judiciary Committee. Prior to the commencement of the Roberts hearings, the chair of that committee, Senator Arlen Specter of Pennsylvania, wrote an op-ed in the New York Times referring to Roe as a "super-precedent". He revisited this concept during the hearings, but neither Roberts nor Alito endorsed the term or the concept.

Persuasive Precedent

Persuasive precedent (also persuasive authority) is precedent or other legal writing that is not binding precedent but that is useful or relevant and that may guide the judge in making the decision in a current case. Persuasive precedent includes cases decided by lower courts, by peer or higher courts from other geographic jurisdictions, cases made in other parallel systems (for example, military courts, administrative courts, indigenous/tribal courts, state courts versus federal courts in the United States), statements made in dicta, treatises or academic law reviews, and in some exceptional circumstances, cases of other nations, treaties, world judicial bodies, etc.

In a "case of first impression", courts often rely on persuasive precedent from courts in other jurisdictions that have previously dealt with similar issues. Persuasive precedent may become binding through its adoption by a higher court.

In civil law and pluralist systems, as under Scots law, precedent is not binding but case law is taken into account by the courts.

Lower Courts

A lower court's opinion may be considered as persuasive authority if the judge believes they have applied the correct legal principle and reasoning.

Higher Courts in Other Circuits

A court may consider the ruling of a higher court that is not binding. For example, a district court in the United States First Circuit could consider a ruling made by the United States Court of Appeals for the Ninth Circuit as persuasive authority.

Horizontal Courts

Courts may consider rulings made in other courts that are of equivalent authority in the legal system. For example, an appellate court for one district could consider a ruling issued by an appeals court in another district.

Statements Made in Obiter Dicta

Courts may consider obiter dicta in opinions of higher courts. Dicta of a higher court, though not binding, will often be persuasive to lower courts. The phrase obiter dicta is usually translated as "other things said", but due to the high number of judges and individual concurring opinions, it is often hard to distinguish from the ratio decidendi (reason for the decision). For these reasons, the obiter dicta may often be taken into consideration by a court. A litigant may also consider obiter dicta if a court has previously signaled that a particular legal argument is weak and may even warrant sanctions if repeated.

Dissenting Opinions

A case decided by a multi-judge panel could result in a split decision. While only the majority opinion is considered precedential, an outvoted judge can still publish a dissenting opinion. Common patterns for dissenting opinions include:

- an explanation of how the outcome of the case might be different on slightly different facts, in an attempt to limit the holding of the majority
- planting seeds for a future overruling of the majority opinion

A judge in a subsequent case, particularly in a different jurisdiction, could find the dissenting judge's reasoning persuasive. In the jurisdiction of the original decision, however, a judge should only overturn the holding of a court lower or equivalent in the hierarchy. A district court, for example, could not rely on a Supreme Court dissent as a basis to depart from the reasoning of the majority opinion. However, lower courts occasionally cite dissents, either for a limiting principle on the majority, or for propositions that are not stated in the majority opinion and not inconsistent with that majority, or to explain a disagreement with the majority and to urge reform (while following the majority in the outcome).

Treatises, Restatements, Law Review Articles

Courts may consider the writings of eminent legal scholars in treatises, restatements of the law, and law reviews. The extent to which judges find these types of writings persuasive will vary widely with elements such as the reputation of the author and the relevance of the argument.

Persuasive Effect of Decisions from Other Jurisdictions

The courts of England and Wales are free to consider decisions of other jurisdictions, and give them whatever persuasive weight the English court sees fit, even though these other decisions are not binding precedent. Jurisdictions that are closer to modern English common law are more likely to be given persuasive weight, for example Commonwealth states (for example Canada, Australia, or New Zealand). Persuasive weight might be given to other common law courts, such as from the United States, most often where the

Chapter 3
Precedent

American courts have been particularly innovative, e.g. in product liability and certain areas of contract law.

In the United States, in the late 20th and early 21st centuries, the concept of a U.S. court considering foreign law or precedent has been considered controversial by some parties. The Supreme Court splits on this issue. This critique is recent, as in the early history of the United States, citation of English authority was ubiquitous. One of the first acts of many of the new state legislatures was to adopt the body of English common law into the law of the state. Citation to English cases was common through the 19th and well into the 20th centuries. Even in the late 20th and early 21st centuries, it is relatively uncontroversial for American state courts to rely on English decisions for matters of pure common (i.e. judge-made) law.

Within the federal legal systems of several common-law countries, and most especially the United States, it is relatively common for the distinct lower-level judicial systems (e.g. state courts in the United States and Australia, provincial courts in Canada) to regard the decisions of other jurisdictions within the same country as persuasive precedent. Particularly in the United States, the adoption of a legal doctrine by a large number of other state judiciaries is regarded as highly persuasive evidence that such doctrine is preferred. A good example is the adoption in Tennessee of comparative negligence (replacing contributory negligence as a complete bar to recovery) by the 1992 Tennessee Supreme Court decision McIntyre v. Balentine (by this point all US jurisdictions save Tennessee, five other states, and the District of Columbia had adopted comparative negligence schemes). Moreover, in American law, the Erie doctrine requires federal courts sitting in diversity actions to apply state substantive law, but in a manner consistent with how the court believes the state's highest court would rule in that case. Since such decisions are not binding on state courts, but are often very well-reasoned and useful, state courts cite federal interpretations of state law fairly often as persuasive precedent, although it is also fairly common for a state high court to reject a federal court's interpretation of its jurisprudence.

Nonprecedential Decisions: Unpublished Decisions, Non-publication and Depublication, Noncitation Rules

Non-publication of opinions, or unpublished opinions, are those decisions of courts that are not available for citation as precedent because the judges making the opinion deem the case as having less precedential value. Selective publication is the legal process which a judge or justices of a court decide whether a decision is to be or not published in a reporter. "Unpublished" federal appellate decisions are published in the Federal Appendix. Depublication is the power of a court to make a previously published order or opinion unpublished.

Litigation that is settled out of court generates no written decision, and thus has no precedential effect. As one practical effect, the U.S. Department of Justice settles many cases against the federal government simply to avoid creating adverse precedent.

Res Judicata, Claim Preclusion, Collateral Estoppel, Issue Preclusion, Law of the Case

Several rules may cause a decision to apply as narrow "precedent" to preclude future legal positions of the specific parties to a case, even if a decision is non-precedential with respect to all other parties.

<u>Res Judicata, Claim Preclusion</u>

Once a case is decided, the same plaintiff cannot sue the same defendant again on any claim arising out of the same facts. The law requires plaintiffs to put all issues on the table in a single case, not split the case. For example, in a case of an auto accident, the plaintiff cannot sue first for property damage, and then personal injury in a separate case. This is called res judicata or claim preclusion ("Res judicata" is the traditional name going back centuries; the name shifted to "claim preclusion" in the United States over the late 20th century). Claim preclusion applies whether the plaintiff wins or loses the earlier case, even if the later case raises a different legal theory, even the second claim is unknown at the time of the first case. Exceptions are extremely limited, for example if the two claims for relief must necessarily be brought in different courts (for example, one claim might be exclusively federal, and the other exclusively state).

Collateral Estoppel, Issue Preclusion

Once a case is finally decided, any issues decided in the previous case may be binding against the party that lost the issue in later cases, even in cases involving other parties. For example, if a first case decides that a party was negligent, then other plaintiffs may rely on that earlier determination in later cases, and need not re-prove the issue of negligence. For another example, if a patent is shown to be invalid in a case against one accused infringer, that same patent is invalid against all other accused infringers invalidity need not be re-proved. Again, there are limits and exceptions on this principle. The principle is called collateral estoppel or issue preclusion.

Law of the Case

Within a single case, once there's been a first appeal, both the lower court and the appellate court itself will not further review the same issue, and will not re-review an issue that could have been appealed in the first appeal. Exceptions are limited to three "exceptional circumstances": (1) when substantially different evidence is raised at a subsequent trial, (2) when the law changes after the first appeal, for example by a decision of a higher court, or (3) when a decision is clearly erroneous and would result in a manifest injustice. This principle is called "law of the case".

Splits, Tensions

On many questions, reasonable people may differ. When two of those people are judges, the tension among two lines of precedent may be resolved as follows.

Jurisdictional Splits: Disagreements Among Different Geographical Regions or Levels of Federalism

If the two courts are in separate, parallel jurisdictions, there is no conflict, and two lines of precedent may persist. Courts in one jurisdiction are influenced by decisions in others, and notably better rules may be adopted over time.

Splits Among Different Areas of Law

Courts try to formulate the common law as a "seamless web" so that principles in one area of the law apply to other areas. However, this principle does not apply uniformly.

Thus, a word may have different definitions in different areas of the law, or different rules may apply so that a question has different answers in different legal contexts. Judges try to minimize these conflicts, but they arise from time to time, and under principles of 'stare decisis', may persist for some time.

Matter of First Impression

A matter of first impression (known as primae impressionis in Latin) is a legal case in which there is no binding authority on the matter presented. Such a case can set forth a completely original issue of law for decision by the courts. A first impression case may be a first impression in only a particular jurisdiction. In that situation, courts will look to holdings of other jurisdictions for persuasive authority.

In the latter meaning, the case in question cannot be decided through referring to and/or relying on precedent. Since the legal issue under consideration has never been decided by an appeals court and, therefore, there is no precedent for the court to follow, the court uses analogies from prior rulings by appeals courts, refers to commentaries and articles by legal scholars, and applies its own logic. In cases of first impression, the trial judge will often ask both sides' attorneys for legal briefs.

In some situations, a case of first impression may exist in a jurisdiction until a reported appellate court decision is rendered.

Application

Development

Early English common law did not have or require the stare decisis doctrine for a range of legal and technological reasons:

- During the formative period of the common law, the royal courts constituted only one among many fora in which in the English could settle their disputes. The royal courts operated alongside and in competition with ecclesiastic, manorial, urban, mercantile, and local courts.

- Royal courts were not organised into a hierarchy, instead different royal courts

(exchequer, common pleas, king's bench, and chancery) were in competition with each other.
- Substantial law on almost all matters was neither legislated nor codified, eliminating the need for courts to interpret legislation.
- Common law's main distinctive features and focus were not substantial law, which was customary law, but procedural.
- The practice of citing previous cases was not to find binding legal rules but as evidence of custom.
- Customary law was not a rational and consistent body of rules and does not require a system of binding precedent.
- Before the printing press, the state of the written records of cases rendered the stare decisis doctrine utterly impracticable.

These features changed over time, opening the door to the doctrine of stare decisis:

By the end of the eighteenth century, the common law courts had absorbed most of the business of their nonroyal competitors, although there was still internal competition among the different common law courts themselves. During the nineteenth century, legal reform movements in both England and the United States brought this to an end as well by merging the various common law courts into a unified system of courts with a formal hierarchical structure. This and the advent of reliable private case reporters made adherence to the doctrine of stare decisis practical and the practice soon evolved of holding judges to be bound by the decisions of courts of superior or equal status in their jurisdiction.

United States Legal System

Stare decisis applies to the holding of a case, rather than to obiter dicta ("things said by the way"). As the United States Supreme Court has put it: "dicta may be followed if sufficiently persuasive but are not binding."

In the United States Supreme Court, the principle of stare decisis is most flexible in constitutional cases:

Stare decisis is usually the wise policy, because in most matters it is more important that the applicable rule of law be settled than that it be settled right. ... But in cases involving the Federal Constitution, where correction through legislative action is practically impossible, this Court has often overruled its earlier decisions. ... This is strikingly true of cases under the due process clause.

——Burnet v. Coronado Oil & Gas Co., 285 U.S. 393, 406–407, 410 (1932) (Brandeis, J., dissenting).

For example, in the years 1946–1992, the U.S. Supreme Court reversed itself in about 130 cases. The U.S. Supreme Court has further explained as follows:

When convinced of former error, this Court has never felt constrained to follow precedent. In constitutional questions, where correction depends upon amendment, and not upon legislative action, this Court throughout its history has freely exercised its power to reexamine the basis of its constitutional decisions.

——Smith v. Allwright, 321 U.S. 649, 665 (1944).

The United States Supreme Court has stated that where a court gives multiple reasons for a given result, each alternative reason that is "explicitly" labeled by the court as an "independent" ground for the decision is not treated as "simply a dictum".

English Legal System

The doctrine of binding precedent or stare decisis is basic to the English legal system. Special features of the English legal system include the following:

The Supreme Court's Ability to Override Its Own Precedent

The British House of Lords, as the court of last appeal outside Scotland before it was replaced by the UK Supreme Court, was not strictly bound to always follow its own decisions until the case London Street Tramways v. London County Council [1898] AC 375. After this case, once the Lords had given a ruling on a point of law, the matter was closed unless and until Parliament made a change by statute. This is the most strict form of the doctrine of stare decisis (one not applied, previously, in common law jurisdictions, where there was somewhat greater flexibility for a court of last resort to review its own precedent).

Chapter 3
Precedent

This situation changed, however, after the issuance of the Practice Statement of 1966. It enabled the House of Lords to adapt English law to meet changing social conditions. In R v G & R 2003, the House of Lords overruled its decision in Caldwell 1981, which had allowed the Lords to establish mens rea ("guilty mind") by measuring a defendant's conduct against that of a "reasonable person", regardless of the defendant's actual state of mind.

However, the Practice Statement has been seldom applied by the House of Lords, usually only as a last resort. As of 2005, the House of Lords has rejected its past decisions no more than 20 times. They are reluctant to use it because they fear to introduce uncertainty into the law. In particular, the Practice Statement stated that the Lords would be especially reluctant to overrule themselves in criminal cases because of the importance of certainty of that law. The first case involving criminal law to be overruled with the Practice Statement was Anderton v. Ryan (1985), which was overruled by R v. Shivpuri (1986), two decades after the Practice Statement. Remarkably, the precedent overruled had been made only a year before, but it had been criticised by several academic lawyers. As a result, Lord Bridge stated he was "undeterred by the consideration that the decision in Anderton v. Ryan was so recent. The Practice Statement is an effective abandonment of our pretention to infallibility. If a serious error embodied in a decision of this House has distorted the law, the sooner it is corrected the better." Still, the House of Lords has remained reluctant to overrule itself in some cases; in R v. Kansal (2002), the majority of House members adopted the opinion that R v. Lambert had been wrongly decided and agreed to depart from their earlier decision.

<u>Distinguishing Precedent on Legal (Rather than Fact) Grounds</u>

A precedent does not bind a court if it finds there was a lack of care in the original "Per Incuriam". For example, if a statutory provision or precedent had not been brought to the previous court's attention before its decision, the precedent would not be binding.

Rules of Statutory Interpretation

One of the most important roles of precedent is to resolve ambiguities in other legal texts, such as constitutions, statutes, and regulations. The process involves, first and foremost, consultation of the plain language of the text, as enlightened by the legislative history of enactment, subsequent precedent, and experience with various interpretations of similar texts.

Statutory Interpretation in the U.K.

A judge's normal aids include access to all previous cases in which a precedent has been set, and a good English dictionary.

Judges and barristers in the U.K. use three primary rules for interpreting the law.

Under the literal rule, the judge should do what the actual legislation states rather than trying to do what the judge thinks that it means. The judge should use the plain everyday ordinary meaning of the words, even if this produces an unjust or undesirable outcome. A good example of problems with this method is R v Maginnis (1987), in which several judges in separate opinions found several different dictionary meanings of the word supply. Another example is Fisher v. Bell, where it was held that a shopkeeper who placed an illegal item in a shop window with a price tag did not make an offer to sell it, because of the specific meaning of "offer for sale" in contract law. As a result of this case, Parliament amended the statute concerned to end this discrepancy.

The golden rule is used when use of the literal rule would obviously create an absurd result. The court must find genuine difficulties before it declines to use the literal rule. There are two ways in which the golden rule can be applied: the narrow method, and the broad method. Under the narrow method, when there are apparently two contradictory meanings to a word used in a legislative provision or it is ambiguous, the least absurd is to be used. For example, in Adler v. George (1964), the defendant was found guilty under the Official Secrets Act of 1920. The act said it was an offence to obstruct HM Forces in the vicinity of a prohibited place. Adler argued that he was not in the vicinity of a prohibited place but was actually in a prohibited place. The court chose not to accept the wording literally. Under the broad method, the court may reinterpret the law at will when it is clear that there is only one way to read the statute. This occurred in Re Sigsworth (1935) where a man who murdered his mother was forbidden from inheriting her estate, despite a statute to the contrary.

The mischief rule is the most flexible of the interpretation methods. Stemming from Heydon's Case (1584), it allows the court to enforce what the statute is intended to remedy rather than what the words actually say. For example, in Corkery v. Carpenter (1950), a man was found guilty of being drunk in charge of a carriage, although in fact he only had a bicycle.

Statutory Interpretation in the United States

In the United States, the courts have stated consistently that the text of the statute is read as it is written, using the ordinary meaning of the words of the statute.

- "In interpreting a statute a court should always turn to one cardinal canon before all others. ... Courts must presume that a legislature says in a statute what it means and means in a statute what it says there." Connecticut Nat'l Bank v. Germain, 112 S. Ct. 1146, 1149 (1992). Indeed, "[w]hen the words of a statute are unambiguous, then, this first canon is also the last: 'judicial inquiry is complete.'"

- "A fundamental rule of statutory construction requires that every part of a statute be presumed to have some effect, and not be treated as meaningless unless absolutely necessary." Raven Coal Corp. v. Absher, 153 Va. 332, 149 S.E. 541 (1929).

- "In assessing statutory language, unless words have acquired a peculiar meaning, by virtue of statutory definition or judicial construction, they are to be construed in accordance with their common usage." Muller v. BP Exploration (Alaska) Inc., 923 P.2d 783, 787–788 (Alaska 1996).

However, most legal texts have some lingering ambiguity—inevitably, situations arise in which the words chosen by the legislature do not address the precise facts in issue, or there is some tension among two or more statutes. In such cases, a court must analyze the various available sources, and reach a resolution of the ambiguity. The "Canons of statutory construction" are discussed in a separate article. Once the ambiguity is resolved, that resolution has binding effect as described in the rest of this article.

Exercises

I. Please match the terms on the left with the definitions on the right. Write the term number in the blank.

Terms **Definitions**

1. Closed memo   A. ____ Final and determinative utterance by court on a lawsuit.

2. Open memo   B. ____ Party with the burden of proof has failed to present a prima facie case for jury consideration so the trial judge orders an entry of a verdict without allowing the jury to consider it, because, as a matter of law, there can be only such verdict.

3. Demurrer   C. ____ Structure of the rules.

4. Bargain   D. ____ An action seeking the return of goods rather than monetary damages.

5. Judgment   E. ____ Writing a memo in which all of the cases are provided.

6. Estoppel   F. ____ Small stand in the front of the class from which the professor lectures.

7. Replevin   G. ____ Writing a memo in which none of the lecture has yet been done.

8. Summary judgment   H. ____ A mutual undertaking, contract, or agreement.

9. Directed verdict   I. ____ The cause, motive, price, or impelling influence which induces a contracting party to enter into a contract.

10. Depositions   J. ____ Allegation that the evidence against the defendant is insufficient in point of law (whether true or not) to make out his case or sustain the issue.

11. Discovery   K. ____ A principle that provides that an individual is barred from denying or alleging a certain fact or state facts because of that individual's previous conduct, allegation, or denial.

12. Legal doctrine   L. ____ Testimony that is given under oath, especially a statement given by a witness that is read out in court in the witness's absence.

Chapter 3
Precedent

13. Legal theory	M. ____	Broad conceptions of purpose underlying an area of law.
14. Torts	N. ____	Case is decided during pretrial by the judge because there is no dispute as to either material fact or inferences to be drawn from undisputed facts, or if only a question of law is involved.
15. Podium/ Lectern	O. ____	The disclosure of bringing to light what was previously hidden.
16. Consideration	P. ____	A legal wrong.

II. Certiorari (leave to appeal), Verbs of Permission and Refusal

Even though two or more terms are regarded as synonymous (having the same or a similar meaning) in English, they may not always be substituted for one another. For example, a noun may only collocate or combine with a specific verb but not its synonym. Look at the legal term certiorari, for example.

Which of the following verbs of permission do you think can combine with certiorari in the example sentence? If you're only becoming familiar with legal English, you may not know the answers, just make your best guess.

    permitted granted allowed gave agreed to

One month ago, this Court _____ certiorari to resolve the issues whether the execution of the presently mentally incompetent offends the English Amendment, and, if it does, what process is due a condemned prisoner who might lack any understanding of the penalty he faces.

Granted almost always combines with certiorari. The English Language Institute, University of Michigan (ELI-UM) legal English corpus contains 30 examples of grant certiorari and no examples of other verbs of permission that collocate or combine with certiorari. Allowed and permitted also combine with certiorari, but rarely.

What about the opposite of grant certiorari? Which of the verbs of refusal that follow collocate with certiorari in the sentence on page 11? Given that certiorari generally collocates with only one verb of permission, is it logical to suppose that it also collocates primarily with one verb of refusal? If you have access to a legal corpus, you may wish to search it for the answer. You can also go the Google Scholar and type in each verb plus certiorari, as in "refuse certiorari". Otherwise, make your best guess.

            refuses   rejects   denies   declines

Relying on Ninth Circuit precedent, the district court finds that Nanosoft's copying is fair use and grants summary judgment in favor of Nanosoft. The Ninth Circuit affirms, and the Supreme Court _____ certiorari.

Leave to appeal is a synonym for certiorari. Is it likely to combine with the same verbs?

By the way, how do you pronounce certiorari?

Chapter 4
Law of the United States

Overview

The law of the United States comprises many levels of codified and uncodified forms of law, of which the most important is the United States Constitution, the foundation of the federal government of the United States. The Constitution sets out the boundaries of federal law, which consists of acts of Congress, treaties ratified by the Senate, regulations promulgated by the executive branch, and case law originating from the federal judiciary. The United States Code is the official compilation and codification of general and permanent federal statutory law.

Federal law and treaties, so long as they are in accordance with the Constitution, preempt conflicting state and territorial laws in the 50 U.S. states and in the territories. However, the scope of federal preemption is limited because the scope of federal power is not universal. In the dual-sovereign system of American federalism (actually tripartite because of the presence of Indian reservations), states are the plenary sovereigns, each with their own constitution, while the federal sovereign possesses only the limited supreme authority enumerated in the Constitution. Indeed, states may grant their citizens broader rights than the federal Constitution as long as they do not infringe on any federal constitutional rights. Thus, most U.S. law (especially the actual "living law" of contract, tort, property, criminal, and family law experienced by the majority of citizens on a day-to-day basis) consists primarily of state law, which can and does vary greatly from one state to the next.

At both the federal and state levels, the law of the United States is largely derived from the common law system of English law, which was in force at the time of the American

Revolutionary War. However, American law has diverged greatly from its English ancestor both in terms of substance and procedure, and has incorporated a number of civil law innovations.

Sources of Law

In the United States, the law is derived from five sources: constitutional law, statutory law, treaties, administrative regulations, and the common law (which includes case law).

Constitutionality

Where Congress enacts a statute that conflicts with the Constitution, the Supreme Court may find that law unconstitutional and declare it invalid.

Notably, a statute does not disappear automatically merely because it has been found unconstitutional; it must be deleted by a subsequent statute. Many federal and state statutes have remained on the books for decades after they were ruled to be unconstitutional. However, under the principle of stare decisis, no sensible lower court will enforce an unconstitutional statute, and any court that does so will be reversed by the Supreme Court. Conversely, any court that refuses to enforce a constitutional statute (where such constitutionality has been expressly established in prior cases) will risk reversal by the Supreme Court.

American Common Law

The United States and most Commonwealth countries are heirs to the common law legal tradition of English law. Certain practices traditionally allowed under English common law were expressly outlawed by the Constitution, such as bills of attainder and general search warrants.

As common law courts, U.S. courts have inherited the principle of stare decisis. American judges, like common law judges elsewhere, not only apply the law, they also make the law, to the extent that their decisions in the cases before them become precedent for decisions in future cases.

The actual substance of English law was formally "received" into the United States in several ways. First, all U.S. states except Louisiana have enacted "reception statutes" which generally state that the common law of England (particularly judge-made law) is the law of the state to the extent that it is not repugnant to domestic law or indigenous conditions. Some reception statutes impose a specific cutoff date for reception, such as the date of a colony's founding, while others are deliberately vague. Thus, contemporary U.S. courts often cite pre-Revolution cases when discussing the evolution of an ancient judge-made common law principle into its modern form, such as the heightened duty of care traditionally imposed upon common carriers.

Second, a small number of important British statutes in effect at the time of the Revolution have been independently reenacted by U.S. states. Two examples that many lawyers will recognize are the Statute of Frauds (still widely known in the U.S. by that name) and the Statute of 13 Elizabeth (the ancestor of the Uniform Fraudulent Transfer Act). Such English statutes are still regularly cited in contemporary American cases interpreting their modern American descendants.

However, it is important to understand that despite the presence of reception statutes, much of contemporary American common law has diverged significantly from English common law. The reason is that although the courts of the various Commonwealth nations are often influenced by each other's rulings, American courts rarely follow post-Revolution Commonwealth rulings unless there is no American ruling on point, the facts and law at issue are nearly identical, and the reasoning is strongly persuasive.

Early on, American courts, even after the Revolution, often did cite contemporary English cases. This was because appellate decisions from many American courts were not regularly reported until the mid-19th century; lawyers and judges, as creatures of habit, used English legal materials to fill the gap. But citations to English decisions gradually disappeared during the 19th century as American courts developed their own principles to resolve the legal problems of the American people. The number of published volumes of American reports soared from 18 in 1810 to over 8,000 by 1910. By 1879 one of the delegates to the California constitutional convention was already complaining: "Now, when we require them to state the reasons for a decision, we do not mean they shall write a hundred pages of detail. We [do] not mean that they shall include the small cases, and impose on the country all this fine judicial literature, for the Lord knows we have got enough of that already."

Today, in the words of Stanford law professor Lawrence Friedman: "American cases rarely cite foreign materials. Courts occasionally cite a British classic or two, a famous old case, or a nod to Blackstone; but current British law almost never gets any mention." Foreign law has never been cited as binding precedent, but as a reflection of the shared values of Anglo-American civilization or even Western civilization in general.

Levels of Law

Federal Law

Federal law originates with the Constitution, which gives Congress the power to enact statutes for certain limited purposes like regulating interstate commerce. The United States Code is the official compilation and codification of the general and permanent federal statutes. Many statutes give executive branch agencies the power to create regulations, which are published in the Federal Register and codified into the Code of Federal Regulations. Regulations generally also carry the force of law under the Chevron doctrine. Many lawsuits turn on the meaning of a federal statute or regulation, and judicial interpretations of such meaning carry legal force under the principle of stare decisis.

During the 18th and 19th centuries, federal law traditionally focused on areas where there was an express grant of power to the federal government in the federal Constitution, like the military, money, foreign relations (especially international treaties), tariffs, intellectual property (specifically patents and copyrights), and mail. Since the start of the 20th century, broad interpretations of the Commerce and Spending Clauses of the Constitution have enabled federal law to expand into areas like aviation, telecommunications, railroads, pharmaceuticals, antitrust, and trademarks. In some areas, like aviation and railroads, the federal government has developed a comprehensive scheme that preempts virtually all state law, while in others, like family law, a relatively small number of federal statutes (generally covering interstate and international situations) interacts with a much larger body of state law. In areas like antitrust, trademark, and employment law, there are powerful laws at both the federal and state levels that coexist with each other. In a handful of areas like insurance, Congress has enacted laws expressly refusing to regulate them as long as the states have laws regulating them (see, e.g., the McCarran-Ferguson Act).

Statutes

The United States Code, the codification of federal statutory law

After the President signs a bill into law (or Congress enacts it over his veto), it is delivered to the Office of the Federal Register (OFR) of the National Archives and Records Administration (NARA) where it is assigned a law number, and prepared for publication as a slip law. Public laws, but not private laws, are also given legal statutory citation by the OFR. At the end of each session of Congress, the slip laws are compiled into bound volumes called the United States Statutes at Large, and they are known as session laws. The Statutes at Large present a chronological arrangement of the laws in the exact order that they have been enacted.

Public laws are incorporated into the United States Code, which is a codification of all general and permanent laws of the United States. The main edition is published every six years by the Office of the Law Revision Counsel of the House of Representatives, and cumulative supplements are published annually. The U.S. Code is arranged by subject matter, and it shows the present status of laws (with amendments already incorporated in the text) that have been amended on one or more occasions.

Regulations

The Code of Federal Regulations, the codification of federal administrative law

Congress often enacts statutes that grant broad rulemaking authority to federal agencies. Often, Congress is simply too gridlocked to draft detailed statutes that explain how the agency should react to every possible situation, or Congress believes the agency's technical specialists are best equipped to deal with particular fact situations as they arise.

Therefore, federal agencies are authorized to promulgate regulations. Under the principle of Chevron deference, regulations normally carry the force of law as long as they are based on a reasonable interpretation of the relevant statutes.

Regulations are adopted pursuant to the Administrative Procedure Act (APA). Regulations are first proposed and published in the Federal Register (FR or Fed. Reg.) and subject to a public comment period. Eventually, after a period for public comment and revisions based on comments received, a final version is published in the Federal Register. The regulations are codified and incorporated into the Code of Federal Regulations (CFR) which is published once a year on a rolling schedule.

Besides regulations formally promulgated under the APA, federal agencies also frequently promulgate an enormous amount of forms, manuals, policy statements, letters, and rulings. These documents may be considered by a court as persuasive authority as to how a particular statute or regulation may be interpreted (known as Skidmore deference), but are not entitled to Chevron deference.

Common Law, Case Law and Precedent

The United States Reports, the official reporter of the Supreme Court of the United States

Unlike the situation with the states, there is no plenary reception statute at the federal level that continued the common law and thereby granted federal courts the power to formulate legal precedent like their English predecessors. Federal courts are solely creatures of the federal Constitution and the federal Judiciary Acts. However, it is universally accepted that the Founding Fathers of the United States, by vesting "judicial power" into the Supreme Court and the inferior federal courts in Article Three of the United States Constitution, thereby vested in them the implied judicial power of common law courts to formulate persuasive precedent; this power was widely accepted, understood, and recognized by the Founding Fathers at the time the Constitution was ratified. Several legal scholars have argued that the federal judicial power to decide "cases or controversies" necessarily includes the power to decide the precedential effect of those cases and controversies.

The difficult question is whether federal judicial power extends to formulating binding precedent through strict adherence to the rule of stare decisis. This is where the act of deciding a case becomes a limited form of lawmaking in itself, in that an appellate court's rulings will thereby bind itself and lower courts in future cases (and therefore also impliedly binds all persons within the court's jurisdiction). Prior to a major change to federal court rules in 2007, about one-fifth of federal appellate cases were published and thereby became binding precedents, while the rest were unpublished and bound only the parties to each case.

As federal judge Alex Kozinski has pointed out, binding precedent as we know it today simply did not exist at the time the Constitution was framed. Judicial decisions were not consistently, accurately, and faithfully reported on both sides of the Atlantic (reporters often simply rewrote or failed to publish decisions which they disliked), and the United Kingdom lacked a coherent court hierarchy prior to the end of the 19th century. Furthermore, English judges in the eighteenth century subscribed to now-obsolete natural law theories of law, by which law was believed to have an existence independent of what individual judges said. Judges saw themselves as merely declaring the law which had always theoretically existed, and not as making the law. Therefore, a judge could reject another judge's opinion as simply an incorrect statement of the law, in the way that scientists regularly reject each other's conclusions as incorrect statements of the laws of science.

In turn, according to Kozinski's analysis, the contemporary rule of binding precedent became possible in the U.S. in the nineteenth century only after the creation of a clear court hierarchy (under the Judiciary Acts), and the beginning of regular verbatim publication of U.S. appellate decisions by West Publishing. The rule gradually developed, case-by-case, as an extension of the judiciary's public policy of effective judicial administration (that is, in order to efficiently exercise the judicial power). The rule of precedent is generally justified today as a matter of public policy, first, as a matter of fundamental fairness, and second, because in the absence of case law, it would be completely unworkable for every minor issue in every legal case to be briefed, argued, and decided from first principles (such as relevant statutes, constitutional provisions, and underlying public policies), which in turn would create hopeless inefficiency, instability, and unpredictability, and thereby undermine the rule of law.

Here is a typical exposition of that public policy in a 2008 majority opinion signed by Associate Justice Stephen Breyer:

Justice Brandeis once observed that "in most matters it is more important that the applicable rule of law be settled than that it be settled right." Burnet v. Coronado Oil & Gas Co. [...] To overturn a decision settling one such matter simply because we might believe that decision is no longer "right" would inevitably reflect a willingness to reconsider others. And that willingness could itself threaten to substitute disruption, confusion, and uncertainty for necessary legal stability. We have not found here any factors that might overcome these considerations.

It is now sometimes possible, over time, for a line of precedents to drift from the express language of any underlying statutory or constitutional texts until the courts' decisions establish doctrines that were not considered by the texts' drafters. This trend has been strongly evident in federal substantive due process and Commerce Clause decisions. Originalists and political conservatives, such as Associate Justice Antonin Scalia have criticized this trend as anti-democratic.

Under the doctrine of Erie Railroad Co. v. Tompkins (1938), there is no general federal common law. Although federal courts can create federal common law in the form of case law, such law must be linked one way or another to the interpretation of a particular federal constitutional provision, statute, or regulation (which in turn was enacted as part of the Constitution or after). Federal courts lack the plenary power possessed by state courts to simply make up law, which the latter are able to do in the absence of constitutional or statutory provisions replacing the common law. Only in a few narrow limited areas, like maritime law, has the Constitution expressly authorized the continuation of English common law at the federal level (meaning that in those areas federal courts can continue to make law as they see fit, subject to the limitations of stare decisis).

The other major implication of the Erie doctrine is that federal courts cannot dictate the content of state law when there is no federal issue (and thus no federal supremacy issue) in a case. When hearing claims under state law pursuant to diversity jurisdiction, federal trial courts must apply the statutory and decisional law of the state in which they sit, as if they were a court of that state, even if they believe that the relevant state law is irrational or just bad public policy. And under Erie, deference is one-way only: state courts are not bound by federal interpretations of state law.

Although judicial interpretations of federal law from the federal district and intermediate appellate courts hold great persuasive weight, state courts are not bound to follow those interpretations. There is only one federal court that binds all state courts as to the interpretation of federal law and the federal Constitution: the U.S. Supreme Court itself.

State Law

The fifty American states are separate sovereigns, with their own state constitutions, state governments, and state courts. All states have a legislative branch which enacts state statutes, an executive branch that promulgates state regulations pursuant to statutory authorization, and a judicial branch that applies, interprets, and occasionally overturns both state statutes and regulations, as well as local ordinances. They retain plenary power to make laws covering anything not preempted by the federal Constitution, federal statutes, or international treaties ratified by the federal Senate. Normally, state supreme courts are the final interpreters of state constitutions and state law, unless their interpretation itself presents a federal issue, in which case a decision may be appealed to the U.S. Supreme Court by way of a petition for writ of certiorari. State laws have dramatically diverged in the centuries since independence, to the extent that the United States cannot be regarded as one legal system as to the majority of types of law traditionally under state control, but must be regarded as 50 separate systems of tort law, family law, property law, contract law, criminal law, and so on.

Most cases are litigated in state courts and involve claims and defenses under state laws. In a 2012 report, the National Center for State Courts' Court Statistics Project found that state trial courts received 103.5 million newly filed cases in 2010, which consisted of 56.3 million traffic cases, 20.4 million criminal cases, 19.0 million civil cases, 5.9 million domestic relations cases, and 1.9 million juvenile cases. In 2010, state appellate courts received 272,795 new cases. By way of comparison, all federal district courts in 2010 together received only about 282,000 new civil cases, 77,000 new criminal cases, and 1.5 million bankruptcy cases, while federal appellate courts received 56,000 new cases.

Local Law

States have delegated lawmaking powers to thousands of agencies, townships, counties, cities, and special districts. And all the state constitutions, statutes and regulations (as well as all the ordinances and regulations promulgated by local entities) are subject to judicial interpretation like their federal counterparts.

It is common for residents of major U.S. metropolitan areas to live under six or more layers of special districts as well as a town or city, and a county or township (in addition to the federal and state governments). Thus, at any given time, the average American citizen is subject to the rules and regulations of several dozen different agencies at the federal, state, and local levels, depending upon one's current location and behavior.

Exercises

I. Please match the terms on the left with the definitions on the right. Write the term number in the blank.

Terms

1. Compensation

Definitions

A. ____ Conduct which falls below the standard established by law for the protection of others against unreasonable risk of harm.

2. Negligence

3. Uniform Commercial Code (UCC)

4. Federal Rules of Civil Procedure

5. Model Penal Code

6. Proscenium

7. Intestate

8. Testate
9. Lawsuit
10. Administrator

11. Hypo (hypothetical)
12. Legalisms

13. Law Review
14. Cite checking

15. Shepardizing

B. ____ Criminal statue drafted in the '60s by the American Law Institute (ALI), a group of legal scholars, and since adopted by a number of states.

C. ____ One who has made a will.

D. ____ Researching to determine if a case has been overruled.

E. ____ Body of procedural rules which govern all civil actions in U.S. District Courts.

F. ____ A scenario which never occurred but could.

G. ____ A periodic publication of law schools containing lead articles on topical subjects by law professors, judges or attorneys, and case summaries by law review member-students. Staff is made up of honor or top law students.

H. ____ Payment of damages; making whole.
I. ____ Stage in the front of the classroom.
J. ____ Laws drafted by the National Conference of Commissioners on Uniform State Laws and the ALI governing commercial transactions. Parties have been adopted by all states.

K. ____ A case before a court.
L. ____ Doing research to confirm that the legal references are correct.

M. ____ Dying without a will.
N. ____ Working for a judge as a researcher and writer.

O. ____ A person appointed by the court to manage the assets and liabilities of a decedent.

16. Judicial clerkship   P. ____ Strict, literal or excessive conformity to the law.

17. Note   Q. ____ Specialized language of the legal profession that has been replaced by plain talk.

18. Legalese   R. ____ An abstract; a memorandum.

II. Good Law, Bad Law

Antonyms are words that have the opposite meaning, such as top and bottom, full and empty, tall and short. Generally, we would say that good and bad are opposites. Is that always the case? What about the expression good law? Is its opposite bad law? Look at these excerpts from legal materials. What meaning(s) does good law have? What about bad law? In which of these eight excerpts could good and bad be considered opposites?

Read the examples that follow and explain.

1. Garcia remains good law, its reasoning has not been repudiated, and it has not been challenged here.

2. Good intentions, unsupported by well informed policy choices, often result in bad law.

3. Developing "good law" on which people may rely — for example, mechanisms to secure credit or protect intellectual property — allows much higher levels of economic performance.

4. [W]e must acknowledge that Aguilar, as well as the portion of Ball addressing Grand Rapids' Shared Time program, are no longer good law.

5. (Dissent) [N]othing can disguise the reality that, until today, Aguilar had not been overruled. Good or bad, it was in fact the law.

6. (Concurrence) Barnhart was bad law when decided and must be overruled. It takes more courage to admit a mistake than to stick our heads in the sand of stare decisis and adhere to a holding which perpetuates a recognized injustice.

Chapter 5
Reading Legal Cases

Legal cases or opinions are decisions written by the court for publication. In general, these opinions contain the court's ruling on specific legal controversies. A legal case has a number of predictable, identifiable components that reveal its functions and shape its structure. Successful case reading requires familiarity with these components. In American law schools, students are usually assigned a casebook rather than a textbook. Casebook may be 1,000 or more pages in length and contain several hundred leading cases from the area of law being studied. These cases, which are generally abridged, are used to illustrate one or more points of law. Cases begin with the following important information: the parties, the court that decided the case, the date, the citation, and the name of the judge or justice.

The Parties

Cases in civil law may be divided into two main groups: cases in law and cases in equity. Cases in law are legal conflicts in which the plaintiff seeks damages or compensation for loss he or she has suffered. Cases in equity, on the other hand, offer other types of remedies nor offered at common law, such as an injunction (preventing a party from doing something or requiring a party to do something). Cases generally begin with the names of the opposing parties in the case — the plaintiff, who brings the action to court because he or she believes he or she has been aggrieved or injured, and the defendant, who is named by the plaintiff in the suit and who receives and responds to the plaintiff's complaint. Law students and professors abbreviate these designations by using the Greek letters Π (pi) for plaintiff and Δ (delta) for defendant. Cases in equity may refer to the parties as the petitioner (the one who petitions the court) and the respondent. After the lower court hears the case and finds for (decides in favor of) one of the parties, the other party may choose to appeal. The parties are generally referred to as the appellant (the party filing the appeal) and the appellee (the party responding to the appeal) or petitioner and respondent.

Unlike the state and federal reporters in which legal cases are published, casebooks do not list all parties in the heading nor do they label the parties. They also eliminate first names and abbreviate company names, for example, Hawkins v. McGee and Palsgraf v. Long Island R. Co. The legal abbreviation for versus is v., which is pronounced like the letter of the alphabet, v. On appeal, the first person listed in the case heading is generally, but nor always, the appellant. Sometimes the name of the original plaintiff remains first.

The Court

Under the names of the parties is the name of the court that made the decision and the date on which the case was decided. When reading legal cases, it is important to find out (1) whether the case was heard in federal or state court, (2) what court in the hierarchy of courts decided the matter, and (3) the date that the case was decided.

Federal or State Courts

Generally, state have exclusive jurisdiction over state matters. However, not all cases involving state law are heard in state courts. There is a class of cases called diversity claims, in which the plaintiff and the defendant are from different states. Article III, Section 2 of the U.S. Constitution allows for controversies "between Citizens of different states" to be heard in federal court. To avoid prejudicing a party from one state in another state, the case can, in some circumstances, be removed to federal court. To file a diversity claim, the amount in controversy (the damages or compensation sought by the plaintiff) must be more than $75,000 (28 U.S.C. 1332). This amount is increased from time to time by the U.S. Congress. In diversity cases, the law of the state in which the action took place is applied (used).

Thus, when reading legal cases, one cannot always assume that a case heard in federal

Chapter 5
Reading Legal Cases

court addresses a federal issue. Likewise, it cannot always be assumed that a case heard in state court deals with a state issue. This is because state courts may have concurrent jurisdiction over some federal subject matter.

Court Location and Hierarchy

State cases include the name of court and state, such as Supreme Court of New Hampshire or Court of Appeals of New York. Federal district cases specify the district, such as the Eastern District of New York. U.S. court of appeals cases name the circuit, such as United States Court of Appeals, Second Circuit. The Second Circuit includes the states of New York and Vermont (see Fig.3). Sometimes law students read cases from other common law countries, such as Canada or England. The location in the heading may be well known or may become obvious when reading the case. If not, most English dictionaries have a section on place names. However, sometimes the location of the court is not clearly stated, such as Court of Exchequer, which is an English court. Information on foreign courts can be found in the section on Tables under Foreign Jurisdictions in The Bluebook: A Uniform System of Citation.

The level of a court in the state court hierarchy is generally clear from the heading, such as the Supreme Court of New Hampshire. New York, along with several other states, is an exception to this general rule because its mid-level court is the Supreme Court of New York and its highest court is the Court of Appeals of New York.

The Date

The name of the court is followed by the date, such as Appellate Court of Illinois, First District, 1987. The date of the case is important because both state and federal courts may overrule or void prior decisions. If the case was decided recently, it is likely still good law. In other words, it still serve as precedent for deciding similar cases. However, if it is an older case, some research is necessary to determine if the case has been overruled and therefore no longer has binding authority.

The Citation

Following the court and date is the citation, which indicates in which reporter(s) (publication(s)) the case can be found, such as 84 N.H.114,146 A.641. The names of the reporters are abbreviated. In this example, N.H. stands for New Hampshire Reports, which is an official state publication, and A. stands for Atlantic Reporter, which is published by West Publishing Co., a private publisher. The Bluebook: A Uniform System of Citation lists the full forms and abbreviations of all reporters in the United States under United States Jurisdictions. The volume number (84/146) precedes the name of the reporter and the page number follows it (114,641).

The Name of the Judge or Justice

The text of the case begins with the name of the judge or justice who wrote the opinion or decision for the majority, such as Cardozo, C.J. (C.J. stands for Chief Justice; J. stands for Justice or Judge.) Many names go unrecognized by the average law student. However, the names of famous Supreme Court justices, such as John Marshall, Oliver Wendell Holmes, Benjamin Cardozo, Earl Warren, Thurgood Marshall, and Sandra Day O'Connor, and even some lower court judges, such as Richard Posner, may be familiar to legal scholars and students, practitioners, and even laypersons. Per curiam is occasionally found in place of the name of the judge. It means that the opinion was written "by the court" and no author is identified. Per curiam opinions are often unanimous.

The body of a legal case contains the opinion of the majority of the judges, also referred to as the court. It generally contains the issue, the substantive facts or the facts, the procedural facts or procedural history, the rule(s), the holding, and the reasoning. The majority opinion is followed first by the concurring opinions and then by the dissenting opinions. The other components are not arranged in a set order. However, information that provides background for the decision, such as the facts, issue, and the procedural history, is typically found in the first part of the body of the case, while the reasoning occurs later in the case. The issue and holding sometimes occur as a pair at the beginning of the case. The

Chapter 5
Reading Legal Cases

holding is often found at the end of the case as a conclusion to the court's reasoning.

The Issue

In the United States, court make decisions only when there is a specific case in controversy. The plaintiff brings the defendant to court because the plaintiff believes he or she has legal claim (cause of action) against the defendant. For the case to proceed, there must be a legal issue or question that the court can remedy. If not, the case is dismissed. A claim that is insufficient on its face (as it is written) is referred to as a frivolous claims.

The issue is the legal question raised by the plaintiff that the court will answer. Generally, the issue is stated in the form of an indirect question. Case readers may have no trouble spotting the issue if it is clearly stated in the first section of the body of the case; however, sometimes the issue may be implied, leaving the reader to construct the actual legal question.

In the American legal system, issue at trial are usually different from those presented on appeal. This is because cases can generally be appealed only as a matter of law. In other words, the issue has something to do with whether the lower court(s) erred or made an error in applying the law. For example, in a civil case, the judge may have granted a motion to dismiss the case even though the plaintiff had a valid legal claim or may have submitted incorrect instructions to the jury. Law students read mainly appellate cases since they often highlight important legal questions.

It is possible to glimpse how the court has answered a legal question (yes or no) by looking for one of the following words at the very end of the case: affirmed, reversed, or reversed and remanded. In this final position, affirmed means that the court upholds or agrees with the decisions of the last court to hear the case. It tells the reader that the appellant does not prevail and the decision in favor of the appellee is let stand. Reversed means it disagree with the last court's opinion. Reversed and remanded means that the court is sending the case back to the lower court with a mandate, that is, instructions to the lower court to apply a different rule or set up a new trial. It is possible that the court has upheld the decision of the trail court while reversing the decision of the appellate court; however, this will not be evident when glancing at the end of the case.

In addition to the issue, a case contains three important histories or stories. The first two are the substantive facts and the procedural history or procedural facts. The third, precedent, is discussed under Reasoning.

The Substantive Facts

The substantive facts or the facts of the case, which are also referred to by law students and professors as the fact pattern, tell the history or story of the participants in a law suit. Cases on appeal generally contain a recitation of the facts that have been decided at trial by the jury or judge based on the evidence presented by the parties. The fact pattern includes but is not limited to all relevant facts relating to the legal issue. The facts must be sufficient or adequate to prove that there is a legal claim. By reading the facts, an experienced reader is often able to discern the issue, even if it has not yet been stated.

The Procedural Facts or Procedural History

The procedural history, also called the procedural facts, summarizes the history of the case in the court system. It tells the reader in what court(s) the case has already been heard, the decision of the lower court(s), and the reasons that the court(s) decided the case in the way it did.

Rule(s)

The rule refers to the specific law or legal principle the court applies in a legal dispute. To answer the legal question posed by the issue, the court identifies and interprets the rule that governs the particular area of law and applies it to the facts of the case. Courts are bound by primary sources of law, which include common law principles, statues, constitutions, and regulations, but not secondary sources, such as model codes, treaties, and articles from law reviews, which are scholarly legal journals.

Chapter 5
Reading Legal Cases

The rule or the applicable section of the rule may be stated in the body of the case or in a footnote. Skillful case readers are able not only to identify the rule but also understand the court's interpretation of the rule in the particular case. In addition, they can quickly perceive disagreements between the parties as to what rule should be applied in a particular case or how the rule should be applied.

Holdings

As previously mentioned, the issue before the court is often stated in the form of a question. The holding is the answer to the legal question or issue. It is generally defined as the general legal principle drawn from a specific controversy. It is also sometimes defined as the application of the legal rule that governs a case to the substantive facts of the case. The legal principle announced in a case may serve as authority or precedent for deciding future similar cases. In the case, the holding is often signaled by the words We hold, We conclude, or We find. (See Reading 5, Briefing a Legal Case—The Holding.)

Reasoning

The reasoning of the court refers to the court's analysis of the case. It reveals the court's thinking on a particular issue. While the holding may give little or no indication of the court's logic, in the analysis the court articulates its rationale for deciding a case in a particular way. In its analysis, the court may also include other opinions, called dicta (sing. dictum), that are not directly relevant to the decision. Dicta are generally stated in hypothetical terms and, while not binding, may be looked to as persuasive authority.

In its analysis, the court turns to precedent for justification of its decision. Precedent, the third type of history found in a legal opinion, refers to a body of cases decided over a period of time in the past that have a similar or analogous set of facts as the current or instant case. These cases set forth certain legal principles that the court must generally apply to the present case, that is, that serve as binding authority in the instant case.

Often, one party may attempt to persuade the court to distinguish a particular case or

set of cases from the instant case while the other may attempt to show the court how the cases are similar or analogous. In its reasoning, the court responds by providing reasons why it has chosen or rejected certain cases as precedent.

Concurring and Dissenting Opinions

If the decision of the court is unanimous, the case ends at this point. However, if it is not, it is generally followed by concurring and dissenting opinions. Concurring opinions follow the majority opinion. They are written by court members who agree with the decision of he majority but do not agree with the reasoning. Dissenting opinions follow. There may be more than one minority opinion if each dissenter writes a separate opinion. In addition to arguing for a different decisions and analysis of the case, the dissenter may reveal additional substantive facts not mentioned by the majority. If the majority overrules a group of precedents, the dissenter may defend the prior stance of the court. Or, if the majority upholds these precedents, the dissenting opinion may foreshadow the future direction of the court in which these precedents are overruled.

From an abridged version of a case, it may be difficult to know how many members of the court heard a case and how the entire court voted. Judges may recuse or remove themselves from a case for bias — links to or feelings about the parties in the case. Cases before the U.S. Supreme Court are generally heard by nine members. If there are two concurring opinions and three dissents, it means that there is no majority opinion, only a plurality opinion with six members of the court voting the same way but only four using the same reasoning or rationale to decided the case. In cases where there are only eight justices (one justice having recused himself or herself) and the vote is four to four, the appellate decision stands. State supreme courts generally have seven members. Federal courts of appeals generally have a three-judge panel unless the judges in a circuit sit en banc (together).

Future Precedent

The present case, having been decided, can become primary authority. It then serves as precedent for similar future cases unless there is a change in the law.

Syllabus and Headnotes

Published cases are often preceded by a syllabus, or summary of the case, and headnotes, which are topical references to parts of the case. However, these are generally omitted from casebooks used by law student.

The Restatements

The Restatements are a series of publications conceived by the American Law Institute, a private organization. The Restatements endeavor to unify common law rules on a national scale to bring about consistency in the common law among the states. They are written and revised with input from legal scholars, lawyers, judges, and other experts in the field. Restatements exist for three first-year law classes — property, torts and contracts — as well as others areas, such as trusts and security. Restatements are presented in the form of rules. Following the rules are Comments with a Rationale, Illustrations, and the Reporter's Note, which discusses changes and additions to the Restatement over time. A Statutory Note may be included as well.

It is important to note that the Restatements are secondary authority and are not binding on any court. However, if a state court relies on a section of a Restatement to decide a case, that section becomes primary authority. The Comments may also become primary authority. If they do not, the court may consider them persuasive authority.

In Case 2, the court refers to the Comments from the Restatement (second) of Torts in its discussion of the issue.

Briefing Cases

Case briefs are useful tools for law students. A brief is an organized way to express the material contained in any case. Case briefs are individual tools that students use to better understand and remember any case for class participation and exam preparation. While you

will develop your own style of case briefing over time, begin with this format.

1. Introductory Materials — case name, citation, court, authoring judge or justice.

2. Facts:

   a. Procedural Posture — this is the history of the case through the legal system. Include everything that has happened in the courts.

   b. Substantive Facts — this is the human story or dispute that brings the parties before the court. What is the personal, business or other problem that made the parties seek legal intervention.

3. Issue — this is the question that the parties bring before the court. Make this a narrow, factually specific legal question.

4. Holding — this is the narrow, factually specific legal answer that the court gives to the question that the parties ask. State how the court decided this particular controversy.

5. Rule — this is the broad legal principle for which the case stands. State whether court articulated a new legal principle or ruled upon existing legal principles. Discuss how this case added to the body of existing law in the jurisdiction.

6. Rationale — this is the court's reasoning. Discuss how the court explained its decision. The court may use several lines of reasoning. If so, you should explain each one thoroughly.

7. Dissenting Opinions — discuss alternate reasoning on this issue by other members of the court.

8. Evaluation — this section should contain your thoughts, ideas and questions about the case.

Exercises

I. Claim

Claim is frequently followed by the prepositions *of*, *for*, *to*, and *against*, among others. Which prepositions would precede the words in the right-hand column? Place a check (√) in the column in which the term belongs.

See the hints for help in completing this task.

A CLAIM OF	A CLAIM FOR	A CLAIM TO	A CLAIM AGAINST
1.			_____ the insurer
2.			_____ negligence
3.			_____ fire damages
4.			_____ a third party
5.			_____ the exclusive use of the family residence
6.			_____ injunctive relief
7.			_____ his deceased wife's property
8.			_____ ineffective assistance of counsel
9.			_____ Individual municipal officials

Hints

1. Upon learning after he retired that he suffered from a work-related hearing loss, respondent Brown filed a timely claim for disability benefits under the Longshore and Harbor Workers' Compensation Act.

2. The trial court found that the plaintiff's claim against the City of Westland and Westland Sports Arena was barred on the ground of governmental immunity.

3. On the basis of the information submitted to the court, the applicant is more likely than not to succeed under its claims of forgery or material fraud...

4. Plaintiff... brought this suit against her employer, Westward Communications ("Westward"), alleging claims for sexual harassment, constructive discharge and retaliation under Title VII of the Civil Rights Act of 1964.

5. We agree with the trial court that White Log failed as a matter of law to establish a claim to the mineral rights by adverse possession.

II. Read and brief the *Groner* case using the briefing format described above. Look up definitions of any unfamiliar words contained in the case.

Groner v. Hedrick
Regional Reporter
169 Atlantic Reporter, 2d series 302

Official Reporter Cite: 403Pa.148

Caption of the case:

Bertha GRONER, Appellant. v. Frank W. HEDRICK and Dorothy Ann Hedrick

Court deciding the case: Supreme Court of Pennsylvania, March 28, 1961;

      Rehearing Denied April 20, 1961

Action by housekeeper for injuries received when knocked down by the defendants' Great Dane which had jumped on her. The Court of Common Pleas of Chester County at No.60, April Term, 1959, Samuel Lichtenfield, J., entered a judgment for the defendants notwithstanding the verdict, and the housekeeper appealed. The Supreme Court, No. 91 January Term, 1961, Bok, J., held that the evidence presented a jury question as whether housekeeper had assumed risk of being jumped upon by the dog.

Reversed and remanded with directions to dispose of motion for new trial.

Bell and Cohen, JJ, dissented.

1. Animals 74(5)

Evidence showed that the owners of Great Dane had knowledge that he might jump up on people.

2. Animals 74(8)

Evidence presented a jury question as to whether housekeeper, knocked down when employers' Great Dane had jumped on her, had assumed risk of being jumped upon by the dog.

Reilly & Fogwell, G. Clinton Fogwell, Jr., West Chester, Jacques H. Fox, Johnson, Fox, McGoldrick & Prescott, Upper Darby, for appellant.

MacElree, Platt & Marrone, Richard Reifsnyder, West Chester, MacElree, West

Chapter 5
Reading Legal Cases

Chester, of counsel, for appellees.

Before CHARLES ALVIN JONES, C.J., and BELL, MUSMANNO, BENJAMIN R. JONES, COHEN, BOK and EAGEN, JJ.

BOK, Justice.

First Friend, as Kipling called Wild Dog, was in this case a large Great Dane named "Sleepy". It jumped upon the plaintiff, who was seventy-four years old, five feet two in height, and 105 pounds in weight, and knocked her down so that she broke her arm and leg. The jury gave her $17,000 but the court below entered judgment for defendants n.o.v., on the theory that plaintiff had assumed the risk of Sleep's temperament. A motion for a new trial was also filed but not disposed of.

What happened was that defendants hired plaintiff to come and be housekeeper and companion for Mrs. Stanley, Mrs. Hedrick's mother, while Mrs. Hedrick went to Europe. Mr. Hedrick stayed behind. The term of employment was five weeks at $100 or $125, and the accident happened after she had been on the job four weeks. She carried a little whip "because he acted as if he was inclined to jump. I was afraid he would jump and knock me over." She also took hold of things when the dog was near, to steady herself, and once, when she told Mr. Hedrick that she was afraid that Sleepy would jump on her, he replied: "Be careful; he might." He jumped or brushed against her on several occasions. She said: "I don't think he was vicious, I'm not sure", and that nothing but his jumping indicated that he was trying to hurt her. He did not growl. Another witness, who said that the dog had jumped on her twice, called him "friendly".

On the day of the accident, plaintiff and her patient were preparing to sit down to lunch when Mrs. Stanley asked to let Sleepy in, in order to keep him off the highway. She called him from the porch, and "when he got beside me I started to go inside the house with him, through the living room door, and that is when he just turned suddenly and just jumped on me*** he just went past me, then he suddenly jumped." By jumping she meant that the dog "raised up with his front paws against here*** left shoulder, left

85

chest." He often put his paws up when plaintiff sat on the sofa, and she kept a rolled magazine to keep him away.

[1] We have no doubt that enough appears to establish defendant's negligence, and indeed this point has not been argued. A large, strong, and over-friendly dog may be as dangerous as a vicious one, and our recital of the dog's behavior at home is enough to bring knowledge to his owners, when considered together with its size and their apparent knowledge that it might jump up on people. Andrew v. Smith, 1936, 324 Pa. 445, 188 A. 146. In Fink v. Miller, 1938, 330Pa. 193,198A. 666, the opinion refers to the dog's viciousness or playfulness as undisclosed by the evidence. We can find no Pennsylvania case of harm by *mansuetae natura*, or tame and domesticated animals, resulting from their excessive affection. Since intention forms no part of an animal's assault and battery, the mood in which it inflicts harm is immaterial, so far as the owner's duty goes. An Alabama case argues what seems to us the correct rule. Owen v. Hampson, 1952, 258 Ala. 228, 62 So.2d 245, 248, in which the Court said:

> Based on a review of our cases, as well as those from other jurisdictions, it is our opinion that the law makes no distinction between an animal dangerous from playfulness, but puts on the owner of both the duty of restraint when he knows of the animal's propensities. Crowley v. Groonell, 73 Vt. 45, 50 A. 546, 55 L.R.A. 876: State v. McDermott, 49 N.J.L. 163, 6 A. 653; Knowles v. Mudler, 74 Mich. 202, 41 N. W. 896; Hicks v. Sullivan, 122 Cal. App. 635, 10 P.2d 516; Mercer v. Marston, 3 La. App.97; Hartman v. Aschoffenburg, La. App., 12 So. 2d 282.

In 3 C.J.S. 148 c, p. 1250, under the title Animals the rule is stated thus:

"A vicious propensity is a propensity or tendency of an animal to do any act that might endanger the safety of the persons and property of others in a given situation. Although an animal is actuated solely by mischievousness or playfulness, rather than maliciousness or ferociousness, yet, if it has a tendency to do a dangerous or harmful act, it has a vicious propensity within the meaning of the rule holding the owner or keeper liable for injuries resulting from vicious propensities of which he has knowledge."

See Restatement, Torts, 518(1), and Stevenson v. United States Express Co., 1908, 221 Pa. 59, 70 A.275, where the temperament of a horse was held to be a matter for the jury.

We regard the rule as different so far as the victim's reaction to the animal is concerned. People trust a dog sooner than a tiger and they would trust a friendly dog before a vicious one. In life the firmest friend, Byron said of the dog: the first to welcome, foremost to defend. It is likely that plaintiff would have acted very differently if Sleepy had been a growler and a biter. A bite is a bite, but a dog's display of affection may be greater or less. And plaintiff had successfully evaded the animal's amiable lunges for four weeks.

Hence, when we give her the benefit of all favorable facts and inferences, as we are told to do while considering judgment n.o.v. by such cases as Rutovitsky v. Magliocco, 1959, 394 Pa. 387, 147 A. 2d 153, we think that the entry of summary judgment was error. In Esher v. Mineral R.R. & Mining Co. (No. 1), 1905, 28 Pa. Super. 387, the Court said:

> "Where the facts are disputed, where there is any reasonable doubt as to the inference to be drawn from them, or when the measure of duty is ordinary and reasonable care and the degree varies according to the circumstances, the question cannot in the nature of the case be considered by the court; it must be submitted to the jury."

The Superior Court then added:

> "It cannot be successfully contended that the risk of injury from the vicious mule was so obvious that Esher ought not to have continued in the service of the company in the tunnel where the mule was used or that if he did so he assumed the risk of injury. If he knew the vicious disposition of the mule, it was still the province of the jury to determine whether from the character of his duties he assumed the risk of injury form this source."

The court below quotes Section 521 of the Restatement of Agency 2nd:

> "In the absence of a statue or an agreement to the contrary, a master is not liable to a servant for harm caused by the unsafe state of the premises or other

conditions of the employment, if the servant, with knowledge of the facts and understanding of the risks, voluntarily enters or continues in the employment."

[2] We think that it was for the jury to say whether plaintiff, under the economic pressure of the job, had knowledge of the facts and understanding of the risks, when the facts and the risks were dependent upon Sleepy's mood, and hence whether she can be held to have assumed them, There are too many variable factors in the dog and in the person and in the enclosing circumstances. Even this court has taken advanced position of trust about dogs, when we said in Andrews v. Smith, supra (324 Pa. 455, 188 A. 146, 148):

"Of all animals, dogs have probably been the longest domesticated and the vast majority of them can be allowed their freedom without imperiling the public safety."

The judgment is reversed and the record is remanded with the directions to dispose of the motion for a new trial.

BELL, Justice (dissenting)

The majority and I agree that a dog is man's best friend; after that we part. It is likely that dogs were originally tamed and used for protection, later for the chase, then for "beasts of burden", and now principally for companionship and affection. A dog exhibits obedience but not affection by lying in the corner. Those who understand or love dogs know that very often they show their affection by putting their paws on or licking or playfully jumping onto persons they like or love. I cannot understand how a Court can equate a dog's act of affection with viciousness. It will come as a bitter blow to all doglovers, and their numbers are legion, to learn that man's best friend is malum in se and that the only dog they can safely keep, even in their own home, is a sleeping dog or a dead dog.

Assuming, arguendo, that this dog's affectionate actions amounted to legal misconduct, plaintiff admittedly knew well the dog's dangerous propensities and clearly and certainly assumed the risk.

Chapter 6
The Civil Litigation Process

Key Motions

When reading cases in civil law, law students frequently encounter the terms dismissal, summary judgment, directed verdict, and judgment notwithstanding the verdict (J.N.O.V). The terms are names of four important motions available to one or both parties as a case makes its way through the court system. A motion, simply put, is a request made to the court. The basic purpose for making all four motions is the same: to ask the court to dispose of the case by deciding for the moving party. In other words, as the case proceeds through the court system, either party has the opportunity to ask the court to stop the process by making a final decision in its favor.

Motion to Dismiss

A civil case begins with a summons and complaint. The summons notifies the defendant that a lawsuit against him or her has begun and requires the defendant to respond to charge made by the plaintiff. In the complaint the plaintiff alleges (asserts) facts that, if true, form the basis of a legal controversy or cause of action. Upon receiving a summons and complaint, the defendant has the option of responding to the claim or filing a motion to dismiss. If the defendant does not think the complaint contains enough information to show that there is a legal basis for suit, he or she can file a motion to dismiss the case. Federal Rules for Civil Procedure (Fed.R.Civ.P.) are followed in the federal court system. Each state has its own state rules. Fed.R.Civ.P.12(b)(6) allows the court to dismiss the case for the plaintiff's "failure to state a claim upon which relief can be granted." In considering the motion, the court assumes that the plaintiff can prove that facts he or she alleges. But if the alleged facts do not establish or reach the level of a legal claim under any legal theory — that is, there is no legal claim to connect the facts to — the court grants the motion, the process ends, and the case is dismissed. The plaintiff, however, may have the opportunity to file an amended complaint.

If the motion is not granted, the defendant responds to the complaint by alleging facts that, if true, either contradict the facts that the plaintiff alleges or provide an affirmative defense (e.g., the statute of limitations has run and thus the action is time barred). The defendant may also file a counterclaim against the plaintiff or a cross-claim against another defendant.

<u>Terms That Also Refer to Motion to Dismiss Include:</u>

demurrer

dismissal

non-suit

failure to state a claim (upon which relief can be granted)(Fed.R.Civ.P.)

failure to state a cause of action

Fed.R.Civ.P.12(b)(6)

12(b)(6)motion

Motion for Summary Judgment

If the court does not grant a motion to dismiss, the case proceeds to the discovery stage. During discovery, both the plaintiff and defendant have the right to gather information to support their positions. For instance, parties may request documents and other physical evidence. They may also seek out key players in the case, such as the opposing party or potential witnesses for the opposing party, and interview them. One way of gathering testimony is by means of a deposition. During a deposition, deponents, (people giving a deposition) answer questions presented orally under oath. Attorneys for both sides are present during a deposition but generally the judge is not. Any party may also attend the deposition. Deponents' statements are transcribed and may also be videotaped. Another

Chapter 6
The Civil Litigation Process

way to gather information during discovery is by means of interrogatories, which are written questions to be answered under oath by the other party or a witness.

A case proceeds to trial if there is conflicting evidence. The case may involve only a question of law. In other words, there may be no genuine issue of material fact. Both parties may stipulate to the facts — that is, tell the court they generally agree about what happened. At this stage, both parties have the opportunity to file a motion for summary judgment requesting that the court apply the law in their favor. If "the pleadings [the claim and answer to the claim], depositions, answers to interrogatories, and admissions on file, together with the affidavits, if any, show that there is no genuine issue as to any material fact and that [one of the moving parties] is entitled to a judgment as a matter of law" (Fed. R.Civ.P.56(c)), then the court applies the law and grants a motion for summary judgment. If, for example, the plaintiff produces enough evidence to show that he or she has met the burden of proving all the elements of his or her claim (has made out a prima facie case) and that the defendant has not been able to provide evidence to support an affirmative defense, the court will grant the plaintiff does not meet his or her burden of proving all elements, the defendant prevails. Or if the plaintiff meets his or her burden of proof but the defendant produces enough evidence to support an affirmative defense, the court will decide in favor of the defendant by granting his or her motion for summary judgment; that is, the defendant prevails. The party who loses the motion, if not satisfied, may appeal the decision.

<u>Terms that Refer to Motion for Summary Judgment Include:</u>

summary judgment

summary disposition

judgment as a matter of law

Rule 56 (c) (Fed.R.Civ.P.)

Directed Verdict

The court will generally not grant a motion for summary judgment if the facts are contradictory, meaning that the parties do not agree about the facts. In these circumstances, the case may then proceed to trial. The jury serves as the fact finders or triers of fact. It is the jury's role to determine the credibility of the evidence at trial. The plaintiff, as the complainant, is the first to present his or her side of the story. It is generally the burden or responsibility of the plaintiff to prove his or her case against the defendant. After the plaintiff rests (finishes presenting evidence in his or her favor), the defendant can file a motion for a directed verdict. The defendant's rationale for requesting a directed verdict is that the plaintiff, given the facts presented, does not have enough evidence to support his or her claim. In other words, the evidence is not legally sufficient to decide for the plaintiff. "If during a trial by jury a party has been fully heard on the issue and there is no legally sufficient evidentiary basis for a reasonable jury to find for that party on that issue, the court may determine the issue against that party and may grant a motion for judgment as a matter of law..." Fed.R.Civ.P.50(a)(1). If the judge grants the motion, the process ends and the defendant as the moving party wins the suit. If, however, the motion is denied, the defendant now has the opportunity to present evidence in his or her favor. After hearing the defendant's evidence, both parties can file a request for a directed verdict. If the court grants the motion of one of the parties, the other can appeal.

Terms That Refer to Motion for Directed Verdict Include:

motion for directed verdict

judgment as a matter of law (Fed.R.Civ.P.)

Rule 50 (a)(Fed.R.Civ.P.)

Judgment Notwithstanding the Verdict

If the court denies motions for a directed verdict, the jury will convene to deliberate. The judge gives the jury instructions on what law to apply in the case. The role of the jury is to decide the facts and apply the law. After the jury announces its verdict, the losing party can file a motion for judgment notwithstanding the verdict. If the evidence is not legally sufficient or contrary to the law and no reasonable person could decide for the non-moving party, the judge will grant the motion to set aside (vacate, reverse) the jury's verdict. The losing party may then appeal or make a request for a new trial if he or she thinks there have been errors at trial. If on appeal, the judge's J.N.O.V, is set aside, the decision of the jury is reinstated, and there is no necessity of a new trial. If, on the other hand, the judge grants a directed verdict, rather than a J.N.O.V. that is set aside on appeal, a new trial is necessary because the jury deliberations did not take place at trial.

Under the Federal Rules of Civil Procedure, directed verdict and judgment notwithstanding the verdict are both referred to as judgment as a matter of law because they are basically the same motion.

Terms for Motion for Judgment Notwithstanding the Verdict Include:

judgment now

judgment non obstante veredicto (J.N.O.V.)

renewed request for motion for judgment after trial (Fed.R.Civ.P.)

judgment as a matter of law (Fed.R.Civ.P.)

Rule 50 (b)(Fed.R.Civ.P.)

Summary of the Civil Litigation Process

Pre-Trial

1. The plaintiff files a summons and complaint.

2. The defendant may request a motion to dismiss.

3. If the judge denies the motion to dismiss, the defendant responds to the complaint.

4. Both parties undertake discovery by means of depositions and/or interrogatories.

5. Either party may file a motion for summary judgment during pre-trial.

6. If the judge denies the motions for summary judgment, the case goes to trial.

Trial

1. The plaintiff presents evidence to the jury.

2. At the conclusion of the plaintiff's evidence, the defendant may file a motion for directed verdict (motion as a matter of law).

3. If the judge denies the motion for directed verdict, the defendant presents evidence to the jury.

4. Either party may request a motion for directed verdict.

5. If the motions for directed verdict are denied, the jury deliberates and reaches a decision.

Post-Trial

1. The losing party may request a motion for judgment notwithstanding the verdict (renewed motion as a matter of law).

2. If the judge grants the motion, the decision of the jury is reversed.

3. If the losing party preserves its right to appeal (through objections), it may file an appeal or a request for a new trial.

4. If, on appeal, the court finds that the judge erred in granting a motion to dismiss, a motion for summary judgment, or a motion for a directed verdict, the appellant still has an opportunity to prevail.

5. If, on appeal, the court finds that the judge erred in granting a motion for judgment notwithstanding the verdict, the decision of the jury stands.

Exercises

I. Please match the terms on the left with the definitions on the right. Write the term number in the blank.

Terms

1. Bench trial

2. Jury trial

3. En banc decision

Definitions

A. ____ Organizing time to fit in many activities.

B. ____ Test necessary for entrance to Law School; measures analytical and logical skills.

C. ____ Classes required for graduation; first year classes

Chapter 6
The Civil Litigation Process

4. Civil action

D. ____ Session when the entire membership of the court will participate in the decision rather than the regular quorum.

5. Criminal action

E. ____ Week before classes officially start in which first years become acquainted with the school.

6. Auditing class

F. ____ Case decided before a judge instead of a jury.

7. Time management

G. ____ Textbook that has never been used.

8. Arguments

H. ____ Action brought to enforce, redress, or protect private rights.

9. Opening statements

I. ____ Taking a class but not receiving a grade for it.

10. Core classes

J. ____ Going over the term's or year's material.

11. Review session

K. ____ Class that discusses the Federal Rules of Civil Procedure.

12. Grade scale

L. ____ Remarks addressed by attorney judge or jury on the merits of case or on points of law.

13. Used textbook

M. ____ Textbook that had been used before; not brand new.

14. New textbook

N. ____ Outline or summary of nature of case and of anticipated proof presented by attorney to jury at start of trial. Before any evidence is submitted.

15. Civil procedure

O. ____ Commercial outline of textbooks.

16. Constitutional law

P. ____ Law based on the United States Constitution and violations of rights granted by it.

17. Orientation

Q. ____ Trial held before a jury.

18. Law School Admissions Text (LSAT)

R. ____ An action, suit, or cause instituted to punish an infraction of the criminal laws.

19. Hornbooks

S. ____ A mark indicating a degree of accomplishment in school, ranging from A to F.

95

II. Incur, Suffer, Support, Sustain, Uphold

Legal terms, like other words in English, can have several meanings. The context in which a legal term occurs often determines its meaning. Only one of these verbs listed can be used in all of the following contexts. Circle that verb. Then fill each of the blanks with another verb from the list that can be used in its place.

    incur   suffer   support   sustain   uphold

1. The judge evaluated the Government's evidence and determined that it was legally insufficient to _____ a conviction.

2. The plaintiff's child _____ injuries when an explosion rocked a public school classroom.

3. Determining that the arbitrator had committed no error of law or clear error of fact, the court _____ his decision. The Court of Appeals for the District of Columbia Circuit reversed.

4. Holland-America also appeals from the district court's order… granting An-Son's post-judgment motion for attorneys fees and expenses _____ in litigating this action.

5. Public support has been insufficient to _____ a solid public health infrastructure.

6. Tenant hereby acknowledges that late payment by Tenant to Landlord of rent…will cause Landlord to _____ costs not contemplated by this Lease.

Part II

An Introduction to American Laws

Chapter 7
Constitutional Law

United States constitutional law is the body of law governing the interpretation and implementation of the United States Constitution.

Interpreting the Constitution and the Authority of the Supreme Court

Beginning

United States constitutional law defines the scope and application of the terms of the Constitution. It covers areas of law such as the relationship between the federal government and state governments, the rights of individuals, and other fundamental aspects of the application of government authority in the United States. It is a field of law that is broad and complex. Some constitutional scholars maintain that the authors of the Constitution intended that it be vague and subject to interpretation so that it could be adapted to the needs of a changing society. Others maintain that the provisions of the Constitution should be strictly construed and their provisions applied in a very literal manner.

The Power of Judicial Review

Early in its history, in Marbury v. Madison, 5 U.S. 137 (1803) and Fletcher v. Peck, 10 U.S. 87 (1810), the Supreme Court of the United States declared that the judicial power granted to it by Article III of the United States Constitution included the power of judicial review, to consider challenges to the constitutionality of a State or Federal law. According to this jurisprudence, when the Court measures a law against the Constitution and finds the law wanting, the Court is empowered and indeed obligated to strike down that law. In this role, for example, the Court has struck down state laws for failing to conform to the Contract Clause (see, e.g., Dartmouth College v. Woodward) or the Equal Protection

Clause (see, e.g., Brown v. Board of Education), and it has invalidated federal laws for failing to arise under the Commerce Clause of the Constitution (see, e.g., United States v. Lopez).

Scope and Effect

The Supreme Court's interpretations of constitutional law are binding on the legislative and executive branches of the federal government, on the lower courts in the federal system, and on all state courts. This system of binding interpretations or precedents evolved from the common law system (called "stare decisis"), where courts are bound by their own prior decisions and by the decisions of higher courts. While neither English common law courts nor continental civil law courts generally had the power to declare legislation unconstitutional (only the power to change law), the United States Supreme Court has long been understood to have the power to declare federal or state legislation unconstitutional.

Prudential Limit — the Principles of Justiciability

Before deciding a constitutional question, the Supreme Court may consider whether the court can avoid the constitutional question by basing its decision on a non-constitutional issue at dispute. For example, if a federal statute is on shaky constitutional footing but has been applied to the challenging party in a manner that does not implicate the basis for the constitutional claim, the Supreme Court will not decide whether the statute might be unconstitutional if it were applied differently. Or, when reviewing a decision of a state's highest court, the Court may avoid the constitutional question if the state court's decision is based on an independent and adequate state-law grounds.

Federal courts consider other doctrines before allowing a lawsuit to go forward:

Actual dispute — the lawsuit concerns a "case or controversy" under the meaning of Article III, Section 2 of the U.S. Constitution.

Standing — the party bringing the suit must have (1) a particularized and concrete injury, (2) a causal connection between the complained-of conduct and that injury, and (3) a likelihood that a favorable court decision will redress the injury.

Ripeness — a party will lack standing where his/her case raises abstract, hypothetical or conjectural questions.

Mootness — a party is seeking redress over a case that no longer has a basis for dispute, though there are limited exceptions.

Political question — the issues raised in the suit are unreviewable because the Constitution relegates it to another branch of government.

Consistent with these doctrines, the Court considers itself prohibited from issuing advisory opinions where there is no actual case or controversy before them. [See Muskrat v. United States, 219 U.S. 346 (1911)]. These doctrines, because they apply to all federal cases whether of constitutional dimension or not, are discussed separately in the article on federal jurisdiction.

Differing Views on the Role of the Court

There are a number of ways that commentators and Justices of the Supreme Court have defined the Court's role, and its jurisprudential method:

The Late Associate Justice Antonin Scalia and current Associate Justice Clarence Thomas are known as originalists; originalism is a family of similar theories that hold that the Constitution has a fixed meaning from an authority contemporaneous with the ratification (although opinion as to what that authority is varies; see discussion at originalism), and that it should be construed in light of that authority. Unless there is a historic and/or extremely pressing reason to interpret the Constitution differently, originalists vote as they think the Constitution as it was written in the late 18th Century would dictate.

Associate Justice Felix Frankfurter was a leading proponent of so-called judicial restraint, in that he believed that the Supreme Court should not make law (which, by invalidating or significantly altering the meaning of Congressional bills, Frankfurter felt they were), and so believers in this idea often vote not to grant cases the writ of certiorari. Associate Justice Stephen Breyer generally advocates a quasi-purposivist approach, focusing on what the law was supposed to achieve rather than what it actually says, and measuring the possible outcomes of voting one way or another.

Other Justices have taken a more instrumentalist approach, believing it is the role of the Supreme Court to reflect societal changes. They often see the Constitution as a living, changing and adaptable document; thus their legal rationale will sometimes be in stark contrast to originalists. Compare, for example, the differing opinions of Justices Scalia and Ruth Bader Ginsburg, who is a more instrumentalist justice.

Finally, there are some Justices who do not have a clear judicial philosophy, and so decide cases purely on each one's individual merits.

Debate continues over which, if any, of these interpretive strategies is "better". Complicating the analysis is the lack of direct correspondence between the various interpretive strategies and contemporary notions of "conservatism" or "liberalism".

Federalism

In essence, the Constitution is a compromise between two extremes feared by the framers: the development of a British-like monarchy on one end of the spectrum, and the ineffectiveness of an overly decentralized government on the other. The balance reached was the model of federalism: a binary structure of management composed of divided powers between the governments of each of the states and a centralized federal government.

Supporters of federalism believed that a division of power between federal and state governments would decrease the likelihood of tyranny, which on a federal level would be much more concerning than its occurrence locally. The framers felt the states were in the best position to restrict such movements. Another frequently raised value of federalism is the notion that since the states are much closer to the people, they can be more responsive to and effective in resolving the localized concerns of the public. Accordingly, the Constitution explicitly enumerates the powers given to the federal government and bestows the remaining discretion to the states.

In order to create a cohesive government, the framers felt certain powers must have belonged to a centralized authority. Conducting foreign affairs, for example, would be severely curtailed if not embarked upon in a nationally uniform manner. Similarly, a standardized currency was of prime importance for a robust and capable economy. As a result, the powers to raise armies, create treaties, and to regulate commerce with foreign nations and among the states, among others, were given to the federal government.

Powers Granted by the Constitution to the Federal Government

The Federal Commerce Power

Congress is authorized to "regulate commerce with foreign nations, and among the several states, and with the Indian tribes" under Article I, Section 8, Clause 3 of the Constitution.

Important early cases include United States v. E.C. Knight Co. (1895) which held that the federal Sherman Act could not be applied to manufacture of sugar because "commerce succeeds to manufacture, and is not a part of it". Essentially, the Court cabined commerce as a phase of business distinct from other aspects of production.

In the Shreveport Rate Cases (1914), the Court permitted congressional regulation of railroad lines because Congress was regulating the "channels of commerce" and although the regulation was on intrastate rail lines, the effect of the intrastate lines was direct so as to concern interstate commerce. In Schecter Poultry, the Court invalidated a federal statute seeking to enforce labor conditions at a slaughterhouse for chickens; the Court held the relationship between labor conditions and chickens was too indirect — that chickens come to rest upon arrival at the slaughterhouse (thereby ending the stream of commerce), so whatever happened in the slaughterhouse was not Congress's business.

In these early cases, the Court approached problems formalistically — from cabining commerce to a specific zone to a direct/indirect test. This continued in the cow case, Stafford v. Wallace, where the court articulated a "Stream of Commerce" test; essentially, Stream of Commerce conceptualizes commerce as a flow mostly concerned with the transportation and packaging of goods and not including acquisition of raw materials at the front end and retail of those goods at the tail end.

However, with the Great Depression, there was political pressure for increased federal government intervention and the Court increasingly deferred to Congress. A seminal case was NLRB v. Jones and Laughlin where the Court adopted a realist approach and reasoned that interstate commerce is an elastic conception which required the Court to think of problems not as falling on either side of a dichotomy but in a more nuanced fashion.

Expansion of Congress's commerce clause power continued with Wickard in 1942 involving a farmer's refusal to comply with a federal quota. Wickard articulated the aggregation principle: that effects of the entire class matter rather than composites of the class, so even if the single farmer did not substantially affect interstate commerce, all farmers — the class to which he belonged — do — they compete with the national market.

With recent cases like Lopez and Morrison, there has been a return to formalism — i.e. legal tests created by the Court to determine if Congress has overstepped its bounds. In both those cases, the federal statutes were invalidated. But in Gonzalez v. Raich (post Lopez and Morrison), principles of Wickard were resurrected, leaving the future of commerce clause doctrine uncertain.

The Spending Power

Clause 1 of Article I, section 8 grants Congress the power to tax and spend "to provide for the common defense and general welfare of the United States", subject to the qualification that all taxes and duties be uniform across the country.

Other Federal Powers

Other federal powers specifically enumerated by Section 8 of Article I of the United States Constitution (and generally considered exclusive to the federal government) are:

- to coin money, and to regulate its value;
- to establish laws governing bankruptcy;
- to establish post offices (although Congress may allow for the establishment of non-governmental mail services by private entities);
- to control the issuance of copyrights and patents (although copyrights and patents may also be enforced in state courts);
- to govern the District of Columbia and all other federal properties;

Chapter 7
Constitutional Law

- to control naturalization (and, implicitly, the immigration) of aliens;
- to enforce "by appropriate legislation" the Thirteenth, Fourteenth, and Fifteenth Amendments to the United States Constitution (a function of the Constitution's Necessary and Proper clause);
- to propose, by a two-thirds vote, constitutional amendments for ratification by three-fourths of the states pursuant to the terms of Article V.

Powers Reserved by the States

Although, for all practical purposes (as proved by the fact of the U.S. Civil War), the federal government does not actually govern by the "consent of the states", some of the more important powers reserved by the states to themselves in the Constitution are: the power, by "application of two-thirds of the legislatures of the several states", to require Congress to convene a constitutional convention for the purpose of proposing amendments to or revising the terms of the Constitution (see Article V).

Suits Against States: Effect of the 11th Amendment

The Eleventh Amendment to the United States Constitution defines the scope of when and in what circumstances a state may be taken to federal court. Taken literally, the Amendment prohibits a citizen from suing a state in federal court through the sovereign immunity doctrine. However, the Court has articulated three exceptions: (1) Particular state officials may be sued, (2) States can waive immunity or consent to suit, and (3) Congress may authorize suits against a state through the abrogation doctrine. However, concerning this latter exception, the Supreme Court has held in Seminole Tribe v. Florida that Congress may not, outside of the Fourteenth Amendment, authorize federal lawsuits against states in abrogation of the Eleventh Amendment's guarantee of sovereign state immunity.

Intergovernmental Immunities and Interstate Relations

The United States government, its agencies and instrumentalities, are immune from state regulation that interferes with federal activities, functions, and programs. State laws and regulations cannot substantially interfere with an authorized federal program, except for minor or indirect regulation, such as state taxation of federal employees.

Limiting the Power of the Three Branches—the System of "Checks and Balances"

Boundaries of Power: Congress Versus the Executive

Many powers of Congress and of the President are specifically enumerated by the Constitution.

Enumerated powers of Congress

Article I, Section 8 of the Constitution enumerates many explicit powers of Congress. See Enumerated powers.

Enumerated powers of the President

Several important powers are enumerated to the President under Article II, Section 2. These include:

- Commander-in-chief of the armed forces;
- Power to pardon offenses against the United States;
- Power to make treaties (with consent of the Senate); and the
- Power to appoint judges, ambassadors, and other officers of the United States (often requiring Senate consent);

The Presidential Veto Power

The Presentment Clause (Article I, Section 7, cl. 2–3) grants the president the power to veto Congressional legislation and Congress the power to override a presidential veto with a supermajority. Under the clause, once a bill has been passed in identical form by both houses of Congress, with a two-thirds majority in both houses, it becomes federal law.

First, the president can sign the bill into law. In this scenario there is Congressional agreement. Second, if not in agreement, the president can veto the legislation by sending the bill back to Congress, within ten days of reception, unsigned and with a written statement of his objections. Third, the president can choose not to act at all on the bill, which can have one of two effects, depending on the circumstances. If Congress is in session, the bill automatically becomes law, without the president's signature, only with a two-thirds majority of both houses. If, however, Congress adjourned during that 10-day period, the bill fails to become law in a procedural device known as the "pocket veto". The bill becomes "mute".

The president approves or rejects a bill in its entirety; he is not permitted to veto specific provisions. In 1996, Congress passed, and President Bill Clinton signed, the Line Item Veto Act of 1996, which gave the president the power to veto individual items of budgeted expenditures in appropriations bills. The Supreme Court subsequently declared the line-item veto unconstitutional as a violation of the Presentment Clause in Clinton v. City of New York, 524 U.S. 417 (1998). The Court construed the Constitution's silence on the subject of such unilateral presidential action as equivalent to "an express prohibition", agreeing with historical material that supported the conclusion that statutes may only be enacted "in accord with a single, finely wrought and exhaustively considered, procedure", and that a bill must be approved or rejected by the president in its entirety. The Court reasoned that a line-item veto "would authorize the President to create a different law — one whose text was not voted on by either House of Congress or presented to the President for signature", and therefore violates the federal legislative procedure prescribed in Article I, Section 7.

Foreign Affairs and War Powers

The president has power as commander-in-chief to control the army. Article I grants congress the power to declare war and raise and support the army and the navy. However, Article II grants the president the power as commander-in-chief. The Supreme Court rarely addresses the issue of the president's use of troops in a war-like situation. Challenges to the president's use of troops in a foreign country are likely to be dismissed on political question grounds. The Supreme Court does not review political questions like who to go to war with or how to handle rebellions since that is the power of the Federal Executive and Legislative branches.

Appointment and Removal of Executive Personnel

Article II, Section 2 grants the President the power, with the "advice and consent of the Senate", to appoint "ambassadors, ... judges of the Supreme Court, and all other officers of the United States, whose appointments are not otherwise provided for" in the

Constitution. This includes members of the cabinet, top-level agency officials, Article III judges, US Attorneys, and the Chairman of the Joint Chiefs, among many other positions. Under the modern interpretation of "advice and consent", a presidential appointment must be confirmed by majority vote in the Senate in order to take effect. Thus, in practice, the President holds the power to nominate, while the Senate holds the power to confirm.

Article II, Section 2 gives Congress the discretion to vest the appointment of "inferior officers" in either the President alone, the heads of departments, or the lower federal courts. Congress may not appropriate this role for itself, and Senate confirmation is not required for these positions.

The President has the authority to remove most high-level executive officers at will. Congress, however, may place limitations on the removal of certain executive appointees serving in positions where independence from the presidency is considered desirable, such as stipulating that removal may only be for cause.

Legislative and Executive Immunity

Legislative Immunity

Members of the Senate and of the House of Representatives have absolute immunity for all statements made on the floor of Congress (Art. I Sec. 6).

Executive Immunity

As a general rule, sitting presidents enjoy immunity from civil suit for damages arising from actions taken while in office. This rule was significantly curtailed by the Supreme Court's decision in Clinton v. Jones, which held that sitting Presidents could in fact be sued for actions undertaken before taking office or for actions which are unrelated to the presidential office.

The Takings Clause

Generally speaking, the Fifth Amendment prevents the government from taking private property "for public use without just compensation". This prohibition on takings is applicable to the 50 states through the Fourteenth Amendment. A governmental taking includes not only physical appropriations of property but also government action that significantly reduces property or impairs its use.

A government "taking" must be distinguished from a government "regulation". With a taking, the government must fairly compensate the property owner when the property is taken for public use. If the government regulates property, it does not have to pay any compensation. A "taking" will be found if there is an actual appropriation or destruction of a person's property or a permanent physical invasion by the government or by authorization of law. The courts may also find a taking where a governmental regulation denies a landowner of all economic use unless principles of nuisance or property law that existed when the owner acquired the land make the use prohibitable.

Freedom of Expression

In the United States, freedom of speech and expression is strongly protected from government restrictions by the First Amendment to the United States Constitution, many state constitutions, and state and federal laws. The Supreme Court of the United States has recognized several categories of speech that are given lesser or no protection by the First Amendment and has recognized that governments may enact reasonable time, place, or manner restrictions on speech. The First Amendment's constitutional right of free speech, which is applicable to state and local governments under the incorporation doctrine, only prevents government restrictions on speech, not restrictions imposed by private individuals or businesses unless they are acting on behalf of the government. However, laws may restrict the ability of private businesses and individuals from restricting the speech of others, such as employment laws that restrict employers' ability to prevent employees from disclosing their salary with coworkers or attempting to organize a labor union.

The First Amendment's freedom of speech right not only proscribes most government restrictions on the content of speech and ability to speak, but also protects the right to receive information, prohibits most government restrictions or burdens that discriminate between speakers, restricts the tort liability of individuals for certain speech, and prevents the government from requiring individuals and corporations to speak or finance certain types of speech with which they don't agree.

Criticism of the government, political advocacy, and advocacy of unpopular ideas that people may find distasteful or against public policy are almost always permitted. Categories of speech that are given lesser or no protection by the First Amendment include obscenity (as determined by the Miller test), fraud, child pornography, speech that incites imminent lawless action, and regulation of commercial speech such as advertising. Within these limited areas, other limitations on free speech balance rights to free speech and other rights, such as rights for authors over their works (copyright), protection from imminent or potential violence against particular persons, restrictions on the use of untruths to harm others (slander), and communications while a person is in prison. When a speech restriction is challenged in court, it is presumed invalid and the government bears the burden of convincing the court that the restriction is constitutional.

The right to freedom of expression includes the right to take and publish photographs of strangers in public areas without their permission or knowledge.

Freedom of Religion

In the United States, freedom of religion is a constitutionally protected right provided in the religion clauses of the First Amendment. Freedom of religion is also closely associated with separation of church and state, a concept advocated by Colonial founders such as Roger Williams, William Penn and later founding fathers such as James Madison and Thomas Jefferson.

"Separation of church and state" is paraphrased from Thomas Jefferson and used by others expressing an understanding of the intent and function of the Establishment Clause and Free Exercise Clause of the First Amendment to the Constitution of the United States which reads: *"Congress shall make no law respecting an establishment of religion, or prohibiting the free exercise thereof..."*

The phrase "separation between church & state" is generally traced to a January

Chapter 7
Constitutional Law

1, 1802 letter by Thomas Jefferson, addressed to the Danbury Baptist Association in Connecticut, and published in a Massachusetts newspaper. Jefferson wrote,

"I contemplate with sovereign reverence that act of the whole American people which declared that their legislature should 'make no law respecting an establishment of religion, or prohibiting the free exercise thereof,' thus building a wall of separation between Church & State."

Jefferson was echoing the language of the founder of the first Baptist church in America, Roger Williams who had written in 1644,

"A hedge or wall of separation between the garden of the church and the wilderness of the world."

Article Six of the United States Constitution also specifies that "no religious Test shall ever be required as a Qualification to any Office or public Trust under the United States."

Jefferson's metaphor of a wall of separation has been cited repeatedly by the U.S. Supreme Court. In *Reynolds v. United States* (1879) the Court wrote that Jefferson's comments "may be accepted almost as an authoritative declaration of the scope and effect of the First Amendment." In *Everson v. Board of Education* (1947), Justice Hugo Black wrote: "In the words of Thomas Jefferson, the clause against establishment of religion by law was intended to erect a wall of separation between church and state."

However, the Court has not always interpreted the constitutional principle as absolute, and the proper extent of separation between government and religion in the U.S. remains an ongoing subject of impassioned debate.

Religion in the United States is characterized by a diversity of religious beliefs and practices. Various religious faiths have flourished within the United States. A majority of Americans report that religion plays a very important role in their lives, a proportion unique among developed countries.

Historically, the United States has always been marked by religious pluralism and diversity, beginning with various native beliefs of the pre-colonial time. In colonial times, Anglicans, Roman Catholics and mainline Protestants, as well as Jews, arrived from

Europe. Eastern Orthodoxy has been present since the Russian colonization of Alaska. Various dissenting Protestants, who left the Church of England, greatly diversified the religious landscape. The Great Awakenings gave birth to multiple Evangelical Protestant denominations; membership in Methodist and Baptist churches increased drastically in the Second Great Awakening. In the 18th century, deism found support among American upper classes and thinkers. The Episcopal Church, splitting from the Church of England, came into being in the American Revolution. New Protestant branches like Adventism emerged; Restorationists and other Christians like the Jehovah's Witnesses, the Latter Day Saint movement, Churches of Christ and Church of Christ, Scientist, as well as Unitarian and Universalist communities all spread in the 19th century. Pentecostalism emerged in the early 20th century as a result of the Azusa Street Revival. Scientology emerged in the 1950s. Unitarian Universalism resulted from the merge of Unitarian and Universalist churches in the 20th century. Beginning in 1990s, the religious share of Christians is decreasing due to secularization, while Buddhism, Hinduism, Islam, and other religions are spreading. Protestantism, historically dominant, ceased to be the religious category of the majority in the early 2010s.

The majority of U.S. adults self-identify as Christians, while close to a quarter claim no religious affiliation. According to a 2014 study by the Pew Research Center, 70.6% of the adult population identified themselves as Christians, with 46.5% professing attendance at a variety of churches that could be considered Protestant, and 20.8% professing Roman Catholic beliefs. The same study says that other religions (including Judaism, Buddhism, Hinduism, and Islam) collectively make up about 6% of the population. According to a 2012 survey by the Pew forum, 36% of U.S. adults state that they attend services nearly every week or more. According to a 2016 Gallup poll, Mississippi with 63% of its adult population described as very religious (say that religion is important to them and attend religious services almost every week) is the most religious state in the country, while New Hampshire with only 20% as very religious is the least religious state.

Chapter 7
Constitutional Law

Exercises

I. Multiple-choice Questions:

Questions 1–2 are based on the following fact situation:

The town of LeMaize, Iowa, faced financial difficulties and its city council sought new ways to raise revenue. In addition to its usual resort to "sin taxes" on alcohol and tobacco, the council passed a new sin tax, aimed at electronic game arcades frequented by local juveniles. The tax is a one-cent per game tax imposed on the manufacturers of the games based on the estimated number of plays over a machine's lifetime.

There are no electronic game manufacturers in Iowa.

1. Which of the following constitutional provisions would support the best argument ***against*** the enforcement of the tax?

    A. The Equal Protection Clause

    B. Substantive due process

    C. The Privileges and Immunities Clause of Article IV

    D. The Commerce Clause

2. Which of the following would most likely be found to have standing to challenge the tax?

    A. The Taxbite Federation, a civic watch-dog and good government group.

    B. Tommy P. Wizard, owner of "Gunga's Den", a game arcade located in LeMaize.

    C. The Rally Manufacturing Company of Chicago, Illinois, a manufacturer of electronic games that sells its games in LeMaize.

    D. Judie DeLinquente, a 16-year-old girl who regularly plays electronic games at Gunga's Den and other LeMaize arcades.

3. The town of Madison has two high schools. Madison High is the public school, and St. Anne's High is a parochial school. Shortly before the school year began, Yvette

Poulet, the French teacher at Madison High, died suddenly. Although the Board of Education made an honest effort, they could find no one in the area qualified and willing to teach French at Madison High. Faced with the prospect of canceling all French classes at Madison High, the board agreed to a friendly proposal offered by Father Finegan, the principal of St. Anne's. Paula Renard, a qualified French teacher and a layperson, was a full-time employee of St. Anne's. Finegan proposed that Renard could spend half her time teaching French at Madison High, if the Board Education reimbursed St. Anne's for half of Renard's salary and half of her benefits package (including health insurance premiums and retirement fund payments). Ms. Renard began the school year teaching two French classes at St. Anne's in the morning and two French classes at Madison High in the afternoon. The Board of Education began forwarding monthly checks to St. Anne's to cover 50% of Renard's salary and benefits.

Assuming that there are no problems with jurisdiction or standing, if Atheists and Other Americans Again Religious Education, a group favoring complete separation of church and state, files suit in federal district court to block the payment of funds to St. Anne's, they will:

    A. Lose, because the arrangement is for a secular purpose, has a primary effect of neither advancing nor inhibiting religion, and does not unduly entangle a governmental body with religion.

    B. Lose, because the arrangement has a secular purpose.

    C. Win, because the arrangement violates the Establishment Clause of the First Amendment.

    D. Win, because it is unconstitutional to transfer public funds to a parochial school.

4. Which of the following acts would be improper for the United States Senate to perform?

    A. Adjudicating a border dispute between states.

    B. Defining certain qualifications for being a member in good standing of the

United States Senate.

C. Sitting in joint session with the House of Representatives.

D. Passing a resolution directing the president to pursue a particular course of foreign policy.

5. The International Wildlife Welfare Federation, a highly respected conversation organization, placed the pfu bird on its endangered species list. Congress responded to this by passing legislation banning the hunting of pfu birds within the United States. The range of the pfu bird is quite limited, and Montoming is one of a few states in which the pfu bird can be found. Hunters from many other states have traditionally travelled to Montoming during its pfu bird hunting season, bringing considerable revenue into the state. A Montoming statute allows hunting of the pfu bird during a two-week period in November and charges a $50 license fee for Montoming residents and a $250 fee for hunters from other states. The bag limit is one pfu bird per licensed hunter.

The Montoming statute allowing pfu bird hunting is:

A. Valid, because states have the right to control their own natural resources and wildlife.

B. Valid, because the power exercised is reserved to the states by the Tenth Amendment.

C. Invalid, because of the Supremacy Clause.

D. Invalid, because of the Commerce Clause.

6. The legislature of State Green was concerned about the problems caused by overpopulation. Therefore, it enacted a statute providing for criminal penalties for any person who is the biological parent of more than two children. The stated purpose of the statute is to preserve the state's natural resources and improve the quality of life for the state's residents. Jane and John Doe, a married couple, have just had their third child. They have been arrested and convicted under the statute.

Which of the following is the strongest argument for voiding the convictions of Mr. and Mrs. Doe?

A. The statute is an invalid exercise of the state's police power because there is no rational basis for concluding that the challenged statute would further the government's stated interests.

B. The statute places an unconstitutional burden on the fundamental privacy interests of married persons.

C. The statute places too great a discretion in state officials to determine who will be permitted to bear children.

D. The statute denies married persons equal protection of law.

7. The town of Equinox, a medium-sized industrial municipality in the northeast, occasionally suffered from air pollution problems due to the typical sources of urban air pollution. The Equinox town council passed the "Equinox Anti-Air Pollution Ordinance", to be effective October 1. The ordinance contained many exhortations to "voluntary compliance", but the only section of the law with any "teeth" read: "Anyone who burns trash, garbage, leaves or similar matter in the open within the confines of the town of Equinox shall be subject to arrest, and may be jailed for up to a maximum of 15 days or fined up to a maximum of $500, or both; however, nothing in this ordinance shall prevent the use of outdoor barbecue grills for the preparation of food."

On the night of October 31, Jezebel, self-proclaimed "Priestess of the Mother Goddess", and three of her "acolytes" raked large quantities of leaves into a big pile in the center of Jezebel's backyard. At the stroke of midnight, they ignited the leaves and danced around the flaming pyre, chanting invocations to the Mother Goddess. Although Jezebel and her followers were careful in building the fire, so that there was no danger that it could spread to any structure in the neighborhood, Gantry, a neighborhood, reported the fire to the police and fire departments. The firefighters doused the fire and Jezebel and her followers were charged under the antipollution ordinance. At trial, Jezebel told the court that she was merely observing one of the important tenets of her faith. The trial judge summarily fined her $250 and fined her three followers $50 each.

Jezebel appealed to the federal courts, asserting that her freedom to practice her religion has been infringed by Equinox.

Will the fines be upheld?

    A. Yes, because Jezebel does not belong to a traditional established religion.

    B. Yes, because the ordinance was adopted to reduce air pollution and not to prohibit religious practices.

    C. No, because the town could accomplish its goal through less restrictive means.

    D. No, because the ordinance is not necessary to promote a compelling interest.

8. Although relations between the United States and the Despotate of Ruritania were tense, and a number of "incidents" over the past few years had on occasion brought the two nations to the brink of war, the United States continued to maintain diplomatic relations with Ruritania. The most recent incident occurred when the state of Michisota tried and convicted Jacques Plastique, a subject of Ruritania, of crimes arising from the bombing of a crowded theater by personnel of a nearby United States Air Force base. Several persons were killed and many more wounded in the bombing. Plastique received the death penalty, but none of his appeals had yet been heard when agents of the Ruritanian secret police seized the American ambassador on the streets of the capital city and imprisoned him in a jail notorious for its inhumane conditions. The United States complained vigorously to the Ruritanian government and also brought its case before the United Nations. However, the Despot of Rurutania steadfastly refused to release the ambassador, whom he claimed was guilty of spying and endangering the security of Rurutania. The President determined that the only way he could ensure the safety of the ambassador was to enter into a distasteful executive agreement with the Despot. Under the terms of the executive agreement, signed by both the President and the Despot, the ambassador would be flown to a neutral country and released to the United States authorities on condition that Plastique was likewise released from prison and flown to a neutral country for release to Ruritanian officials. The President asked Bombast, the

Governor of Michisota, to order Plastique's release from the state penitentiary so that State Department officers could fly him to a neutral country. The Governor felt it would be politically damaging to release Plastique, and she refused to do so.

Which of the following is the best argument that the President can use to compel Governor Bombast to release Plastique?

  A. Under the President's foreign policy power, the President may negotiate executive agreements with foreign governments that have priority over inconsistent state laws.

  B. The power of the President to appoint ambassadors implies that he has the right to do anything in his power to protect them.

  C. The requirement in the Constitution that the President "faithfully execute" the laws means that the President is the final arbiter on questions of division of authority between federal and state governments.

  D. Under the President's plenary power over foreign affairs, ambassadors are agents of the President and he has the power to protect them.

9. A Camptown city ordinance states that anyone wishes to speak in a public park must have a permit to do so issued by the city. The ordinance grants the mayor the discretion to issue or deny such permits based upon the mayor's judgment of whether the speech would be "in the public interest". The mayor has never denied a permit to anybody desiring to speak on a political topic.

Dermot, a person with something to say, went to a public park in Camptown, where he made a 10-minute speech accusing the mayor and the city council of gross incompetence and urging voters to "throw the rascals out" at the next election. Dermot had not applied for a permit. After Dermot completed his oration, the police arrested Dermot and charged him with violating the permit ordinance.

Would a conviction of Dermot be constitutional?

  A. Yes, because Dermot did not have a permit to speak, and a municipality has the right to regulate the time, place, and manner of speech.

B. Yes, because the mayor would have issued the permit, because Dermot's speech was on a political topic.

C. No, because the ordinance is void on its face.

D. No, but only if Dermot could prove that the mayor would not have issued him a permit to speak.

10. The state of Sunny has a climate that is unusually pleasant and mild, with only a few days of really chilly weather in the winter. The federal government owned a building in Solar, Sunny's second city in terms of population but its first in terms of history and commerce. The federal building in Solar housed the regional offices of some federal agencies, as well as a federal records archive. The building was old, but functional, and a typical example of National Recovery Act architecture from the 1930s. The furnace heating the building in winter was quite outmoded, but because the weather in Sunny was so mild there was never a strong drive to ask Congress or the General Services Administration to allocate money for a new heating plant when other needs seemed far more pressing. However, on the approximately two or three days each winter that it was necessary to operate the furnace at full blast, it emitted a noticeable quantity of smoke and particulate matter. The amount of pollutants exuded into Sunny's air on those days was far in excess of the state's stringent environmental regulations.

If the state attempts to enforce its environmental standards and compel the federal building to comply, the likely result of any litigation of the question in federal court is:

A. Sunny wins, because under the state's police powers it has the right to regulate the quality of its own air.

B. Sunny wins, because the states and the federal government have joint responsibility for clean air and the federal government should give full faith and credit to Sunny's laws and regulations in the area.

C. The United States wins, because the Supremacy Clause of Article VI prevents the state from imposing its regulations on the federal government.

D. The United States wins, because the emissions from the building occur so seldom as to be minimal and the state cannot assert sufficient harm to the health of its citizens as a basis for interference.

II. Essay Question:

What were the basic principles on which the Constitution was framed? What is meant by the "separation of power" and "checks and balances" in the Federal Government?

Chapter 8
Contract Law

Overview

A contract is a legally enforceable agreement between two or more parties where each assumes a legal obligation that must be completed. Legal issues involving contracts arise most often when one party fails to perform the legal obligation it has agreed to do. When a party breaches a contract by failing to perform, the other party can often sue for money damages, or, in some limited cases, can ask the court to force the other party to perform as promised.

Simply put, a contract is an agreement between two or more people or entities that creates a legal duty or responsibility. Entities entering a contract might include individual people, companies, corporations and organizations, but there are a few conditions that must be met for the contract to hold water in the courtroom. Specifically, a legally enforceable contract must contain some key ingredients:

- Offer and acceptance
- Consideration
- A meeting of the minds regarding the legal subject of the contract (e.g., both parties intend on the purchase and sale of a car for an agreed price)
- Legal capacity (competency)

Here's a further breakdown:

- Subject: A contract needs to have definite terms that spell out all the details and a clearly defined offer. These specifics are referred to as the contract's subject. Consider purchasing a used car from a dealer. The sales agreement is the subject and likely includes information such as price, warranty, and transfer of title or ownership.

- Consideration: There needs to be a valid cause to enter the contract. Consideration of a contract is the reason, motive, price or whatever objective there is to have a contract. In many cases, the consideration is money, but it also might include acceptance of liability or a promise not to do something. A non-disclosure agreement (NDA), for example, contractually rules out sharing information that might otherwise be fair game. This is often established during the meeting of the minds.

- Competency: Everyone involved must be competent. This means that a person who is severely mentally disabled can't enter an enforceable contract. Additionally, contracts entered by minors usually can't be enforced until they reach age 18 or whatever the majority age is where they reside.

Examples of Contracts

It's not hard to find examples of contracts in everyday life. Many aspects of daily life involve contracts, including buying property, applying for a car loan, signing employment-related paperwork, and agreeing to terms and conditions when buying products and services or using computer software. In fact, you enter contracts daily without even thinking about it. You are entering an implied contract every time you make a purchase at your favorite store, order a meal at a restaurant, receive treatment from your doctor or even checkout a book at your library. Other examples of contracts are more concrete or express. You're entering a contract when you drop your car off at the shop for service, accept a new job or sign a check.

No matter whether you're running a small business, applying for a job, leasing an apartment or swiping a credit card to pay for lunch, contracts are a part of life, and being well-informed about contract basics can help you be confident when making all kinds of legal decisions.

Contracts and the Law

A business contract is one of the most common legal transactions you will be

Chapter 8
Contract Law

involved in when running a business. No matter what type of business you run, having an understanding of contract law is a key to creating sound business agreements that will be legally enforceable in the event that a dispute arises. The following is a discussion of the law of contracts.

Laws that Govern Contracts

At its most basic level, a contract is:

- An agreement
- That is legally enforceable

Contracts are usually governed and enforced by the laws in the state where the agreement was made. Depending upon the subject matter of the agreement (i.e. sale of goods, property lease), a contract may be governed by one of two types of state law:

The Common Law. The majority of contracts (i.e. employment agreements, leases, general business agreements) are controlled by the state's common law — a tradition-based but constantly evolving set of laws that is mostly judge-made, from court decisions over the years.

The Uniform Commercial Code (UCC). The common law does not control contracts that are primarily for the sale of goods. Contracts for the sale of goods are controlled by the Uniform Commercial Code (UCC), a standardized collection of guidelines that govern the law of commercial transactions. Most states have adopted the UCC in whole or in part, making the UCC's provisions part of the state's codified laws pertaining to the sale of goods.

Creation of a Contract

In the eyes of the law, a contract arises when there is an offer, acceptance of that offer, and sufficient "consideration" to make the contract valid:

An offer allows the person or business to whom the offer is made to reasonably expect that the offering party is willing to be bound by the offer on the terms proposed. The terms of an offer must be definite and certain.

An acceptance is a clear expression of the accepting party's agreement to the terms of

the offer.

Consideration is a legal term given to the bargained-for exchange between the parties to the contract — something of some value passing from one party to the other. Each party to the contract will gain some benefit from the agreement, and will incur some obligation in exchange for that benefit.

Types of Contracts

The law recognizes contracts that arise in a number of different ways:

A bilateral contract is the type of agreement most people think of as a traditional contract — a mutual exchange of promises among the parties. In a bilateral contract, each party may be considered as both making a promise, and being the beneficiary of a promise.

A unilateral contract is one in which the offer requests performance rather than a promise from the person accepting the offer. A unilateral contract is formed when the requested act is complete. A classic example of a unilateral contract is a "reward" advertisement, offering payment of money in exchange for information or the return of something of value.

An express contract is formed by explicit written or spoken language, expressing the agreement and its terms.

An implied contract is formed by behavior of the parties that clearly shows an intent to enter into an agreement, even if no obvious offer and/or acceptance were clearly expressed in words or writing.

Written vs. Oral, Implied vs. Express

Contracts can also be the source of legal disputes when they are not written clearly. Parties who misunderstand the terms of their agreement may sue each other and have a court settle the argument. Additionally, when a company signs a contract and later goes out of business or is unable to fulfill its promises, the other party may have to pursue legal action in civil or bankruptcy court to obtain relief.

Contracts can be oral or written, implied or express, depending on what the situation at hand calls for. While an oral contract-basically a verbal agreement made out loud in conversation — might suffice in some instances, most enforceable contracts should be expressly written into a tangible document.

Contracts can also be implied or express. Written contracts are generally considered express, which means the subject is clearly stated and all details are included. Consider a car rental contract. When you're renting a car, you agree to pay a certain amount for the use of the car over a specific period of time and agree to pay certain, predetermined fees in case the car is returned late or in different condition than it is received.

Other situations where an express, written contract will likely be required include:

- The transfer or sale of real estate, such as when selling a house or land, or perhaps if leasing office space or an apartment;
- The sale of goods or services worth more than $500, such as when hiring someone to put a new roof on your house or when buying a car;
- An agreement for something that will require more than a year to perform, for example a year-long maintenance contract for your home or a non-disclosure agreement that will last at least 12 months.

On the other hand, implied contracts are just as they sound — the details are assumed. Consider ordering a latte at your favorite coffee shop. You just entered an oral contract with the barista taking your order, even though the subject wasn't clearly verbalized or expressly explained. By ordering the drink, it was assumed that you were willing to pay for it.

Will Your Contract Be Enforced Under the Law?

If you are involved in a business agreement, one of the first things to determine is whether the promise or agreement at issue will be considered an enforceable contract under the law. While contracts usually involve promises to do something (or refrain from doing something), not all promises are contracts. How does the law determine which promises are enforceable contracts and which are not?

Is the Agreement a Contract?

In a dispute, the court must initially determine whether the agreement constitutes a contract or not. In order for an agreement to be considered a valid contract, one party must make an offer and the other party must accept it. There must be a bargained-for exchange of promises, meaning that something of value must be given in return for a promise (called "consideration"). In addition, the terms of a contract must be sufficiently defined for a court to enforce them.

Enforcement and Contract Defenses

If a court determines that a contract exists, it must decide whether that contract should be enforced. There are a number of reasons why a court might not enforce a contract, called defenses to the contract, which are designed to protect people from unfairness in the bargaining process, or in the substance of the contract itself.

If there is a valid defense to a contract, it may be voidable, meaning the party to the contract who was the victim of the unfairness may be able to cancel or revoke the contract. In some instances, the unfairness is so extreme that the contract is considered void, in other words, a court will declare that no contract was ever formed. What are some of the reasons a court might refuse to enforce a contract?

1. Capacity to Contract

In order to be bound by a contract, a person must have the legal ability to form a contract in the first place, called capacity to contract. A person who is unable, due to age or mental impairment, to understand what she is doing when she signs a contract may lack capacity to contract. For example, a person under legal guardianship due to a mental defect completely lacks the capacity to contract. Any contract signed by that person is void.

A minor generally cannot form an enforceable contract. A contract entered into by a minor may be canceled by the minor or their guardian. After reaching the age of majority (18 in most states), a person still has a reasonable period of time to cancel a contract entered into as a minor. If the contract is not canceled within a reasonable period of time (determined by state law), it will be considered ratified, making it binding and enforceable.

Courts are usually not very sympathetic to people who claim they were intoxicated when they signed a contract. Generally a court will only allow the contract to be voided if the other party to the contract knew about the intoxication and took advantage of the person, or if the person was somehow involuntarily drugged.

2. Undue Influence, Duress, Misrepresentation

Coercion, threats, false statements, or improper persuasion by one party to a contract can void the contract. The defenses of duress, misrepresentation, and undue influence address these situations:

- Duress: A party must show that assent or agreement to the contract was induced by a serious threat of unlawful or wrongful action, and that she had no reasonable alternative but to agree to the contract.
- Undue Influence: Undue influence is often defined as unfair persuasion by a person who, because of his or her relation to the victim, is justifiably assumed by the victim to be one who will not act in a manner that is inconsistent with the victim's welfare.
- Misrepresentation: A misrepresentation may be a false statement of fact; the deliberate withholding of information which a party has a duty to disclose; or an action that conceals a fact (for example, painting over water damage when selling a house).

3. Unconscionability

The unconscionability defense is concerned with the fairness of both the process of contract formation and the substantive terms of the contract. When the terms of a contract are oppressive or when the bargaining process or resulting terms shock the conscience of the court, the court may strike down the contract as unconscionable.

A court will look at a number of factors in determining if a contract is unconscionable. If there is a gross inequality of bargaining power, so the weaker party to the contract has no meaningful choice as to the terms, and the resulting contract is unreasonably favorable to the stronger party, there may be a valid claim of unconscionability. A court will also look at whether one party is uneducated or illiterate, whether that party had the opportunity to ask questions or consult an attorney, and whether the price of the goods or services under the contract is excessive.

4. Public Policy and Illegality

Rather than protecting the parties to a contract as other contract defenses do, the defenses of illegality and violation of public policy seek to protect the public welfare and the integrity of the courts by refusing to enforce certain types of contracts. Contracts to engage in illegal or immoral conduct would not be enforced by the courts.

5. Mistake

In order to cancel a contract for mistake, both parties must have made a mistake as to a basic assumption on which the contract was based, the mistake must have a material effect upon the agreed exchange, and must relate to facts existing at the time the contract is made. In addition, the party seeking to avoid the contract must not have contractually assumed the risk of mistake.

Parties sometimes attempt to claim mistake as a defense to a contract when they have failed to read the contract and later become aware of terms they dislike. Failure to read the contract is not a defense. A person who signs a contract is presumed to know what it says, and is bound to the terms she would have known about, had she read the contract.

Breach of Contract and Lawsuits

In a perfect world, agreements would be entered into, both sides would benefit and be pleased with the outcome, and no disputes would arise. But in the real world of business, delays happen, financial problems can crop up, and other unexpected events can occur to hinder or even prevent a successful contract from being carried out.

What Is a Breach of Contract?

A business contract creates certain obligations that are to be fulfilled by the parties who entered into the agreement. Legally, one party's failure to fulfill any of its contractual obligations is known as a "breach" of the contract. Depending on the specifics, a breach can occur when a party fails to perform on time, does not perform in accordance with the terms of the agreement, or does not perform at all. Accordingly, a breach of contract will usually be categorized as either "material" or "immaterial" for purposes of determining the appropriate legal solution or "remedy" for the breach.

Breach of Contract: An Example

Let's assume that R. Runner contracts with Acme Anvils for the purchase of some of its products, for delivery by the following Monday evening. If Acme delivers the Anvils to Runner on the following Tuesday morning, such a breach of the contract would likely be deemed immaterial, and R. Runner would likely not be entitled to money damages (unless he could show that he was somehow damaged by the late delivery).

However, assume now that the contract stated clearly and explicitly that "time is of the essence" and the anvils MUST be delivered on Monday. If Acme delivers after Monday, its breach of contract would likely be deemed "material", and R. Runner's damages would be presumed, making Acme's liability for the breach more severe, and likely relieving Runner of the duty to pay for the anvils under the contract.

What Happens After a Contract Is Breached?

When a breach of contract occurs or is alleged, one or both of the parties may wish to have the contract enforced on its terms, or may try to recover for any financial harm caused by the alleged breach.

If a dispute over a contract arises and informal attempts at resolution fail, the most common next step is a lawsuit. If the amount at issue is below a certain dollar figure (usually $3,000 to $7,500 depending on the state), the parties may be able to resolve the issue in small claims court.

Courts and formal lawsuits are not the only option for people and businesses involved in contract disputes. The parties can agree to have a mediator review a contract dispute, or may agree to binding arbitration of a contract dispute. These out-of-court options are two methods of "alternative dispute resolution".

Remedies for a Breach of Contract

When an individual or business breaches a contract, the other party to the agreement is entitled to relief (or a "remedy") under the law. The main remedies for a breach of contract are:

- Damages,
- Specific Performance, or
- Cancellation and Restitution

Damages

The payment of damages — payment in one form or another — is the most common remedy for a breach of contract. There are many kinds of damages, including the following:

Compensatory damages aim to put the non-breaching party in the position that they had been if the breach had not occurred.

Punitive damages are payments that the breaching party must make, above and beyond the point that would fully compensate the non-breaching party. Punitive damages are meant to punish a wrongful party for particularly wrongful acts, and are rarely awarded in the business contracts setting.

Nominal damages are token damages awarded when a breach occurred, but no actual money loss to the non-breaching party was proven.

Liquidated damages are specific damages that were previously identified by the parties in the contract itself, in the event that the contract is breached. Liquidated damages should be a reasonable estimate of actual damages that might result from a breach.

Specific Performance

If damages are inadequate as a legal remedy, the non-breaching party may seek an alternative remedy called specific performance. Specific performance is best described as the breaching party's court-ordered performance of duty under the contract. Specific performance may be used as a remedy for breach of contract if the subject matter of the agreement is rare or unique, and damages would not suffice to place the non-breaching party in as good a position as they would have been had the breach not occurred.

Cancellation and Restitution

A non-breaching party may cancel the contract and sue for restitution if the non-breaching party has given a benefit to the breaching party. "Restitution" as a contract remedy means that the non-breaching party is put back in the position it was in prior to the breach, while "cancellation" of the contract voids the contract and relieves all parties of any obligation under the agreement.

Exercises

I. Multiple-choice Questions:

Questions 1–2 are based on the following fact situation:

Oboe owned a large apartment complex. She contracted with Piper to paint the porches for $5,000. The contract was specifically made subject to Oboe's good faith approval of the work. Piper finished painting the porches. Oboe inspected the job and believed in good faith that Piper had done a bad job. Piper demanded payment, but Oboe told Piper that the paint job was poor and refused to pay. Piper pleaded that he was desperately in need of money. Oboe told Piper, "Okay, I've got a soft heart; I'll give you a check for $4,500, provided that you repainted the porches." Piper reluctantly agreed, and Oboe gave Piper a check in the amount of $4,500. Piper went to his bank, indorsed the check "under protest, Piper," and deposited the check in his account. Piper never returned to repaint the porches.

Oboe sues Piper for specific performance, demanding that Piper repaint the porches. Piper counterclaims for $500, which Piper believes he is still owed on his contract to paint the porches.

1. Will Piper prevail in his claim for $500 against Oboe?

    A. Yes, because he indorsed the check "under protest".

    B. Yes, but only if he repaints the porches.

    C. Yes, because he performed the contract by painting the porches the first time.

    D. No, even if he repaints the porches.

2. Will Oboe prevail in her action for specific performance?

   A. Yes, because there has been a novation.

   B. Yes, because she honestly believed Piper did a poor job.

   C. No, because Oboe had a preexisting legal duty to pay Piper.

   D. No, because Piper's services are not unique.

3. On September 4, the *Metropolis Sentinel-Herald-Examiner* printed an advertisement paid for by Mortimer's Mechanics, an auto repair business, that included the following statement:"Special! Wednesday, September 5 only! Anyone ordering our regular complete four-cylinder engine tune-up, at the regular price of $249.95 (plus parts and lubricants), will receive in addition to the tune-up, at absolutely no additional cost, his or her choice of either (1) an all expenses paid bus trip to Fresno, California, complete with motel accommodations for three days and two nights, or (2) a set of Singu knives, with a knife and scissors sharpener, plus a fruit and vegetable peeler!" The next day , Mortimer's was inundated with tune-up customers, and by 3:15 p.m. it had exhausted its entire supply of Singu knives and accessories. At 3:17 p.m., Nancy pulled her import sedan into Mortimer's service bays, jumped out, and said to the mechanic on duty, "Give me your complete four-cylinder engine tune-up plus a set of those wonderful Singu knives, plus accessories!" The mechanic, knowing that no Singu knives were available, briefly tried to talk Nancy into a trip to Fresno, which proved unavailing. He then looked quickly under Nancy's hood and pronounced her engine "in tip top condition — no tune-up needed here". Finally, when Nancy insisted that her car had been burning a quart of oil a week and frequently lost power going downhill, the mechanic stated that there was not enough time left before closing to complete the tune-up, and that Nancy should try Mike's Motors down the street. In fact, it would have taken about four hours to complete a tune-up on Nancy's car, and Mortimer's closed at 5 p.m. that day, its regular closing time. Nancy drove home without a tune-up and without any Singu knives.

Chapter 8
Contract Law

What is Mortimer's strongest defense against a breach of contract action brought by Nancy?

    A. A tune-up of Nancy's car could not have been completed in the time available before the shop closed.

    B. The advertisement in the newspaper was merely an invitation to offer, and Mortimer's had the right to refuse to accept any offer made.

    C. Sine Nancy never expressly tendered payment of the $249.95, there was no acceptance of Mortimer's offer.

    D. Nancy's unwillingness to travel to Fresno indicated lack of good faith on her part.

4. XYZ Corp., a general contractor, wished to bid on a construction project and solicited bids from a variety of subcontractors. Four electrical subcontractors, Alpha, Beta, Gamma, and Delta, submitted bids to XYZ. The bids were as follows: Alpha—$75,000; Beta—$85,000; Gamma—$90,000; and Delta—$95,000.

As XYZ was making out its bid on the construction project based upon the low bid submitted by Alpha, XYZ's president called Alpha and told him, "We won't be able to do it with your present bid, but if you can shave off $5,000, I'm sure that the numbers will be there for us to get that project." Alpha responded, "No way! In fact, that bid we submitted was based on a $15,000 error; we can't do it for a cent less than $90,000." XYZ lost the construction job and subsequently sued Alpha.

Alpha is liable for:

    A. Breach of contract, because the mistake was not so unreasonably obvious as to make acceptance of Alpha's bid unconscionable.

    B. Breach of contract, because the mistake was unilateral.

    C. Nothing, because Alpha rejected XYZ's counteroffer.

    D. Nothing, because even though Alpha lacked authority to renege on its bid, XYZ suffered no damages since no bidder was willing to do the work for $70,000.

Questions 5-6 are based on the following fact situation:

Osman, a homeowner, wanted Khaled, a contractor, to make some improvements on Osman's house. They made a written contract whereby Khaled would do the improvement for $5,000. Shortly after the contract was signed, Khaled told Osman, "When the job is finished, give the money to my daughter, Nadja. Nadja is getting married soon and I want her to have a nice wedding present from me." Nadja was aware that Khaled made this statement to Osman. Nadja married, but soon thereafter Khaled told Osman, "Pay me the $5,000 for the home improvement job. I think my son-in-law may have a gambling problem and that the money would probably just be used to play the ponies."

5. Against whom, if anyone, may Nadja enforce the agreement to pay her $5,000?

   A. Osman.

   B. Khaled.

   C. Either Osman or Khaled.

   D. Neither Osman nor Khaled.

6. What is the best argument in favor of Nadja's being able to enforce a contract for $5,000 in her favor?

   A. Statute of Frauds.

   B. Parol evidence rule.

   C. Nadja was an intended third-party beneficiary.

   D. Nadja married in reliance on a promise.

7. Phlo was looking for an apartment to rent, and she was interested in a particular apartment because of its very distinctive features in a building managed by Deed's Real Estate Company, but she was also interested in a number of other apartments in town. Because she wanted some time to make up her mind, she contacted Deeds, president of Deed's Real Estate, and asked him to reserve her right to rent the particular apartment. After some discussion they made the following agreement:

Phlo is to pay Deeds $200 on June 1. Upon timely receipt by Deeds of Phlo's payment, Phlo shall have the right to inform Deeds that she wishes to rent the apartment any time on or before July 1. If Phlo fails to notify Deeds that she wants the apartment on or before July 1, Deeds shall keep the $200. However, if Phlo does notify Deeds that she desires the apartment, Deeds has 15 days in which to accept or reject Phlo's application. If the application is accepted, Deeds will apply the $200 to the first month's rent. If the application is rejected, Deeds will refund the $200 to Phlo.

Phlo paid Deeds $200.

On June 9, Deeds rented the apartment to Tony. On June 1, Phlo told Deeds that she wanted the apartment. Deeds told Phlo, "The apartment has been rented; here's your $200 back."

Assuming that Phlo wants the court to compel Deeds to rent her apartment, and that the court determines that Deeds has breached his agreement with Phlo, would it be appropriate for the court to order Deeds to rent the apartment to Phlo?

    A. Yes, but only because Deeds should not have rented the apartment to Tony before July 2.

    B. Yes, but only because Deeds should not have rented the apartment to Tony before July 16.

    C. No, because the contract was unconscionable.

    D. No, because Phlo has not suffered irreparable harm.

8. Bernasie, the sole proprietor of Bernaise Distributors, a food service and food brokerage concern, entered into oral negotiations with Hollandaise, president and chief executive officer of Holsauce, a corporation that manufactured gourmet food products for restaurants and select retail outlets. Bernaise wished to secure an exclusive distributorship for Holsauce products in the six New England states. At the end of the first stage of oral negotiations between Bernaise and Hollandaise, both parties agreed on the major points of their arrangement, but a few points of disagreements remained. Both, however, were anxious to begin distribution of Holsauce products in New England and so Hollandaise assured Bernaise, "Don't worry about it; we'll work there things

out." Assuming from this that he would be the New England distributor for Holsauce, Bernaise went out and leased larger facilities, bought a number of trucks, hired 30 new workers, and expanded his management staff by hiring, among others, an experienced distribution manager who was given a two-year contract with a high salary. Shortly after Bernasie had done these things, Hollandaise informed him that Bechamel Distributors, and not Bernaise, would receive the New England distributorship.

If Bernaise prevails in a suit against Holsauce and Hollandaise, it will most likely because the court applies which of the following theories?

A. Implied-in-fact contract.

B. Promissory estoppel.

C. Unjust enrichment.

D. Quasi-contract.

Questions 9-10 are based on the following fact situation:

Richelle owns and operates an electronic equipment store. On December 6, Richelle sent a letter to Morris, a manufacturer of small computers, asking for the price on a specific type of computer, the Morristronic 606. Morris replied by letter, enclosing a catalog giving the prices and describing all of his available computers, along with various accessories. Morris's letter stated that the terms of sale were cash within 30 days of delivery. On December 14, Richelle ordered the Morristronic 606. She enclosed a check for the amount of the listed price of the Morristronic 606, which was $4,000.

Immediately upon receipt of Richelle's order and check, Morris sent Richelle a letter indicating that there had been a mistake in the catalog as to the price of the Morristronic 606, which should have quoted the price as $4,300. Morris went on to state that they would ship the computer to Richelle if Richelle would pay the additional $300 upon receipt of the machine.

On December 31, Richelle replied: "Ship me the Morristronic 606 and I'll pay the additional $300, but it must be delivered on or before January 19 as it's promised to a customer for January 20."

Morris shipped the Morristronic 606, but made no specific reply to Richelle's December 31 letter.

The machine did not actually arrive to Richelle until February 14. Richelle accepted the computer from the carrier, but promptly wrote a letter to Morris, stating: "Since you didn't deliver the computer on time, I'm not going to pay the extra $300. I'm also putting you on notice that if I lose any money because of your late shipment, I'm going to hold you liable for that amount."

Richelle delivered the computer to her customer on February 15. The customer accepted the Morristronic 606 and paid for it.

9. Richelle's letter of December 14 in which the $4,000 check was enclosed can be characterized as:

    A. Not an acceptance, because Morris's first communication stated terms calling for cash within 30 days after delivery.

    B. Not an acceptance, because of the mistake as to price.

    C. Not an acceptance, because Morris's first communication did not constitute an offer.

    D. An acceptance.

10. Assume for purposes of this question and the questions following that a contract arose on December 14. Is Richelle's promise to pay $300 more than the price listed in the catalog enforceable?

    A. No, because Morris did not ship the computer so that it would arrive at Richelle's store by January 19.

    B. No, because it was only a counteroffer, which Morris did not accept.

    C. No, because had a preexisting legal obligation to ship the computer to Richelle.

    D. Yes, it is enforceable.

II. Essay Question:

At the wedding of Tom and Mary, Tom's father, Frank, told them that he wanted them to live with him and to care for him for the rest of his life. He said, "If you agree to do this, I will deliver to you, within a year, a deed to my home." Tom and Mary told Frank they accepted his offer and promised to look after Frank with loving care in Frank's home. They immediately moved in with him. Soon after moving into Frank's home, Tom and Mary used their own money to add a new wing to the house, pay the outstanding property taxes, and pay off an existing mortgage of $25,000. One year after Tom and Mary moved into the home, Tom reminded Frank of his promise to convey the property to them. Frank became angry, refused to execute the deed, and ordered Tom and Mary to leave the premises.

Tom and Mary consult you concerning the rights and the remedies that may be available to them.

How would you advise them? Discuss.

Chapter 9
Tort Law

A tort is an act or omission that gives rise to injury or harm to another and amounts to a civil wrong for which courts impose liability. In the context of torts, "injury" describes the invasion of any legal right, whereas "harm" describes a loss or detriment in fact that an individual suffers.

Overview

The primary aims of tort law are to provide relief to injured parties for harms caused by others, to impose liability on parties responsible for the harm, and to deter others from committing harmful acts. Torts can shift the burden of loss from the injured party to the party who is at fault or better suited to bear the burden of the loss. Typically, a party seeking redress through tort law will ask for damages in the form of monetary compensation. Less common remedies include injunction and restitution.

The boundaries of tort law are defined by common law and state statutory law. Judges, in interpreting the language of statutes, have wide latitude in determining which actions qualify as legally cognizable wrongs, which defenses may override any given claim, and the appropriate measure of damages. Although tort law varies by state, many courts utilize the Restatement of Torts (2nd) as an influential guide.

Torts fall into three general categories: intentional torts (e.g., intentionally hitting a person); negligent torts (e.g., causing an accident by failing to obey traffic rules); and strict liability torts (e.g., liability for making and selling defective products — see Products Liability). Intentional torts are wrongs that the defendant knew or should have known would result through his or her actions or omissions. Negligent torts occur when the defendant's actions were unreasonably unsafe. Unlike intentional and negligent torts, strict liability torts do not depend on the degree of care that the defendant used. Rather, in strict liability cases, courts focus on whether a particular result or harm manifested.

There are numerous specific torts including trespass, assault, battery, negligence, products liability, and intentional infliction of emotional distress. There are also separate areas of tort law including nuisance, defamation, invasion of privacy, and a category of economic torts.

How Are Torts Classified?

Torts may be classified into three broad categories:
- Intentional torts such as battery
- Unintentional torts such as negligence in a slip and fall case
- Strict liability torts such as those involving ultrahazardous materials that are dangerous in and of themselves

Torts are categorized under civil laws, rather than criminal laws. This means that some torts may involve conduct that is not necessary illegal, but causes harm to another person. However, some tort cases may involve an overlap with criminal laws (such as assault).

What Are Some Examples of Torts?

- Some common examples of torts include:
- Negligence-related claims
- Civil assault/civil battery
- Wrongful death claims
- Trespassing
- Products liability and dangerous products
- Intentional inflection of emotional distress

Probably the most common type of tort lawsuit is negligence. In order to prove negligence, the victim needs to prove that the defendant breached a duty of care owed to them, and that the breach was the cause of their injuries or losses.

For instance, if the defendant had a duty to keep their shop floor clean, but failed to do so, the plaintiff may be able to sue them if they were injured due to a slip on the dirty shop floor.

Joint Tortfeasors

Joint tortfeasors, seen as equally liable for the committing of a tort, usually can be combined under one indictment. This is known as a "joinder of defendants". In a case similar to this, one significant reasoning behind its institution besides the commonality that the defendants share in their joint action, is that of "judicial economy". In reference to this term, the court is making the decision that placing all defendants under one sole indictment will be the most appropriate option in terms of efficiency and, ultimately, cost-effectiveness for the judicial system itself. Due to the mounting quantities of cases arising daily, this practice is employed as a worthwhile alternative, especially when an occasion such as that of joint tortfeasors comes about.

Intentional Torts

A "tort" is some kind of wrongful act that causes harm to someone else. This definition covers a wide range of actions, and the legal field of torts is split up into many different subcategories. One of the ways torts are split up is by the mental state of the person that does the wrongdoing. When the person that acts wrongly actually intends to perform the action, it becomes what is known as an "intentional tort".

The easiest example of an intentional tort is a punch to the face. In that case, the actor intended to make a fist and slam it into his victims face, and the actor also intended to harm his victim. However, the person who performs an intentional tort need not intend the harm. For example, if you surprise someone with an unstable heart condition, and the fright causes that person to have a heart attack, you commit an intentional tort, even if you did not intend to scare that person into a heart attack.

Typical Intentional Torts

Battery: This is the legal term for hitting someone, which comes from the verb "to batter". This covers a surprising range of activities, including sending projectiles into someone else's body, as in firing a gun.

Assault: An assault is an attempted battery, or threatening injury when no battery takes place.

False Imprisonment: The technical definition of false imprisonment is "confinement without legal authority". Generally, no one is allowed to restrict another person's movement against her will. There are two major exceptions to this. Police generally have authority to detain people they reasonably suspect of crimes. The other exception is called the "shopkeeper's privilege", which allows shopkeepers to keep people they suspect of shoplifting for a reasonable amount of time.

Intentional Infliction of Emotional Distress: This is a particularly difficult tort to prove in court. In order to prove a claim of intentional infliction of emotional distress, a plaintiff has to prove that someone else engaged in extreme or outrageous conduct, with the intent of frightening someone else, and caused severe emotional distress or bodily harm.

Fraud: This is the legal term for lying to someone. In order to succeed in a suit for fraud, plaintiffs generally have to prove that the speaker knew that he was saying something false, that the other person would believe him, that the other person would rely on that information, and that the other person would be harmed by relying on this information.

Defamation: The term defamation refers to an abusive attack on a person's character or to make false claims against someone in order to damage their good name. There are two forms of defamation that can be used: libel and slander. An unreasonable person may abuse the right of privilege in order to commit defamation against another person. Slander and libel involve intentionally making a false statement that ends up damaging the reputation of another. Slander involves verbal statements, while libel deals with published written statements. (Note: slander and libel, which are different types of defamation, are sometimes referred to as "quasi-intentional" torts because it isn't always necessary to establish the mindset of the defendant in these kinds of claims.)

Invasion of Privacy: The exact nature of invasion of privacy varies by state, but there are generally four types of invasions of privacy. Invasion of solitude, in which someone

Chapter 9
Tort Law

interferes with someone else's right to be left alone; Public disclosure of private facts; False light, in which someone publishes not true, but not defamatory facts about someone else; and appropriation, which is the unauthorized use of someone else's likeness for profit.

Trespass: Trespass comes in two forms: trespass to land, and trespass to chattel, or personal property. In either case, trespass means using the property without permission of the owner.

Conversion: Conversion is when someone takes someone else's property and "converts" it to their own. In the criminal world, this is known as stealing.

Intentional Torts vs. Crimes

Many intentional torts are also crimes. The difference between the two is subtle but very important. A tort — intentional or otherwise — can result in a civil suit. This is a lawsuit brought by one private citizen against another. The loser of a civil suit may be found "liable", and can be subject to a judgment ordering the payment of monetary damages to the prevailing party. Even wrongful death or battery cases involve monetary damages.

Crimes, on the other hand, are very different. Criminal proceedings are brought by the state (meaning the government, not just a particular state) against a party accused of violating a criminal statute. Criminal cases are not about damages. They are about protecting the public welfare and punishing the guilty for their transgressions.

Battery is a prime example of an act that is often both an intentional tort and a crime. State and federal law classifies battery as a crime. A party accused of battery can stand trial, and if a jury of their peers finds that all the elements of criminal battery have been met, and the person is guilty of battery beyond a reasonable doubt, incarceration can occur. Regardless of the outcome of criminal proceedings, the battered party may file a civil suit seeking monetary damages from the accused.

One of the most famous illustrations of an intentional tort that is also a crime is the OJ Simpson trial. OJ Simpson was famously found not guilty of murder. However, subsequent to criminal proceedings, the families of the victims sued Simpson in civil court for wrongful death. Civil trials have a lower burden of proof than criminal trials, and as a result Simpson was held liable for the victims' deaths and was ordered to pay millions of dollars in damages to their families.

Unintentional Torts

Negligence is the unintentional failure to live up to the community's ideal of reasonable care, having nothing to do with moral care. An individual who has behaved negligently is one who has not lived up to a certain imputed duty or obligation to conform to a certain standard of conduct for the protection of others against unreasonable risk of harm. However, if the defendant could not reasonably foresee any injury as the result of a certain conduct, there is no negligence and thus no liability.

Negligence: Standard of Conduct

There are certain elements that are required to prove that a defendant acted negligently. There is a specific code of conduct which all people are expected to follow and there is a duty of the public to act in a certain way, which reduces the risk of harm to others. Negligence can only be claimed by an injured plaintiff, whose interests have actually been interfered with. This portrays that a plaintiff must prove his injuries, and prove that they were caused by the defendant. This proximate cause is the link between the defendant's actions and the plaintiff's injuries. There is a statute of limitations in negligence cases, however, there are several rules, such as discovery and continuing negligence, which may excuse a plaintiff from the statute of limitations.

Negligence Proof

The necessity for a negligence case to be tried in a court of law is essential and evident. Tort law, like any other law, is tough to decide upon when an enforcement or violation issue arises, and is furthermore tedious. In negligence cases, a court appoints a jury to make a decision upon a case based on the direct or circumstantial evidence that is available to them. The burden of proof a plaintiff faces in a case, relates to four elements of proof that must exist in order for them to be able to prove that a negligent act not only existed, but the fact that the act by a defendant, led to the injury sustained by the plaintiff. The elements necessary for a cause of action under the tort of negligence are (1) a duty or standard of care recognized by law, (2) a breach of that duty or failure to exercise reasonable care, (3) causation resulting from said breach resulting in (4) some harm to the plaintiff. No cause of action in negligence is recognized if any of these elements are absent from the case.

Malpractice

Malpractice, or mala praxis, applies to professional negligence that takes different forms in different fields. Professionals are believed to have a higher degree of knowledge, skills, or experience than a reasonable person and are consequently required to use that capacity. Professionals are required to act as would a reasonably skilled, prudent, competent, and experienced member of that same profession.

Negligence Per se

There is no actionable negligence unless there is a legal duty of care. However, in the case of legislative acts, plaintiffs must merely establish that they are within the limited class of individuals intended to be protected by the statute. Once it is decided that a statute is applicable, most courts hold that an unexcused violation is conclusive as to the issue of negligence. Thus, it is negligence per se for one to violate a speeding ordinance, and the issue of negligence does not go to a jury, nor are issues of causation relevant. The violation of the ordinance is proof of negligence in itself.

Duty to Aid

While as a general rule under the common law there is no duty to aid or protect, courts have ruled that when a special relationship is found to exist, there comes with that a duty to aid or protect another. Such a relationship exists in regard to parent and child, lifeguard and swimmer, bartender and patron, counselor and camper, and many, many others. In addition, if one puts another in peril, assumes a duty through contract, or begins to assist and then backs out, one has a duty to aid and if breached, an action for negligence could and likely would ensue. Thus, although persons seeing another in distress may have no obligation to be Good Samaritans, if they choose to do so, they incur the duty of exercising ordinary care.

Owners & Occupiers

The ordinary principles of negligence do not govern occupiers' liability to those entering their premises. Thus, the duty the land occupier or possessor in title owes to a trespasser is less than the duty the possessor owes to the general public under the ordinary principles of negligence. The amount of duty owed by possessors in terms of importance is first to (1) invitees, then (2) licensees, and finally the very lowest of duties is owed to (3) trespassers.

An invitee is either a public invitee or a business visitor. A public invitee is a member of the public who enters land for the purpose for which the land is held open to the public, for example, a customer who enters a store. A business visitor enters land for a purpose directly or indirectly connected with business dealings with the possessor of title. A landowner owes the invitee a duty to exercise ordinary care under the usual principles of negligence liability.

One who enters or remains on land by virtue of the possessor's implied or express consent is a licensee, for example, a door-to-door salesman or a social guest, such as a neighbor entering the property for a purely social purpose. Police officers and firefighters are also usually classified as licensees. While a possessor of land generally owes the licensee only the duty to refrain from willful or wanton misconduct, the possessor is under a duty to give warning to licensees of known dangers.

A trespasser is one who enters and remains on the land of another without the possessor's expressed or implied consent. Licensees or invitees may become trespassers when they venture into an area where they are not invited or expected to venture, or if they remain on the premises for longer than necessary. The only duty that is owed to a trespasser by an occupier of the land is to refrain from willful or wanton misconduct. However, in regard to an adult trespasser whose presence has been discovered or who habitually intrudes on a limited area, there is still owed a duty of reasonable care. In relation to a child trespasser, who may be enticed to enter upon a property to swim in a pool or jump on a trampoline, there is also owed a duty of reasonable care.

Proximate Cause

The name given to the direct cause of an accident, or incident leading to injury, is referred to as "proximate". The term proximate has long been known to mean near, or in the vicinity of, not actual. For the plaintiff to support a negligence action there must be a reasonable connection between the negligent act of the defendant and the damage suffered by the plaintiff. For tort liability, however, proof of factual causation is not enough. Tort liability is predicated on the existence of proximate cause, which consists of both: (1) causation in fact, and (2) foreseeability. A plaintiff must prove that his or her injuries were the actual or factual result of the defendant's actions. Causation in fact may be established directly or indirectly, but there still must be foreseeability.

But for Test

Courts normally use a "but for" test to establish causation in fact. But for the defendant's alarm not going off, the defendant would not have gotten into the accident with the plaintiff. In addition to this element, of course, there must also be a foreseeability element to fully establish proximate cause. Thus, the question before the court in a negligence case is whether the conduct has been so significant and important a cause that the defendant should be legally responsible. In most instances, then, causation in fact alone will not suffice for liability.

Limited Duty

In legal terms, duty is seen as an individuals obligation to act in a manner conducive to the well being of everyone around them, such as the prevention of any "foreseeable injury to a victim". To account for the many factual variations that will inevitably occur with accidents and instances of negligence, the law has found that for an appropriate and legitimate allowance for causation, there must be some boundary set for the consequences of an act. Therefore, an individual is only responsible for those consequences that are reasonably foreseeable, and will be relieved of liability for injuries that are not reasonably related to the negligent conduct. We found that the court, in West v. East Tennessee

Pioneer Oil Co., 172 S.W.3d 545 (Sup. Ct. Tenn. 2005) ruled that a duty of care was created when employees at a gas station allowed and assisted a clearly inebriated customer to gas up his car, which led to a serious accident shortly thereafter. The court reasoned that the foreseeable probability of harm vastly outweighed the burden or duty that the court was placing on the defendants, which was to merely to refrain from allowing and assisting the motorist to fill up his car.

Contributory Negligence

Contributory negligence is a defense that exists when the injured persons proximately contributed to their injuries by their own negligence. When proven, contributory negligence will usually bar any recovery by the plaintiff. The defense of assumption of the risk occurs when the plaintiffs had knowledge of the risk and made the free choice of exposing themselves to it. For example, baseball fans who sit in unscreened seats at the ballpark know that the balls and even bats may strike them. Thus, they implicitly agree to take a chance of being injured in this manner.

Comparative Negligence

A major shortcoming of contributory negligence, however, is that the entire loss is placed on one party even when both are negligent. For this reason, most states now utilize a comparative negligence standard, where total liability is determined by comparing the amount of negligence on behalf of the plaintiff with the amount of negligence on behalf of the defendant. Under the doctrine of comparative negligence, a negligent plaintiff may be able to recover a portion of the cost of an injury. Specifically, comparative negligence divides the damages between the parties by reducing the plaintiff's damages in proportion to the extent of the person's contributory fault. Thus, in a pure comparative negligence jurisdiction, a plaintiff adjudged 80% responsible for his injuries would still be able to collect 20%, while in a contributory negligence jurisdiction; such a plaintiff would be awarded nothing.

Res ipsa loquitur

Plaintiffs can also recover in negligence by proving that a manufacturer's conduct violated the reasonable person standard and proximately caused injury. In product liability suits, it is often difficult to prove the defendant's act or omission that caused the plaintiff's injury. Thus, in the interests of justice, courts developed the doctrine of res ipsa loquitur ("the thing speaks for itself"). This doctrine permits plaintiffs to circumstantially prove negligence if the following facts are proved: (1) the defendant had exclusive control over the allegedly defective product during manufacture, (2) under normal circumstances, the plaintiff would not have been injured by the product if the defendant had exercised ordinary care, and (3) the plaintiff's conduct did not contribute significantly to the accident.

While res ipsa loquitur does not necessarily lead to definitive proof of negligence, it does permit jurors to infer a fact for which there is no direct, explicit proof — the defendant's negligent act or omission. Specifically, the trial judge will instruct the jurors that the law permits them to consider the inferred fact as well as the proved facts in deciding whether the defendant was negligent.

Imputed Negligence

Vicarious liability represents a venue in which individuals may be "vicariously" held accountable for the actions of individuals other than themselves. Imputed negligence results when one person (the agent) acts for or represents another (the principal) by the latter's authority and to accomplish the latter's ends. A common example is the liability of employers for the torts that employers commit in the scope of their employment. Generally, an employee would not be within the scope of employment if (1) the employee is en route to or from home, (2) if the employee is on an undertaking of his own, (3) if the acts are prohibited by the employer, or (4) if the act is an unauthorized delegation by the employer. While employers are not usually liable for the acts of independent contractors, there are certain exceptions to this nonliability, for example, if an employer is negligent in hiring a contractor who assigns a nondelegable duty.

Misrepresentation & Nondisclosure

Misrepresentation and nondisclosure form two fundamental bases for many actions represented under tort law. Any case where false or hidden information plays a significant part, essentially implies a standard of care that reflects the negligence addressed by tort.

To phrase it more simply, the fact that information has been withheld or misrepresented directly implies a negligent situation. This means that among the various subsections of tort law, cases of misrepresentation and nondisclosure can prove to be the easiest to form a legal consensus of opinion on whether negligence has happened, due to the very idea that the act itself is a negligent action.

Misrepresentation and nondisclosure can take many forms, but generally they refer to an act or service. they are usually rendered for compensation that do not fulfill their terms of promise, either because they misrepresent their ability to perform, or fail to disclose elements that prevent adequate performance (like a unknown side effect for a product, or a conflict of interest in a case of service).

There are many remedies one may seek when a case of misrepresentation can be seen to have occurred, though the extent to which they fall under tort law or other forms of legal action are highly dependent on the specific legal system, as well as the nature of the misrepresentation. In nearly all cases, there is an obligation on the provider of a product or service to provide information either by law, or by request, so as to adhere to all legal standards of accurate representation.

No-fault Liability Statute

Under a modified no-fault liability statute, an injured person normally has no right to file suit to recover money damages for personal injuries and lost wages below a statutorily specified threshold. Instead, the injured party is compensated by his/her own insurance company. The effect of these statutes has been to reduce the cost of automobile insurance by saving litigation costs, including attorneys' fees, and by allowing little or no recovery for the pain and suffering and emotional stress that accompany an automobile accident.

Negligence Defenses

Contributory negligence is one of the most commonly used negligence defenses. The defendant attempts to deny the plaintiff the right to action, by claiming that the plaintiff's own negligence played a large role in his injuries. In contributory negligence, both parties are guilty of negligence, but the plaintiff is not awarded any damages. The last clear chance rule is an exception to the contributory negligence defense which permits the plaintiff more freedom in taking action against a defendant when the plaintiff is also guilty of negligence. The last clear chance refers to an instance where the defendant had the last clear chance to avoid injuring the plaintiff, but did not take the opportunity. In cases where both the plaintiff and the defendant are both guilty of some degree of negligence, contributory negligence places liability solely on the plaintiff.

Strict Liability

In addition to intentional torts and negligence, there is a third type of tort called strict liability or absolute liability. This imposes liability on defendants without requiring any proof of lack of due care. Strict liability in tort is applied in cases involving what the common law recognized as abnormally dangerous activities and, more recently, in product liability cases.

One who is involved in abnormally dangerous activities is legally responsible for harmful consequences that are proximately caused. A few illustrative dangerous instrumentalities commonly associated with dangerous activities include poisons, toxic chemicals, explosives, nuclear fuel and waste, and vicious animals.

Product defects include defects in design, manufacturing defects, and warning defects. A person who has been injured by a product defect may be able to recover based on strict liability, as well as breach of warranty and negligence. In fact, much of the use of strict liability in product liability cases occurred because of dissatisfaction with the negligence and warranty remedies. It was argued that if consumers too often bore the brunt of all injuries, then it would be more economically prudent to shift the cost of injuries to manufacturers, since manufacturers could purchase insurance and could distribute the costs of the premiums among those who purchased their products.

In contrast to the plaintiff who relies on breach of warranty and negligence remedies, a plaintiff who relies on strict liability has to prove that the product was unreasonably dangerous and defective and that the defect proximately caused the injury.

Distinguishing Torts from Other Bases of Liability

Torts are distinguishable from crimes, which are wrongs against the state or society at large. The main purpose of criminal liability is to enforce public justice. In contrast, tort law addresses private wrongs and has a central purpose of compensating the victim rather than punishing the wrongdoer. Some acts may provide a basis for both tort and criminal liability. For example, gross negligence that endangers the lives of others may simultaneously be a tort and a crime.

Some actions are punishable under both criminal law and tort law, such as battery. In that case, ideally tort law would provide a monetary remedy to the plaintiff, while criminal law would provide rehabilitation for the defendant, while also providing a benefit to society by reforming the defendant who committed assault.

Tort law is also distinct from contract law. Although a party may have a strong breach of contract case under contract law, a breach of contract is not typically considered a tortious act.

Remedies

The law recognizes torts as civil wrongs and allows injured parties to recover for their losses. Remedies in a tort case will of course be different depending on the type of violation involved, and depending on how the victim was injured or suffered losses. Injured parties may bring suit to recover damages in the form of monetary compensation or for an injunction, which compels a party to cease an activity. In certain cases, courts will award punitive damages in addition to compensatory damages to deter further misconduct.

In the vast majority of tort cases, the court will award compensatory damages to an injured party that has successfully proven his or her case. Compensatory damages are typically equal to the monetary value of the injured party's loss of earnings, loss of future earning capacity, pain and suffering, and reasonable medical expenses. Thus, courts may award damages for incurred as well as expected losses.

When the court has an interest in deterring future misconduct, the court may award punitive damages in addition to compensatory damages. For example, in a case against a manufacturer for a defectively manufactured product, a court may award punitive damages to compel the manufacturer to ensure more careful production going forward.

In some cases, injured parties may bring suit to obtain an injunction rather than monetary relief. The party seeking an injunction typically must prove that it would suffer considerable or irreparable harm without the court's intervention.

Tort Reform

As plaintiff's injuries continue to mount, there have been increased arguments for tort reform, focusing on limitations or caps placed on jury awards. Specifically, many advocates of reform believe that trial attorney greed is at the core of the problem, while others assert that the high rewards are directly responsible for our seemingly unstoppable increases in health care costs. On the other hand, opponents point out that these reforms seek to arbitrarily deny injured people the awards that they are entitled to and, in fact, the damage awards are large only in cases in which the injuries are horrific and the tortfeasor's liability is great.

As a result of the increasingly divisive battle to engage in tort reform, many states have tried to lower jury awards by statutorily establishing ceilings on recoveries for noneconomic damages such as pain and suffering. Proponents of tort reform often urge lawmakers to establish financial "caps" on the amount of damages a successful tort plaintiff can receive. The rationale generally given is that doctors cannot afford to pay the cost of malpractice insurance premiums and that establishing ceilings on damage awards will reduce the overall cost of medical care. As we learned in Atlanta Oculoplastic Surgery v. Nestlehutt, 286 Ga. 731 (2010), however, such caps may be ruled as unconstitutional in abridging or infringing on the plaintiff's constitutional right to a jury trial.

Exercises

I. Multiple-choice Questions:

1. Porter worked in a petrochemical plant owned and operated by Cheminc. Porter did routine repair work around the Cheminc plant. As Porter was bending over to work on a fouled machine, a pipe carrying hot oil that was located behind Porter exploded. Porter was sprayed with the oil and suffered severe burns. Porter hired an attorney who made inquiries of the Cheminc plant manager and discovered that the exploding pipe had been manufactured by Pipeco. However, the plant manager refused to tell the attorney when the pipe had been installed in the plant.

If Porter brings a negligence action against Pipeco for his injuries, who will prevail?

   A. Porter, because the pipe manufactured by Pipeco exploded.

   B. Porter, if a reasonable inspection by Pipeco would have revealed a defect in the pipe that caused it to explode.

   C. Pipeco, if the pipe had burst because the oil had corroded it.

   D. Pipeco, because the pipe was in Cheminc's possession when it exploded.

Questions 2—3 are based on the following fact situation:

Hurts U-Drive rented one of its shiny new cars to Driver, for a leisurely cross-country vacation trip which Driver had planned for his family. While driving through a remote stretch of farmland, Driver decided to see how much power the rented car really had, and was driving in excess of 90 m.p.h. when he came to a curve. He applied the brakes and attempted to slow down, but the car went across the double line and struck head-on a station wagon coming in the opposite direction. Sam, the driver, was killed in the accident, and the station wagon was destroyed.

A "permissive use" statute is in effect making the bailor of an automobile liable for personal injury, death, or property damage caused by any person operating the automobile with his consent, up to a maximum of $25,000. The jurisdiction follows traditional contributory negligence and contribution rules.

2. If Sam's estate files suit against Hurts pursuant to the "permissive use" statute, and recovers the full $25,000, what rights if any would Hurts have against Driver?

 A. None, unless the rental agreement obligated Driver to assume any such liability imposed on the renter.

 B. Hurts may obtain contribution from Driver to the extent of $12,500, but not indemnity.

 C. Hurts may obtain indemnity against Driver for the full $25,000.

 D. Hurts may obtain contribution from Driver to the extent of Driver's relative fault, but not indemnity.

3. Assume for purposes of this question only that Sam's estate files against both Hurts and Driver, alleging that Driver was negligent in the operation of the rented automobile, and that Hurts was negligent in renting it to him, having reason to know that Driver was an incompetent and irresponsible driver. If the jury returns a verdict of joint and several liability against both defendants, and assesses damages in the sum of $100,000, how should the judgment be entered?

 A. $50,000 as against each defendant.

 B. $25,000 against Hurts and $ 75,000 against Driver.

 C. $100,000 against Hurts only.

 D. $100,000 against both defendants.

Questions 4–5 are based on the following fact situation:

As a result of interests traceable to his early career as a blacksmith, John's father acquired a large collection of anvils, which ultimately came into John's possession. John loaned the collection to the local museum and hired professional movers to transport the anvils to the second floor of the museum, where they would be displayed. The movers used an old rope and pulley apparatus to lift the anvils on the outside of the building to a second-story window. While one of the largest anvils was being lifted, it slipped and fell, crashing through the roof of Jane's parked car. Jane had just walked out of the drugstore across the street and saw the entire incident. Although the anvil was not even dented, Jane's car was extensively damaged.

4. If John brings a negligence action against the movers for allowing the antique anvil to fall, he can recover:

   A. Nominal damages.

   B. Punitive damages.

   C. Both nominal damages and punitive damages.

   D. Neither nominal damages nor punitive damages.

5. If Jane brings a claim for negligent infliction of emotional distress, she would:

   A. Recover, if there were accompanying physical consequences.

   B. Recover, because she was a foreseeable plaintiff.

   C. Not recover, because she was not within the zone of danger.

   D. Not recover, because there was no impact.

Questions 6—7 are based on the following fact situation:

Gilda Gammaray, a precocious student at Northcentral High School, was an "A" student in her chemistry class and was interested in developing a Science Fair project in the area of chemistry. She was inspired by an experiment conducted in class in which the teacher had the students mix three chemicals together to create a gas that caused the faces of the students to become grossly distorted. Gilda obtained an ample supply of three chemicals and went to an abandoned building located on a street that had heavy pedestrian traffic. She mixed together the chemicals, and the fumes passed across the sidewalk, causing the pedestrians' faces to become grossly distorted, as if they suffered from physical defects. The effect of the gas was temporary and none of the pedestrians suffered any permanent damage. One of the pedestrians exposed to the gas was Parker.

6. If Parker wants to sue Gilda, which of the following best describes the tort she has committed against him?

   A. Assault.

   B. Battery.

C. Intentional infliction of emotional distress.

D. Invasion of privacy.

7. Assume for purposes of this question only that Parker was a rather vain man of middle years, and that in order to further her experiment, Gilda took pictures of the pedestrians affected by the gas and sent the pictures to the local newspaper. The newspaper ran a story describing Gilda's experiment and also ran a picture of Parker in which his face appeared highly contorted. If Parker sues the newspaper for false light publicity, he will:

    A. Prevail, because the picture made him appear to be a grumpy old man.

    B. Prevail, because the newspaper disclosed a private fact.

    C. Not prevail, because he was on a public sidewalk when the picture was taken.

    D. Not prevail, because he suffered no permanent harm.

Questions 8–9 are based on the following fact situation:

Matt looked out his front window one day and saw Rex standing on a narrow ledge on the second story of the house across the street. He also saw a ladder lying on the ground beneath where Rex was stranded. Matt turned away and pulled the drapes, muttering to himself, "Well, I'm not going to watch him fall off there." Later, Howard was walking down the street and saw Rex's situation and determined to help. Howard picked up the ladder and placed it against the side of the house. However, he set it atop a patch of ice. As Rex started down the ladder, a rotten rung broke and Rex fell to the ground and was injured.

8. If Rex sues Matt for damages for his injuries, will he recover?

    A. Yes, because Matt had a duty to aid Rex when he saw that Rex was in peril.

    B. Yes, because a reasonably prudent person would have aided Rex under the circumstances.

    C. No, because Matt took no action to aid Rex.

    D. No, because Rex put himself in a position of peril.

9. If Rex sues Howard, will he recover?

    A. Yes, because Howard's action caused the injury to Rex.

    B. Yes, because Howard assumed the duty of aiding Rex.

    C. Yes, because it was foreseeable that Rex would be injured as a result of Howard's negligent conduct.

    D. No, because Howard's negligence did not cause the injury to Rex.

10. The Runtz Mansion was a large property that had once belonged to one of the founding families of Dodgeville, a city of 75,000 people. The mansion was purchased as a residence by Pangol, a vice president at Dodge State Bank, one of the three major banks in Dodgeville. Pangol was extremely annoyed when he saw a headline in a local newspaper, *The Dodge Herald*, reading: "Local Banker Buys Old Runtz Mansion for 300 Grand." Hoppe, a reporter for the *Herald*, had noticed that the "for sale" sign had been removed from the spacious front lawn of the Runtz Mansion. He had gone to the County Recorder of Deeds' office and discovered the name of the buyer and the amount paid for the property from the deed, which was on file. Hoppe had then called the real estate agent and asked her about Pangol. The agent had told Hoppe that Pangol was a vice president at Dodge State Bank. In addition to the article in the *Herald*, which described the mansion and indicated Pangol's name and occupation and the amount paid for the property, the *Herald* published a picture of the front of the mansion, which one of its staff photographers had taken from the sidewalk in front of the mansion.

    If Pangol sues the *Herald* for invasion of privacy, will he recover?

    A. Yes, because Pangol did not consent to publication of information about himself and his private residence.

    B. Yes, if a reasonable person of ordinary sensibilities would have been upset by publication of the story.

    C. No, because the *Herald* printed public facts.

    D. No, because the story in the *Herald* was true.

II. Essay Question:

One afternoon, Frank Fuller gave his four-year-old son, Steven, permission to visit a neighbor's house. Frank was aware that a pet dog at the neighbor's house was unusually aggressive. Frank watched Steven walk to the neighbor's house. Soon after Steven began his visit at the neighbor's house, the neighbor's dog attacked and injured him.

Steven sued his father for damages on a negligence theory. Frank sought to have the case dismissed on grounds of immunity. The trial court granted that motion.

Steven has appealed to the state's highest court. That court has never before considered this issue. Discuss how it should decide the case, considering how possible resolutions would apply to Steven's case.

Chapter 10
Property Law

Property law is law governing the ownership of property, and the transfer of that property. Property laws specifically deal with the concepts of real property and personal property, which are kept distinct from one another in terms of how the property law treats them. Real property is immovable property, such as land, buildings, and other edifices. Personal property, on the other hand, is movable property, such as personal possessions which are easily exchanged, for example. Property law is in general centered on individual property rights and the protection of those rights. Specifically, then, property laws are designed to ensure that an individual who owns a given object has full rights to do with that object as he or she pleases, assuming that doing so will not harm either another individual or another individual's property. Property law is primarily oriented outwardly, towards the forms of property which were mentioned above, as one's rights to one's own body are considered personal rights, instead of property rights. Property laws also govern the rights of a property owner in giving that property to another, and the rights of individuals to lay claim to a given piece of property after particular arrangements have been reached.

Property law of the modern world is complicated even further by the developing body known as intellectual property law, which deals with one's property over ideas and concepts which might not have any kind of physical instantiation. Intellectual property laws are becoming ever more important to the functioning of the world and the world economy as the Internet becomes more prevalent in societies across the face of the earth.

Classification

Property law is characterised by a great deal of historical continuity and technical

Chapter 10
Property Law

terminology. The basic distinction in common law systems is between real property (land) and personal property (chattels).

Before the mid-19th century, the principles governing the transfer of real property and personal property on an intestacy were quite different. Though this dichotomy does not have the same significance anymore, the distinction is still fundamental because of the essential differences between the two categories. An obvious example is the fact that land is immovable, and thus the rules that govern its use must differ. A further reason for the distinction is that legislation is often drafted employing the traditional terminology.

The division of land and chattels has been criticised as being not satisfactory as a basis for categorising the principles of property law since it concentrates attention not on the proprietary interests themselves but on the objects of those interests. Moreover, in the case of fixtures, chattels which are affixed to or placed on land may become part of the land.

Real property is generally sub-classified into:

- corporeal hereditaments — tangible real property (land)
- incorporeal hereditaments — intangible real property such as an easement of way

Acquisition

Gift

A gift, in the law of property, is the voluntary transfer of property from one person (the donor or grantor) to another (the donee or grantee) without full valuable consideration. In order for a gift to be legally effective, three requirements must be met:

- Intention of donor to give the gift to the donee (donative intent)
- Delivery of gift to donee.
- Acceptance of gift by donee.

Adverse Possession

Adverse possession, sometimes colloquially described as "squatter's rights", is a legal principle that applies when a person who does not have legal title to a piece of property — usually land (real property) — attempts to claim legal ownership based upon a history of possession or occupation of the land without the permission of its legal owner. A title owner has the right to recover possession of their property through legal action, such as an ejectment action. However, in jurisdictions that recognize adverse possession, the person in possession of the land may attempt to gain title to the land based upon the nature of their possession of the land, and the number of years that have passed after they took possession.

Courts have long ruled that when an owner does not exercise their right to recover their property and the statute of limitations on recovery expires, not only is the original owner prevented from exercising their rights on the property, but an entirely new title to the property springs up in the adverse possessor. In effect, the adverse possessor becomes the property's new owner. In the United States, the time limit on an owner being able to recover their property varies widely between individual states, ranging from as low as five years to as many as 40 years.

Chattel property may also be adversely possessed, but owing to the differences in the nature of real and chattel property, the rules governing such claims are rather more stringent, favoring the legal owner rather than the adverse possessor. Claims for adverse possession of chattel often involve works of art.

Although the elements of an adverse possession action are different in every jurisdiction, a person claiming adverse possession is usually required to prove non-permissive use of the property that is actual, open and notorious, exclusive, adverse, and continuous for the statutory period.

Lost Property

The common law distinguished between lost property and mislaid property. Lost property is personal property that was unintentionally left by its true owner. Mislaid property is personal property that was intentionally set down by its owner and then forgotten. For example, a wallet that falls out of someone's pocket is lost. A wallet accidentally left on a table in a restaurant is mislaid.

At common law, a person who found lost personal property could keep it until and unless the original owner comes forward. This rule applied to people who discovered lost property in public areas, as well as to people who discovered lost property on their property. Mislaid property, on the other hand, generally goes to the owner of the property where it was found. Thus, for example, a person who finds a wallet lost in the street may keep it. If, however, a person finds a wallet inside a barbershop, the shop owner might have a better claim to the wallet. The basic theory behind this distinction is that owners of mislaid property are more likely to remember where the property is. Allowing property owners to keep it makes it easier for the true owner to recover the property.

Real property may not be lost or mislaid.

Many jurisdictions have statutes that modify the common law's treatment of lost or abandoned property. Typically, these statutes require lost personal property to be turned over to a government official, and that if the property is not claimed within a set period of time, it goes to the finder and the original owner's rights to the property are terminated.

Abandoned Property

Personal property left by an owner who intentionally relinquishes all rights to its control. Real property may not be abandoned. See Adverse Possession.

At common law, a person who finds abandoned property may claim it. To do so, the finder must take definite steps to show their claim. For example, a finder might claim an abandoned piece of furniture by taking it to her house, or putting a sign on it indicating her ownership.

In the context of intellectual property, abandoned property refers to the relinquishing of intellectual property rights by an owner, thereby allowing others to use the intellectual property without protest. For example, an inventor who does not register a patent to his invention relinquishes the patent rights associated with his invention, allowing others to use his invention freely and without recourse.

Courts may have a difficult time distinguishing whether property is lost, mislaid, or abandoned. Typically, this is a question of fact, which means that the jury usually decides the issue.

Finders

In order to determine whether to grant possession to the finder of lost/mislaid/abandoned property, courts will often look to the type of item and where it was found in order to determine whether the finder of the item has a right to the item.

In general, items which are abandoned or lost will go to the finder, unless the find is made at an owner-occupied residence. A Mislaid items usually belong to the possessor of the place where the item is found. If an employee finds an item in the course of his employment, it belongs to the employer. A finder is a bailee, with a duty to care for the found item.

Law of Shipwrecks

While the doctrine of abandoned property typically only applies to personal property, U.S. law has carved out an application for the doctrine in relation to sunken ships. Under the Abandoned Shipwreck Act of 1987, 43 U.S.C. 2101-2106, abandoned shipwrecks which are within three miles of the United States territorial limits belong to the United States. In turn, the U.S. gives control over the shipwreck to whichever state would be the most appropriate.

Bailment

A "bailment" is a non-ownership transfer of possession. Under English Common Law, the right to possess a thing is separate and distinct from owning the thing. In some jurisdictions, an owner of an object can steal his own property, a curious result of the distinction. In context, an owner who lends someone else an article, then secretly takes it back, can be stealing.

When a bailment is created, the article is said to have been "bailed". One who delivers the article is the bailor. One who receives a "bailed" article is the bailee.

Deed

A deed (anciently "an evidence") is any legal instrument in writing which passes, affirms or confirms an interest, right, or property and that is signed, attested, delivered, and in some jurisdictions, sealed. It is commonly associated with transferring (conveyancing)

Chapter 10
Property Law

title to property. The deed has a greater presumption of validity and is less rebuttable than an instrument signed by the party to the deed. A deed can be unilateral or bilateral. Deeds include conveyances, commissions, licenses, patents, diplomas, and conditionally powers of attorney if executed as deeds. The deed is the modern descendant of the medieval charter, and delivery is thought to symbolically replace the ancient ceremony of livery of seisin.

The traditional phrase signed, sealed and delivered refers to the practice of seals; however, attesting witnesses have replaced seals to some extent. Agreements under seal are also called contracts by deed or specialty; in the United States, a specialty is enforceable without consideration. In some jurisdictions, specialties have a liability limitation period of double that of a simple contract and allow for a third party beneficiary to enforce an undertaking in the deed, thereby overcoming the doctrine of privity. Specialties, as a form of contract, are bilateral and can therefore be distinguished from covenants, which, being also under seal, are unilateral promises.

Estates in Land

Possessory Estate

Also known as a present possessory estate. The holder of this has the present or current right to possess the real property. This may be contrasted with a future interest which is a future right to possess. Present estates are divided into Non-Freehold Estates (in which the tenant does not hold possession — rents or leases) and Freehold Estates (in which the tenant does hold ownership). There are three kinds of Freehold Estates:

Life Estate

A life estate grants the holder use of the estate for the duration of a life, often that of the tenant. At the end of the life, the estate will transfer to another by a reversion (if to the grantor) or remainder (if to another). See future estates.

For example: To A for life, then to B. (A will have the land until death, then the estate will transfer to B).

Additionally, a life estate could be for the life of another. Also known as per autre vie (french for t he life of another), this is the same set up, but the measuring life is another person. For example: To A for the life of B, then to C. A will have the land until B dies, then the land will pass to C.

Fee Tail Estate

The Fee Tail is an antiquated system designed to establish family dynasties which require the land to be passed to the blood heirs. This has been abolished in most jurisdictions.

Fee Simple Estates

Fee Simple Estates are the most common and grant a complete interest in land (it's yours to be used without conditions or limitations). There are two kinds of Fee Simple: Absolute or Defeasible.

Absolute Fee Simple: An absolute fee simple estate is one in which the land is yours to do with as you wish, and it can not be revoked by others (note, this land would still be subject to non-property issues like taxes, or be seized for settlement of an unpaid judgement against you…)

Defeasible Fee Simple: A defeasible fee simple is a fee simple estate that could be removed for a reason established in the granting document. If an event or happening occurs, the transfer could be void. There are three kinds of defeasible fee simple estates:

- Fee Simple Determinable: The estate will be automatically terminated if the stated condition occurs. Established by durational language, fee simple determinable estates are followed by the future estates of a possibility of reverter. For example: To A for as long as the property is used for a museum. A has a fee simple determinable, and will hold the land for as long as it is a museum; the grantor holds a possibility of reverter. If the museum is shut down, the land will automatically be transferred to the grantor.

- Fee Simple Subject to Condition Subsequent: The estate is similar to a fee simple, but has a condition attached. Established by conditional language, these estates are followed by a right of entry. If the triggering event occurs, the holder must take steps to establish possession of the land. For example: To A, but if A does not use the land for a museum, then the grantor has a right of entry. A has a defeasible fee simple estate subject to a condition subsequent, and the grantor has a right of entry. If the land is not used for a museum, then the grantor must take action to recover the land. If the grantor does not take action, the land will remain with A, even after it is not being used as a museum.

- Fee Simple Subject to a Executory Limitation: A fee simple with a stated event, which if it happens, is automatically divested by an executory interest in a transferee (if the event happens, the land automatically goes to a third party). For example: To A so long as the land is used for a museum, but if used for anything else, to B. A holds a defeasible fee simple subject to an executory condition, B holds an executory interest. If the land is not used for a museum, it is automatically transferred to B.

Right of Entry

A future interest that the grantor keeps. It follows an estate subject to a condition subsequent.

Example: From O to A, on the condition that A does not smoke. If A smokes, O has the right to come in and reclaim the land. Note that O must actually take action to get the land back

Concurrent Estates

A concurrent estate or co-tenancy is a concept in property law which describes the various ways in which property is owned by more than one person at a time. If more than one person owns the same property, they are referred to as co-owners. If more than one person leases the same property, they are called co-tenants or joint tenants. Most common law jurisdictions recognize tenancies in common and joint tenancies, and some also recognize tenancies by the entirety. Many jurisdictions refer to a joint tenancy as a joint tenancy with right of survivorship, and a few U.S. states treat the phrase joint tenancy as synonymous with a tenancy in common.

The type of ownership determines the rights of the parties to sell their interest in the property to others, to will the property to their devisees, or to sever their joint ownership of the property. Just as each of these affords a different set of rights and responsibilities to the co-owners of property, each requires a different set of conditions to exist.

Tenancy in Common

Tenancy in common is a form of concurrent estate in which each owner, referred to as a tenant in common, is regarded by the law as owning separate and distinct shares of the same property. By default, all co-owners own equal shares, but their interests may differ in size.

TIC owners own percentages in an undivided property rather than particular units or apartments, and their deeds show only their ownership percentages. The right of a particular TIC owner to use a particular dwelling comes from a written contract signed by all co-owners (often called a "Tenancy In Common Agreement"), not from a deed, map or other document recorded in county records. This form of ownership is most common where the co-owners are not married or have contributed different amounts to the purchase of the property. The assets of a joint commercial partnership might be held as a tenancy in common.

Tenants in common have no right of survivorship, meaning that if one tenant in common dies, that tenant's interest in the property will be part of his or her estate and pass by inheritance to that owner's devisees or heirs, either by will, or by intestate succession. Also, as each tenant in common has an interest in the property, they may, in the absence of any restriction agreed to between all the tenants in common, sell or otherwise deal with the interest in the property (e.g. mortgage it) during their lifetime, like any other property interest.

Destruction of tenancy in common

Where any party to a tenancy in common wishes to terminate (usually termed "destroy") the joint interest, he or she may obtain a partition of the property. This is a division of the land into distinctly owned lots, if such division is legally permitted under zoning and other local land use restrictions. Where such division is not permitted, a forced sale of the property is the only alternative, followed by a division of the proceeds.

If the parties are unable to agree to a partition, any or all of them may seek the ruling of a court to determine how the land should be divided — physically division between the joint owners (partition in kind), leaving each with ownership of a portion of the property representing their share. Courts may also order a partition by sale in which the property is sold and the proceeds are distributed to the owners. Where local law does not permit physical division, the court must order a partition by sale.

Each co-owner is entitled to partition as a matter of right, meaning that the court will order a partition at the request of any of the co-owners. The only exception to this general rule is where the co-owners have agreed, either expressly or impliedly, to waive the right of partition. The right may be waived either permanently, for a specific period of time, or under certain conditions. The court, however, will likely not enforce this waiver because it is a restraint on the alienability of property.

Joint Tenancy

A joint tenancy or joint tenancy with right of survivorship (JTROS, JTWROS or JT TEN WROS) is a type of concurrent estate in which co-owners have a right of survivorship, meaning that if one owner dies, that owner's interest in the property will pass to the surviving owner or owners by operation of law, and avoiding probate. The deceased owner's interest in the property simply evaporates and cannot be inherited by his or her heirs. Under this type of ownership, the last owner living owns all the property, and on his or her death the property will form part of their estate. Unlike a tenancy in common, where co-owners may have unequal interests in a property, joint co-owners have an equal share in the property.

It is important to note, however, that creditors' claims against the deceased owner's estate may, under certain circumstances, be satisfied by the portion of ownership previously owned by the deceased, but now owned by the survivor or survivors. In other words, the deceased's liabilities can sometimes remain attached to the property.

This form of ownership is common between wife and husband, and parent and child, and in any other situation where parties want ownership to pass immediately and automatically to the survivor. For bank and brokerage accounts held in this fashion, the acronym JTWROS is commonly appended to the account name as evidence of the owners' intent.

To create a joint tenancy, clear language indicating that intent must be used — e.g. "to AB and CD as joint tenants with right of survivorship, and not as tenants in common". This long form of wording may be especially appropriate in those jurisdictions which use the phrase "joint tenancy" as synonymous with a tenancy in common. Shorter forms such as "to AB and CD as joint tenants" or "to AB and CD jointly" can be used in most jurisdictions. Words to that effect may be used by the parties in the deed of conveyance or other instrument of transfer of title, or by a testator in a will, or in an inter vivos trust deed.

If a testator leaves property in a will to several beneficiaries "jointly" and one or more of those named beneficiaries dies before the will takes effect, then the survivors of those named beneficiaries will inherit the whole property on a joint tenancy basis. But if these named beneficiaries had been bequeathed the property on a tenancy in common basis, but died before the will took effect, then those beneficiaries' heirs would in turn inherit their share immediately (the named beneficiary being deceased).

To create a joint tenancy, the co-owners must share "four unities":

- Time — the co-owners must acquire the property at the same time.
- Title — the co-owners must have the same title to the property. If a condition applies to one owner and not another, there is no unity of title.
- Interest — each co-owner owns an equal share of the property; for example, if three co-owners are on the deed, then each co-owner owns a one-third interest in the property regardless of the amount each co-owner contributed to the purchase price.
- Possession — the co-owners must have an equal right to possess the whole property.

If any of these elements is missing, the joint tenancy is ineffective, and the joint tenancy will be treated as a tenancy in common in equal shares.

Breaking a joint tenancy

If any joint co-owner deals in any way with a property inconsistent with a joint tenancy, that co-owner will be treated as having terminated (sometimes called "breaking") the joint tenancy. The remaining co-owners maintain joint ownership of the remaining interest. The dealing may be a conveyance or sale of the co-owner's share in the property. The position in relation to a mortgage is more doubtful (see below). For example, if one of three joint co-owners conveys his or her share in the property to a third party, the third party owns a 1/3 share on a tenancy in common basis, while the other two original joint co-owners continue to hold the remaining 2/3s on a joint tenancy basis. This result arises because the "unity of time" is broken: that is, because on the transfer the timing of the new interest is different from the original one. If it is desired to continue to maintain a joint tenancy, then the three original joint co-owners would need to transfer, in the one instrument, the joint interest to the two remaining joint co-owners and the new joint co-owner.

A joint co-owner may break a joint tenancy and maintain an interest in the property. Most jurisdictions permit a joint owner to break a joint tenancy by the execution of a document to that effect. In those jurisdictions which retain the old common law requirements, an actual exchange with a straw man is required. This requires another person to "buy" the property from the joint co-owner for some nominal consideration, followed immediately by a sale-back to the co-owner at the same price. In either case, the joint tenancy will revert to a tenancy in common as to that owner's interest in the property.

A significant issue can arise with the simple document execution method. In the straw man approach, there are witnesses to the transfer. With the document, there may not be witnesses. With either method, as soon as the break occurs, it works both ways. Because there may not be witnesses, the party with the document could take advantage of that fact and hide the document when the other party dies.

If one joint co-owner takes out a mortgage on jointly owned property, in some jurisdictions this may terminate the joint tenancy.

Tenancy by the Entirety

A tenancy by the entirety (sometimes called a tenancy by the entireties) is a type of concurrent estate formerly available only to married couples, where ownership of property is treated as though the couple were a single legal person. (In the State of Hawaii, the option of Tenants by the Entirety ownership is also available to domestic partners in a registered "Reciprocal Beneficiary Relationship"; Vermont's Civil Union statute qualifies parties to a civil union for tenancy by the entirety.) Like a Joint Tenancy with Rights of Survivorship, the tenancy by the entirety also encompasses a right of survivorship, so if one spouse dies, the entire interest in the property is said to "ripen" in the survivor so that sole control of the property ripens, or passes in the ordinary sense, to the surviving spouse without going through probate.

In some jurisdictions, to create a tenancy by the entirety the parties must specify in the deed that the property is being conveyed to the couple "as tenants by the entirety", while in others, a conveyance to a married couple is presumed to create a tenancy by the entirety unless the deed specifies otherwise. Also, besides sharing the four unities necessary to create a joint tenancy with right of survivorship — time, title, interest, and possession — there must also be the fifth unity of marriage. However, unlike a JTWROS, neither party in a tenancy by the entirety has a unilateral right to sever the tenancy. The termination of the tenancy or any dealing with any part of the property requires the consent of both spouses. A divorce breaks the unity of marriage, leaving the default tenancy, which may be a tenancy in common in equal shares. Many US jurisdictions no longer recognize tenancies by the entirety. Where it is recognized, benefits can include the ability to shield the property from creditors of only one spouse, as well as the ability to partially shield the property where only one spouse is filing a petition for bankruptcy relief. If a non-debtor spouse in a tenancy by the entirety survives a debtor spouse, the lien can never be enforced against the property. On the other hand, if a debtor spouse survives a non-debtor spouse, the lien may be enforced against the whole property, not merely the debtor spouse's original half-interest.

In many states, tenancy by the entireties is recognized as a valid form of ownership for bank accounts and financial assets. One must be careful to ensure that the tenancy by the entireties designation is chosen as opposed to other forms of joint ownership such as joint tenancy with rights of survivorship, so that the benefits of tenancy by the entireties status is not lost. For example, under Florida law, if a bank account titling document allows for tenancy by the entireties and joint tenancy with rights of survivorship, if the account is opened as a joint tenancy with rights of survivorship account, the benefits of tenancy by entireties will not attach.

Conveyancing

Bona Fide Purchaser

A bona fide purchaser (BFP) — referred to more completely as a bona fide purchaser for value without notice — is a term used predominantly in common law jurisdictions in the law of real property and personal property to refer to an innocent party who purchases property without notice of any other party's claim to the title of that property. A BFP must purchase for value, meaning that he or she must pay for the property rather than simply be the beneficiary of a gift. Even when a party fraudulently conveys property to a BFP (for example, by selling to the BFP property that has already been conveyed to someone else), that BFP will, depending on the laws of the relevant jurisdiction, take good (valid) title to the property despite the competing claims of the other party. As such, recording one's interest protects an owner from losing that interest to a subsequent buyer who qualifies as a BFP. Moreover, some jurisdictions (so-called "race-notice" jurisdictions) require the BFP himself or herself to record in order to enforce his or her rights. In any case, parties with a claim to ownership in the property will retain a cause of action (a right to sue) against the party who made the fraudulent conveyance.

A BFP will not be bound by equitable interests of which he/she does not have actual, constructive or imputed notice, as long as he/she has made "such inspections as ought reasonably to have been made".

BFPs are also sometimes referred to as "equity's darling". However, as Jeffrey Hackney has pointed out, the title is somewhat misleading; in cases where legal title is passed to a bona fide purchaser for value without notice, it is not so much that equity has any great affection for the purchaser — it is simply that equity refuses to intervene to preserve any rights held by the former beneficial owner of the property. The relationship between the courts of equity and the BFP are better characterised as benign neglect. However, equity still undoubtedly recognises the right of the beneficial owner to claim against the former legal owner where the sale was improper.

Torrens Title

The Torrens title system operates on the principle of "title by registration" (granting the high indefeasibility of a registered ownership) rather than "registration of title". The system does away with the need for proving a chain of title (i.e. tracing title through a series of documents). The State guarantees title and is usually supported by a compensation scheme for those who lose their title due to private fraud or error in the State's operation.

In most jurisdictions, there will be parcels of land which are still unregistered.

The Torrens system works on three principles:

1. Mirror principle — the register reflects (mirrors) accurately and completely the current facts about title to each registered lot. This means that each dealing affecting a lot (such as a transfer of title, a mortgage or discharge of same, a lease, an easement or a covenant) must be entered on the register and so be viewable by cheap online search.

2. Curtain principle — one does not need to go behind the Certificate of Title as it contains all the information about the title. This means that ownership need not be proved by long complicated documents that are kept by the owner, as in the Private Conveyancing system. All of the necessary information regarding ownership is on the Certificate of Title.

3. Indemnity principle — provides for compensation of loss caused by private fraud

or by errors made by the Registrar of Titles.

Estoppel by Deed

Estoppel is a common law doctrine which, when it applies, prevents a litigant from denying the truth of what was said or done. The doctrine of estoppel by deed (also known as after-acquired title) is a particular estoppel doctrine in the context of real property transfers. Under the doctrine, the grantor of a deed (generally the seller of a piece of real property) is estopped (barred) from denying the truth of the deed. The doctrine may only be invoked in a suit arising out of the deed, or involving a particular right arising out of the deed. While rooted in warranty deeds, estoppel by deed has been extended to affect quitclaim deeds if the deed represents that the grantor actually had title.

Examples

1. If O conveys property she doesn't own to A by warranty deed, but O later acquires title to that land, then title immediately passes to A.

2. However, if, as above, O conveys property she doesn't own to A by warranty deed, but O later acquires title to that land, A may elect to treat O's lack of title at the time of the conveyance as a breach of the covenants of seisin and right to convey (two of the six traditional forms of Covenants for Title that are contained in a general warranty deed), and sue O for damages. A cannot be forced to accept O's after-acquired title if she wishes instead to receive damages.

3. If O conveys property she doesn't own to A by quitclaim deed, but O later acquires title to that land, then A owns nothing. This is because O passed her interest to A with a quitclaim deed; at the time of the conveyance, O's interest was nothing, so she passed nothing.

Equitable Conversion

Equitable conversion is a doctrine of the law of real property under which a purchaser of real property becomes the equitable owner of title to the property at the time he/she signs a contract binding him/her to purchase the land at a later date. The seller retains legal title of the property prior to the date of conveyance, but this land interest is considered personal property (a right to the payment of money, rather than a right to the property). The risk of loss is then transferred to the buyer — if a house on the property burns down after the contract has been signed, but before the deed is conveyed, the buyer will nevertheless have to pay the agreed-upon purchase price for the land unless the seller in possession or deemed in possession has failed to protect it. Such issues can and should be avoided by parties by stipulating in the contract who will bear the loss in such occurrences. The above rule varies by jurisdiction, but is the general rule.

Quite Title

An action to quiet title is a lawsuit brought in a court having jurisdiction over property disputes, in order to establish a party's title to real property, or personal property having a title, of against anyone and everyone, and thus "quiet" any challenges or claims to the title.

This legal action is "brought to remove a cloud on the title" so that plaintiff and those in privity with him may forever be free of claims against the property. The action to quiet title resembles other forms of "preventive adjudication", such as the declaratory judgment.

This genre of lawsuit is also sometimes called either a try title, trespass to try title, or ejectment action "to recover possession of land wrongfully occupied by a defendant". However, there are slight differences. In an ejectment action, it is typically done to remove a tenant or lessee in an eviction action, or an eviction after a foreclosure. Nonetheless, in some states, all terms are used synonymously.

<u>Grounds for a Quiet Title Action or Complaint</u>

It comprises a complaint that the ownership (title) of a parcel of land or other real property is defective in some fashion, typically where title to the property is ambiguous — for example, where it has been conveyed by a quitclaim deed through which the previous owner disclaims all interest, but does not promise that good title is conveyed. Such an action may also be brought to dispel a restraint on alienation or another party's claim of a nonpossessory interest in land, such as an easement by prescription.

Other typical grounds for complaint include:

- adverse possession where the new possessor sues to obtain title in his or her own name;
- fraudulent conveyance of a property, perhaps by a forged deed or under coercion;
- Torrens title registration, an action which terminates all unrecorded claims;
- treaty disputes regarding the boundaries between nations;
- tax taking issues, where a municipality claims title in lieu of back taxes owed (or a subsequent purchaser of land at a tax sale files action to gain insurable title);
- boundary disputes between states, municipalities, or private parties;
- surveying errors
- competing claims by reverters, remainders, missing heirs and lien holders (often arising in basic foreclosure actions when satisfied liens are not properly discharged from title due to clerical or recording errors between the county clerk and the satisfied lien holder)

Future Use Control

Restraint on Alienation

A restraint on alienation, in the law of real property, is a clause used in the conveyance of real property that seeks to prohibit the recipient from selling or otherwise transferring his interest in the property. Under the common law such restraints are void as against the public policy of allowing landowners to freely dispose of their property. Perhaps the ultimate restraint on alienation was the fee tail, a form of ownership which required that property be passed down in the same family from generation to generation, which has also been widely abolished.

However, certain reasonable restraints will be given effect in most jurisdictions. These traditionally include:

- A prohibition against partition of property for a limited time.
- The right of first refusal — for example, if Joey sells property to Rachel, he may require that if Rachel later decides to sell the property, she must first give Joey the

opportunity to buy it back.

- The establishment of public parks and gardens, as was the case for The Royal Parks of London in the UK. These public spaces were created under such terms by the Crown Estate; which meant that these parks were held in perpetuity for the public to use.

Rule Against Perpetuities

Black's Law Dictionary defines the rule against perpetuities as "the common-law rule prohibiting a grant of an estate unless the interest must vest, if at all, no later than 21 years (plus a period of gestation to cover a posthumous birth) after the death of some person alive when the interest was created."

At common law, the length of time was fixed at 21 years after the death of an identifiable person alive at the time the interest was created. This is often expressed as "lives in being plus twenty-one years". Under the common-law rule, one does not look to whether an interest actually will vest more than 21 years after the lives in being. Instead, if there exists any possibility at the time of the grant, however unlikely or remote, that an interest will vest outside of the perpetuities period, the interest is void and is stricken from the grant.

The rule does not apply to interests in the grantor himself. For example, the grant "For A so long as alcohol is not sold on the premises, then to B" would violate the rule as to B. However, the conveyance to B would be stricken, leaving "To A so long as alcohol is not sold on the premises". This would create a fee simple determinable in A, with a possibility of reverter in the grantor (or the grantor's heirs). The grant to B would be void as it is possible alcohol would be sold on the premises more than 21 years after the deaths of A, B, and the grantor. However, as the rule does not apply to grantors, the possibility of reverter in the grantor (or his heirs) would be valid.

Rule in Shelley's Case

A rule of law that may apply to certain future interests. Prohibited the conveyance of a future interest to the heirs of the grantee who received the possessory estate. If the grantor tried to convey a future interest to the heirs of the grantee, the interest was considered to be to the grantee and not in the heirs of the grantee. When a particular individual that holds a future interest is alive and may be identified. The heirs of a person who is still alive are unascertained.

Land Use Laws

Laws affecting the use and possession of land itself fall under the umbrella of "land use laws". Sometimes land you own may be used by someone who does not legally own or possess your land. This may include public entities, such as the government or city workers, or individuals who may frequent the land in a variety of settings, such as mail carriers, service workers, and even trespassers. There are special rules concerning land use in all states.

Easements

An easement is a legal term describing a situation in which someone allows another party to use a portion of land that they legally possess. Technically, an easement is defined as a "nonpossessory interest" in another party's property. In other words, a neighbor may need access to a portion of your land but doesn't necessarily want to have an ownership stake. And the landowner — who may not have a problem with his neighbor accessing his land — nevertheless wants to be sure he is not liable for any accidents that may occur on his property. An easement, therefore, is a legal process acknowledging another party's limited use of one's land.

For example, let's say you purchase a vacation property on the beach, but the only way to access it is along a gravel road that cuts through your neighbor's property. You can create an easement with your neighbor in order to use that road for the purpose of accessing your property. The easement document typically indicates the scope of this use.

Easements: Affirmative vs. Negative

The majority of easements are considered either affirmative or negative. If you have an affirmative easement, it means you have the right to do something, while the other party has the responsibility to do something with respect to the parcel. For example, an affirmative easement may give you the right to access a road on your neighbor's property and requires the other party to allow access to the road. Blocking your access to the road, even though technically it's on his or her property, violates the terms of the easement. These are the most common type of easement.

A negative easement, on the other hand, is a legally binding agreement to not do something with respect to a given parcel of land. For instance, someone who has a breathtaking view of the ocean may seek an easement to prevent her neighbor from obstructing that view in any way. These are much less common, particularly since homeowners' associations often address these concerns.

The Use and Termination of an Easement

Easements are created through a written document such as a will or contract, generally referred to as "conveyance in a deed". As with wills and other legal agreements, it must be validated through the proper documentation, signatures, and delivery. In some rare instances, the court will base its decision on the existence of an implied easement that is based on circumstances. If the only way to access a property is through another party's property, and the parties have been in agreement, then a court may create a formal easement based on this fact.

Once it has been created, the easement is legally binding and must be maintained. If you hold an easement on another party's property, you have the right to maintain and improve that parcel of land as long as it doesn't disturb or otherwise interfere with the other party's property rights. Easements may be terminated either through another legal agreement or by proving the "intent to abandon" the easement, if no legal action is taken.

Preservation and Conservation Easements

A conservation easement is a legal agreement between a property owner and another party (often a government entity) restricting development. Typically these types of easements are sought out to protect natural resources, including animal habitat and open space. Usually the landowner either donates or sells the easement, but they must be for

Chapter 10
Property Law

purely conservational purposes and carried out voluntarily. If certain conditions are met, the landowner who grants a conservation easement may be eligible for certain tax incentives.

Preservation easements are very similar, but are intended to protect privately owned historic properties. The property owner who grants the easement likely will be restricted in what it can do with the property, but also receives certain tax incentives (specifically, it is not taxed higher after the property is developed). So if a historic building has a conservation easement — often through charitable donations — the property owner must adhere to certain rules.

Eminent Domain

The term eminent domain refers to the right of a government entity to take private property for public use, with payment of compensation for the land. Different government bodies have different criteria; but generally, it must be able to prove a compelling reason for its planned use. One of the more popular uses of eminent domain is for the building of freeways, but it must be for public (not private) use.

When the government takes land, it must compensate the original property owner fairly. A "fair" price would be comparable to what the property owner may fetch on the open market. Landowners may challenge the government's purported "public use" argument, or argue for a better price.

Eminent Domain and Federal Law

The law of eminent domain originates in the "Takings Clause" of the Fifth Amendment to the U.S. Constitution. The framers of the Constitution were generally wealthy landowners who wanted certain guarantees against tyranny, although they understood that sometimes land would have to be taken for the public good. The Takings Clause states that "private property [should not] be taken for public use, without just compensation". As such, it only applies to private property and must be used for the public good. Interstate highways, to use a common example, typically are considered public goods.

What Is "Just" Compensation?

The Constitution requires that private landowners subject to eminent domain be paid "just" compensation, but what exactly does that mean? Generally, this is based on how much the landowner might expect to get on the open market. The value of the land could be determined by a number of factors, including its size and any resources it may have. Sometimes the government takes land for limited periods of time, which tends to make valuation much more difficult. If the police are able to prove "by a preponderance of the evidence" that the property was being used for criminal activity, then the government generally may seize the property without compensation.

Eminent Domain and Condemnation Proceedings

The government follows a particular process when it takes private land for public use under eminent domain law, beginning with its broader expansion or public improvement plan. Once planners determine which private parcels of land may be affected by these plans, they work with their own appraisers to come up with an appropriate valuation. If the private property owner accepts the offer from the government, the transaction is fairly straightforward. But if the parties are unable to agree on a price, the dispute will get resolved in condemnation proceedings.

If the matter goes into condemnation, the property owner (typically with the help of an attorney and an appraiser) will offer his or her own property valuation. One option for property owners is to dispute the forced sale by challenging the government's proposed use of the land, but these challenges typically fail as long as the use is determined to be "proper" and for the public good. Another option is to suggest that the claim is too broad, which in some limited cases may reduce the scope of the purchase. But the value of the property is generally the main issue when eminent domain cases go into condemnation proceedings.

What Is the Meaning of "Public Use"?

Since invoking eminent domain requires that the taken property be used for public use, it's important to understand what that means from a legal perspective. The term "public use" is not limited to the actual, direct use by the public — as would be the case for parks or roads — but refers to any use that generally confers a benefit to the public. For instance, a parcel of land with an abandoned factory may be obtained and cleared of all structures through eminent domain. Even if the end result is an empty lot, and not everyone "uses" the land, it could be argued that this benefits the community as a whole because of the aesthetic improvement from its removal.

Trespassing

To trespass is to enter someone else's land without their consent. Trespassing isn't always a crime (or actionable in a civil suit), such as in the case of deliveries or other situations where consent may be implied. In order for someone to be liable (either in civil law or criminally), there must be some level of intent. If land is fenced or there is a "no trespassing" sign, then it is assumed that a would-be trespasser knows it is private property.

As mentioned above, trespassing can relate to either a criminal or civil wrong. While police, park rangers, and other peace officers enforce criminal trespass law, property owners may file civil trespass claims against individuals who enter their property without permission or right-of-way. But for both civil and criminal trespassing, some element of intent must be established. Accidentally traversing someone else's property typically does not rise to the level of trespassing, since there was no intent to trespass. There also may be instances where an "implied consent" exists, such as when immediate action is needed to save a life or the use of front walkways by mail carriers.

Knowledge that a piece of property is privately owned and therefore off-limits may be implied in a number of different ways, including fences enclosing the parcel of land; "no trespassing" signs; or verbal warnings from the property owner. Similarly, a property owner may establish express consent by granting permission either in writing or verbally.

Liability for Trespasser Injuries

While property owners have no special duty to protect trespassers, they may be held liable in some instances if trespassers are injured. Essentially, a landowner who knows (or ought to know) that trespassers frequent his or her property is liable injuries caused by unsafe conditions if:

- The owner either created or maintained the unsafe condition;
- The unsafe condition is likely to cause serious injury or death;
- The owner had reason to believe that trespassers would not be aware of the unsafe condition; and
- The owner failed to exercise reasonable care to warn trespassers about the unsafe condition.

So while a home may have a "Beware of Dog" sign prominently displayed as a deterrent to would-be trespassers or burglars, it would be considered a fair warning to trespassers who may ultimately be injured by the dog. The rules are different for children, however, since the law assumes that children are largely naive to certain dangers. Therefore, property owners are responsible for maintaining a property that does not pose a risk to children, even those who enter the property without permission. Swimming pools are a common example, referred to as an "attractive nuisance" in the absence of a proper enclosure or deterrent.

Trespassers' Rights Under Adverse Possession Law

Trespassers may actually gain legal title to otherwise unused parcels of land under certain, limited circumstances. Often referred to as "continuous trespassers' rights", adverse possession laws are meant to encourage the use, care, and development of property. So if someone uses and improves a piece of property openly, paying property taxes, that individual may apply for legal title after a certain period of time has elapsed. Generally, a trespasser must satisfy the following four elements in order to qualify for a claim to the property:

- Hostile Claim — Trespasser must occupy the land, with or without knowledge that it is private property (such as relying on an incorrect deed).
- Actual Possession — Trespasser must physically inhabit the property and treat it as his or her own.
- Open and Notorious — Trespasser may not be evasive; the possession must be obvious.

- Exclusive and Continuous — Trespasser must have been in sole possession of the property for an unbroken period of time.

Trespassing is a complicated and multi-faceted area of the law.

Zoning

Most cities and other local municipalities regulate how a given parcel of land may be used through zoning laws. This is why office buildings are seldom located within residential neighborhoods, or why heavy industry (oil refining, for example) is not found next to shopping malls. Some areas are zoned for mixed uses, such as apartments, offices, and retail shops along a town center.

Zoning regulations often change as cities and counties transform, or sometimes are changed in an effort to encourage more business activity or to make way for a special building project.

Types of Zoning Classifications

There are several different types of zones related to real estate development, which tend to vary by community. The main types of zoning categories include the following:

Residential — This zone is meant for homes, such as houses, apartments, condominiums, and mobile homes; residential zones often address whether farm animals (such as chickens) may be kept and whether home businesses are permitted.

Commercial — This is a broad category that may include offices, restaurants, shopping centers, even apartments.

Industrial — Industrial zones include factories, warehouses, and similar types of establishments.

Agricultural — This zone protects agricultural land for farming and related activities; typically limiting the density of development and minimum acreage for separate plots of land.

Rural — This may include residential areas zoned to allow horses or small livestock.

Historic — Some communities have zoning laws that prevent alterations to historic buildings, often affecting those that qualify for tax incentives.

Aesthetic — Some upscale communities have special zoning laws (similar home owner association rules) covering color schemes, landscaping, building materials, and other aesthetic elements.

Mixed — Some areas are zoned for mixed use in order to encourage a greater density of housing, retail, and office space.

Relief From Zoning Laws

Property owners typically must conform to the zoning laws of their community or risk fines and other other sanctions. But there may be isolated instances where a property owner may feel compelled to dispute a zoning determination, particularly when zoning laws are changed and affect existing properties. There are generally two ways to dispute a zoning ordinance — asking for an exception from the law or challenging the ordinance itself as improper. Whatever the reason for challenging a zoning law, property owners should consult with an attorney before pursuing such an action.

In some cases, a property may be excused from any change in zoning law, which is referred to as "continuing existing use" or "lawful nonconforming use". These exceptions also may be available for property owners who have made a substantial investment in their property. For example, someone who spent a lot of time and money renovating a Victorian house into a high-end restaurant — even if it has yet to open for business — may be eligible for a lawful nonconforming use exemption. But if the public use argument is sufficiently compelling, the exemption may be denied.

Another way to get relief from a zoning law is to request a "variance", in which property owners are granted permission to incorporate specified variations from the zoning laws.

Zoning Laws and Homeowner Rights

If you live in a home located in an area that is zoned for residential use only, you generally may not use it for commercial uses. While you certainly can host a garage sale or let your child sell lemonade on the corner, you cannot open a restaurant in your house in places zoned residential. Similarly, most office buildings may not include housing. Make sure you learn your local ordinances with respect to zoning, as they tend to differ from one neighborhood to the next.

Landlord-Tenant Law

Landlord-tenant law governs the rental of commercial and residential property. It is composed primarily of state statutory and common law. A number of states have based their statutory law on either the Uniform Residential Landlord And Tenant Act (URLTA) or the Model Residential Landlord-Tenant Code. Federal statutory law may be a factor in times of national/regional emergencies and in preventing forms of discrimination.

The basis of the legal relationship between a landlord and tenant is grounded in both contract and property law. The tenant has a property interest in the land (historically, a non-freehold estate) for a given period of time. The length of the tenancy may be for a given period of time, for an indefinite period of time, (e.g., renewable/cancelable on a month to month basis), terminable at any time by either party (at will), or at sufferance if the agreement has been terminated and the tenant refuses to leave (holds over). If the tenancy is tenancy for years or periodic, the tenant has the right to possess the land, to restrict others (including the landlord) from entering upon it, and to sublease or assign the property. The landlord-tenant agreement may eliminate or limit these rights. The landlord-tenant agreement is normally embodied in a lease. The lease, though not historically or strictly a contract, may be subject to concepts embodied in contract law.

The landlord-tenant relationship is founded on duties proscribed by either statutory law, the common law, or the individual lease. What provisions may be contained in a lease is normally regulated by statutory law. Basic to all leases is the implied covenant of quiet enjoyment. This covenant ensure the tenant that his possession will not be disturbed by someone with a superior legal title to the land including the landlord. A breach of the covenant of quiet enjoyment may be actual or constructive. A constructive eviction occurs when the landlord causes the premises to become uninhabitable.

Housing codes were established to ensure that residential rental units were habitable at the time of rental and during the tenancy. Depending on the state, housing code violations may lead to administrative action or to the tenant being allowed to withhold rent. The habitability of a residential rental unit is also ensured by warranties of habitability which are prescribed by common and/or statutory law. A breach of the warranty of habitability or a covenant within the lease may constitute constructive eviction, allow the tenant to withhold rent, repair the problem and deduct the cost from the rent, or recover damages.

Unless the lease states otherwise, there is an assumption that the tenant has a duty to pay rent. State statutes may provide for a reasonable rental value to be paid absent a rental price provision. In commercial leases rent is commonly calculated in part or whole as a percentage of the tenants sales. Rent acceleration clauses that cause all the rent to become due if the tenant breaches a provision of the lease are common in both residential and commercial leases. Summary eviction statutes commonly allow a landlord to quickly evict a tenant who breaches statutorily specified lease provisions. Self-help as a method of eviction is generally restricted. Some states do not even allow it for tenants who have held over after the end of a lease. Landlords are also restricted from evicting tenants in retaliation of action the tenant took in regards to enforcing a provision of the lease or applicable law.

Federal law prohibits discrimination in housing and the rental market.

Nuisance

In the early days of the United States, land was abundant and neighbors were distant. As the population began to grow and urban areas increased, the courts were called upon to resolve property disputes. One of the very first judge-made doctrines applied to property disputes in the United States, the law of nuisance, was inherited from England. This doctrine still finds its way into property disputes today. At the risk of oversimplification, this doctrine is generally raised when a neighboring property owner is acting in a manner that can be described as a nuisance.

The Law of Nuisance

Lawsuits invoking the law of nuisance typically involve neighbors suing their neighbors or a public official suing a property owner for the benefit of the general public. By bringing suit, the plaintiff usually seeks to control or limit the use of the land owned by the defendant.

There are two basic types of nuisance suits. These are private and public nuisance actions. A private nuisance means there has been a loss of the use or enjoyment of property without an actual physical invasion of that property. An action for a physical invasion of property is known as a trespass action. A public nuisance is one that has more far reaching effects. It has the ability to affect the health, safety, welfare, or comfort of the public in general.

No matter what the type of nuisance, to be subject to injunctive relief, the interference with the property must be substantial and continuous. Relief that is injunctive in nature generally requires the defendant to take some specific actions to minimize the negative effect of its operations on the plaintiff, from limiting the hours of the action to placing an all out prohibition on the negative action. In constructing its relief, however, most courts will attempt to balance the relative hardships to both of the parties involved in the action. Especially where an ongoing business, as opposed to an individual, is the defendant in the action, the court will try to minimize the economic impact on the business.

How Courts Decide Cases

In deciding nuisance disputes, several factors influence courts. First, courts will look at the location in which the alleged nuisance is occurring and any applicable zoning restrictions that may apply to that area. For instance, a court may be less likely to place restrictions on a livestock feedlot located in a rural area than on one located at the edge of urban sprawl. On the other hand, no matter how rural, if the feedlot is located in a "residential" zone, a court may be more likely to allow injunctive or other relief. At the same time, the fact that an activity is located in area that is zoned for that type of operation does not mean that it cannot be found to constitute a nuisance. For example, an area may be zoned to allow a mixture of residential and commercial building, and, a court might still find that an "all night" gas station creates a nuisance for the residential property owners in

the area.

There are some other points to consider if you are thinking about bringing a nuisance action. First, a mere fear of future injury will not merit injunctive relief. Further, usually pure aesthetic considerations, such as the "look" of a funeral home in a residential area, will not rise to the level of a nuisance. Finally, where a person specifically purchases property knowing that a given operation is located nearby, the "moving to the nuisance" doctrine will usually prohibit injunctive relief. In this manner, if a person moves into a house located next to a baseball field, this doctrine may prohibit the person from seeking relief from the bright lights and noise.

Exercises

I. Multiple-choice Questions:

1. Ogden is the owner of an apartment house. He executes a deed of the property "to my son, Sam, for his life, and, upon Sam's death, to the children of Sam, except that if Sam becomes bankrupt, to my daughter, Diane, then to the children of Diane, upon Diane's death." Sam is alive and well and not bankrupt at the time of the grant.

Assume for purposes of this question only that Sam becomes bankrupt and the Diane takes possession of the property. The interest of Diane's children, Carla and Cliffy, is best described as:

A. A contingent remainder.

B. A vested remainder subject to total divestment.

C. An executory interest.

D. A vested remainder subject to open.

Questions 2-3 are based on the following fact situation:

Owner holds a fee simple interest in 2,000 acres of land. He wants to develop 1,500 acres as a residential subdivision. He wants to hold the remaining 500 acres for a long period, hoping they will appreciate in value. In the meantime, he plans to use the tract as an inducement in the marketing of the lots in the 1,500-acre subdivision. Owner's market analysis leads him to conclude that the greatest inducement he can offer is to hold the 500 acres as an area in which purchasers in the subdivision can ride horseback, hike, camp, and fish. Business judgment indicates that he can make these 500 acres available for these purposes for 20 years if he can be assured that after such period he will be free to do with the land as he chooses.

2. The best device to implement the purpose of Owner with respect to the 500 acres (assuming that any device chosen will receive judicial recognition and enforcement) is:

    A. Covenant.

    B. Easement.

    C. Leasehold.

    D. Personal contractual obligation of Owner.

3. Assume that at the end of 20 years Owner sells the 500-acre tract to Waste, Inc., which plans to use the tract to dispose of low-level radioactive waste. The statute of limitations for adverse possession and prescriptive rights is 10 years. If the subdivision homeowners seek to enjoin this use, they will:

    A. Prevail, because they have acquired an easement by prescription for recreational use.

    B. Prevail, because they have acquired the tract by adverse possession.

    C. Not prevail, because they have no interest in the property.

    D. Not prevail, because damages, not an injunction, is the appropriate remedy.

4. Theodora owned Grayacre. She sold Grayacre to Buzz, who paid her a fair price for the property. Buzz failed to record the deed and left for an extended trip to the Indian Ocean. Two days after Buzz departed, Theodora was struck by a car. She died in the hospital two hours later, having never regained consciousness. Her will was duly probated, and one provision of the will read, "I leave Grayacre to my daughter, Daphne." Daphne knew nothing about the sale of Grayacre to Buzz, and she properly

recorded her title to Grayacre in the county recorder of deeds office. Daphne wanted to start her own business, and asked the chief loan officer at Greenback Bank & Trust Company to advance her $50,000 to start up. The loan officer felt that Daphne's proposal was somewhat risky, but offered to make the loan if Daphne put up sufficient collateral. Daphne offered a mortgage on Grayacre as collateral. The bank checked the recorder's records showing Daphne to have sole title to Grayacre, and the loan and mortgage were executed.

Daphne opened "Daphne's Duncecaps", a company to manufacture and distribute duncecaps to public schools. Unfortunately for Daphne's business, her idea was not popular with school purchasing agents and Daphne's Duncecaps failed. Daphne was unable to repay her loan to Greenback, and the bank went to court to demand that Grayacre be foreclosed, and any proceeds from the sale be turned over to Greenback in satisfaction of Daphne's debt. Just as Grayacre was about to be sold, Buzz returned from the Indian Ocean, deed in hand. The state in which Grayacre is located has the following statute:

No conveyance or mortgage of an interest in land is valid against any subsequent purchaser for value without notice thereof, unless it is recorded.

May Greenback successfully take Grayacre?

 A. Yes, because Greenback succeeds to Daphne's rights in Grayacre.

 B. Yes, because the bank is a mortgagee for value.

 C. No, because Daphne never owned the land.

 D. No, because the bank knew or should have known that Daphne's business was very risky, and an intelligent loan officer would not have loaded the money in the first place.

Questions 5-7 are based on the following fact situation:

Harold and Wilma, a married couple, own Blackacre as a tenancy by the entirety. Harold transfers to Albert, by quitclaim deed, his interest in Blackacre. Wilma is away at the time of the transfer. When she returns, she mortgages her interest to Charlie.

5. What interest, if any, does Albert have?

   A. No interest.

   B. An undivided one-half interest with the right of survivorship.

   C. An undivided one-half interest held in tenancy in common.

   D. The entire fee.

6. What interest, if any, does Charlie have?

   A. A lien against the entire property.

   B. A secured interest against Wilma's one-half interest as tenant in the entirety with Albert.

   C. A secured interest against Wilma's one-half interest as tenant in the entirety with Harold.

   D. No interest.

7. If Wilma predeceases Harold, leaving a will devising her interest to Charlie, who takes her interest?

   A. Albert.

   B. Charlie.

   C. Harold.

   D. Wilma's heirs.

8. For many years, Allison owned Lot A, a parcel of land bordered on the west by a public road, and Barbara owned Lot B, which is located immediately to the east of Lot A. Barbara also had an easement to cross Lot A to enter the public road adjoining Lot A. Lot B is surrounded by swampland on the north, south, and east. Thus, the only route of ingress to and egress from Lot B over dry land passed through Lot A.

Twelve years ago, Barbara decided to move out of state. Thus, Allison purchased Lot B from Barbara and proceeded to use both lots as a common tract. Ten years later, Allison sold Lot B to Carla.

Does Carla have an easement over Lot A?

   A. Yes, she has an easement in gross.

B. Yes, because her only access to Lot B is across Lot A.

C. No, because the easement was extinguished when Allison purchased Lot B.

D. No, because she has not used the property long enough to gain an easement by prescription.

9. Jet inherited Shaleacre, a parcel of land, from Luz. Bick owned Rockacre, a much larger piece of property, which was adjacent to Shaleacre. Bick began to drill for oil on Rockacre, but all of Bick's exploratory wells were nonproductive "dry holes." Bick was certain that there was oil in the area and he importuned Jet to grant him a lease to drill on Shaleacre. Jet turned down Bick's offer. After Jet's refusal, Bick drilled an exploratory well on Rockacre. However, Bick drilled the well on a slanted angle, so that he was actually drilling under Shaleacre, even though his rig was located on Rockacre. Bick struck oil, but shortly thereafter Jet discovered that the oil was coming from underneath Shaleacre.

Does Jet have an action for damages against Bick?

A. Yes, because Bick has invaded Jet's subterranean rights.

B. Yes, but only of Bick's drilling interferes with Jet's use and enjoyment of Shaleacre.

C. No, because oil is a free-flowing liquid and may be captured wherever it flows.

D. No, because Bick's action does not interfere with Jet's rights to drill for oil on Shaleacre.

10. Barbara purchased a house from Stewart. It turned out that the concrete used to pour the foundation had been improperly mixed and the foundation was crumbling. Barbara discovered that the cost of repairing the defective foundation would be over $10,000. She filed suit against Stewart for the cost of repairs.

Which of the following additional facts, if true, will give Barbara the best chance of winning her suit?

A. The crumbling foundation makes the house unsafe or uninhabitable.

B. Stewart was the builder of the house.

C. Barbara took title to the house by warranty deed.

D. Barbara had no knowledge of the defect when she purchased the house, and the defect was not reasonably apparent.

II. Essay Question:

L and T entered into a written lease of a completely furnished dwelling for a period of one year at a rental of $250 per month, commencing on September 1, 2002. The lease contained a clause allowing T "to give up possession and terminate his liability for rent if the premises, through no fault on T's part, are destroyed or damaged so as to be uninhabitable."

X, the previous tenant of L under a lease that expired August 31, 2002, wrongfully held over and remained on the premises until December 1, 2002, when T took possession. During this period, L refused to take any action to oust X, although repeatedly requested to do so by T.

Shortly after going into possession, T was injured when a bedroom chair collapsed under his weight. Several of the screws pulled loose and came out of the softwood frame. There is no evidence that L knew of the chair's defective construction or that L was negligent.

On March 1, 2003, T paid his rent up to date, surrendered possession, and moved out because the roof had deteriorated and had begun to leak badly. L informed T that he refused to accept the surrender, but he would attempt to relet the dwelling for T's account. On May 1, 2003, T relet the premises to Y for the remainder of the term at a rental of $200 per month.

There are no applicable statues. Discuss any rights and duties of L and T.

Chapter 11
Criminal Law

Overview

In the United States, British common law ruled during colonial times. Common law is a process that establishes and updates rules that govern some nations. Once America became an independent nation, it adopted the U.S. Constitution as "the supreme law of the land". The U.S. continues to employ a common law system, which works in combination with state and federal statutes.

Criminal Law, as distinguished from civil law, is a system of laws concerned with punishment of individuals who commit crimes. Thus, where in a civil case two individuals dispute their rights, a criminal prosecution involves the people as a whole deciding whether to punish an individual for his conduct or lack of conduct (i.e. omission). Just as the people decide what conduct to punish, so the people decide what punishment is appropriate. Accordingly, punishments vary with the severity of the offense—from a simple fine (e.g. for a traffic violation) to loss of freedom (e.g. for murder).

Each state decides what conduct to designate a crime. Thus, each state has its own criminal code. Congress has also chosen to punish certain conduct, codifying federal criminal law in Title 18 of the U.S. Code. Criminal laws vary significantly among the states and the Federal Government. While some statutes resemble the common law criminal code, others, like the New York Penal Law, closely mimic the Model Penal Code (MPC).

A "crime" is any act or omission in violation of a law prohibiting it, or omitted in violation of a law ordering it. The government cannot prosecute an individual for conduct that was not declared criminal at the time the individual acted. The Constitution explicitly forbids in Article 1, Sections 9 and 10 retroactively applicable criminal laws—ex post facto

Chapter 11
Criminal Law

laws.

It is also important to note that a law cannot punish a person simply for their status. As the Supreme Court explained in Robinson v. California, 370 U.S. 660 (1962), any statute that criminalizes the status of a person inflicts a cruel and unusual punishment in violation of the Eight and Fourteenth Amendments. For example, a state could not punish an individual for "being homeless", which would be a status offense, but could punish a homeless individual for trespassing or loitering, which involves some conduct.

In general, Criminal Law asks and answers three questions:

Did an individual commit a crime?

Which crime did an individual commit?

Does the individual have a defense?

Mens Rea

Mens Rea is a fancy way to say "mental state". Culpable Mental State refers to the state of mind of an individual while committing a crime. Generally, a crime requires that a guilty act or omission (the actus reus) be committed with the required degree of guilty mind. Generally, certain acts are crimes only if done with a particular state of mind, and that a certain sort of criminal act is more or less serious depending on the perpetrator's state of mind at the time. The prosecution must prove beyond a reasonable doubt that, the accused did so with the state of mind required for the commission of that particular crime in order to convict the accused. A very few acts that amounts to strict liability offenses are criminal, however they are done. The term, Culpable Mental State is synonymous with mens rea (guilty mind).

Classification of a Crime

The classification of a crime is based on the extent of punishment that can be given for committing it. There are two major types of crimes in the United States: felonies and misdemeanors. The punishment is usually based on the seriousness of the crime. States may differ as to the classification of any particular crime. A crime committed in one state may be classified differently than if it was committed in another state.

A felony is considered a serious crime. Most states and the federal government classify a crime that's punishable by more than one year in prison as a felony. A felony that's punishable by death is considered a capital crime.

A misdemeanor is considered a less serious crime. Most states and the federal government classify a crime that's punishable by less than one year in prison as a misdemeanor. Some states consider a misdemeanor as any crime that's punishable only by fine or a small length of time in jail. If a misdemeanor is considered a very minor offense, such as jaywalking, the crime may be classified as a petty offense.

Police Investigate, Prosecutors File Charges

Many people think that police officers (who investigate crimes) also charge offenders. That is a common misconception. Police gather evidence and sometimes also testify in court. But prosecutors — including district attorneys, United States Attorneys and others — ultimately decide whether a suspect is prosecuted or not.

Criminal Charges

Criminal law operates differently according to what crime the state has charged a defendant with. Each crime has its own set of elements that define it, as well as defenses that may apply and factors that influence sentencing. However, while each crime is different, there are several broad types of crimes that share features and defenses. It can be useful to examine all the crimes in a category in order to understand the laws and defenses and involved.

Homicide

When someone takes the life of another, regardless of intent or other details surrounding the incident, it is called a homicide. Homicide is not always a crime, such as in cases of self-defense or the state-sanctioned execution of certain convicted criminals. Criminal homicides involve either negligence or willful intent, and range from involuntary manslaughter (killing another motorist in a drunk driving accident, for example) to first-degree murder (stalking and killing a member of a rival gang, for instance). Sentences also vary widely, depending on the severity of the crime and other mitigating factors. For example, some states sentence convicted murderers to death but provide psychiatric treatment to those acquitted by reason of insanity.

Murder

First degree murder is the most serious criminal homicide. Typically, first degree murder is both intentional and premeditated. Premeditated can mean anything from a long time plan to kill the victim, to a shorter term plan. The intent of the accused murderer does not need to be focused on the actual victim. If someone planned on killing one victim, but by accident kills someone else, the murder is still intentional and premeditated meaning a first degree murder charge. Here is more information about your state's first degree murder laws.

When there is a lack of premeditation but the killer intended to kill for example, in homicides commonly described as occurring "in the heat of passion" the homicide may draw second degree murder charges or perhaps voluntary manslaughter charges, depending on the state. Here is more information about your state's second degree murder laws.

Manslaughter

Manslaughter generally means an illegal killing that falls short of murder. The lowest form of manslaughter is involuntary manslaughter. This means that the perpetrator did not intend to kill anyone, but still killed the victim through behavior that was either criminally negligent or reckless. One common example is a DUI accident which kills someone. Someone driving drunk is behaving in a criminally reckless manner, even if they had no intent to kill anyone. Here is more information about your state's involuntary manslaughter laws.

Voluntary manslaughter usually means that the offender did not have a prior intent to kill such as when the homicide occurs "in the heat of passion" and without forethought. Depending on the state, this crime may fall under a variant of murder charges, instead of manslaughter. Here is more information about your state's voluntary manslaughter laws.

Legal Homicides

Some homicides are not illegal. Criminal laws carve out exceptions for some killings which would otherwise fall under criminal laws against manslaughter or murder. These are referred to as "justified homicide". One primary example is a killing in justified self-defense or defense of someone else. Such a homicide is deemed justified if the situation called for self-defense and state law allows lethal force in that type of situation. Most state laws allow justified homicide to defend oneself or another from credible threat of serious crimes such as rape, armed robbery and murder.

Drug Charges

Many drug cases involve either drug possession or drug trafficking charges. The difference between the two charges has much to do with the amount of the substance in question. Common controlled substances for which possession charges are brought include: prescription drugs (e.g., oxycodone and Xanax); marijuana; cocaine; heroin; methamphetamine (meth); and methylone (molly).

Property Crimes

Property crime is a category of crime in which the person who commits the crime seeks to do damage to or derive an unlawful benefit or interest from another's property without using force or threat of force. Property crimes are often high-volume crimes. Property crime includes burglary, theft, arson, larceny, shoplifting and vandalism. Others require the actual taking of money or property. Some, such as robbery, require a victim present at the time of the crime. Most property crimes include a spectrum of degrees depending on factors including the amount stolen and use of force or arms in theft related cases, and actual or potential bodily injury in property destruction crimes such as arson.

Theft

The term theft is used widely to refer to crimes involving the taking of a person's property without their permission. But theft has a very broad legal meaning which may encompass more than one category, and multiple degrees, of crimes. Theft is often defined as the unauthorized taking of property from another with the intent to permanently deprive them of it. Within this definition lie two key elements:

(1) a taking of someone else's property; and

(2) the requisite intent to deprive the victim of the property permanently.

The taking element in a theft typically requires seizing possession of property that belongs to another, and may also involve removing or attempting to remove the property. However, it is the element of intent where most of the complex legal challenges typically arise in theft-related cases.

For example, Alex goes to Patrick's computer store, puts two flash drives in his pocket, and walks out the door intent of keeping them. Alex can be charged with theft. Had Alex stolen Patrick's car from the par Larceny.

Larceny is what most people think of as common theft — the taking of someone else's property without the use of force. The Model Penal Code and the laws of several states place larceny and certain other property crimes under the general category of theft. However, there are some states that retain the traditional common-law distinctions in which larceny is its own crime, separate from other property crimes like embezzlement or robbery.

The following elements must be proven in order to obtain a conviction for larceny:

- The unlawful taking and carrying away;
- Of someone else's property;
- Without the consent of the owner; and
- With the intent to permanently deprive the owner of the property.king lot, Alex would likely be charged with grand theft.

Burglary

Burglary is typically defined as the unlawful entry into almost any structure (not just a home or business) with the intent to commit any crime inside (not just theft/larceny). No physical breaking and entering is required; the offender may simply trespass through an open door. Unlike robbery, which involves use of force or fear to obtain another person's property, there is usually no victim present during a burglary.

For example, Dan enters Victor's boathouse through an open window, intending to steal Victor's boat. Finding the boat is gone, Dan returns home. Though he took nothing, Dan has committed burglary.

The crime of burglary has been around for a long time. It originally developed under the common law, but states have incorporated the basic idea of burglary into their penal codes, albeit with some slight modifications. For instance, under the common law definition of burglary, the crime had to take place in the dwelling house of another at night. Most states have subsequently broadened the definition of burglary to include businesses and illegal entries during the day.

Burglary developed to protect a person's interest in their home and to prevent violence, not to protect against theft. Other laws criminalize the taking of property; instead, burglary is meant to safeguard the sanctity of a person's home and to protect against the possible violence that could arise if someone discovers a burglar in their house.

The definition of burglary arises out of state law, and thus, the components of the crime may differ slightly depending on the state. Federal criminal law incorporates the meaning of burglary used by the state that the crime occurred in.

Most states and the Model Penal Code use the same basic definition of burglary, however. In those states, burglary is:

- The unauthorized breaking and entry;
- Into a building or occupied structure;
- With the intent to commit a crime inside.

Each of those elements must be present in order to convict a defendant accused of burglary, so its important to examine each of them a little more closely.

Robbery

Many states define robbery as theft/larceny of property or money through the offender's use of physical force or fear against a victim. Where a deadly weapon such as a gun is used or the victim suffers injury, the robbery may be charged as "armed" or "aggravated". Unlike burglary, the crime of robbery almost always requires the presence of a victim who suffers actual injury, or is threatened with harm.

For example, Dan approaches Victor from behind, demanding Victor's wallet while pressing a hard object into his back. Fearing that Dan has a gun, Victor gives up his wallet. If Dan did use a gun, or if Victor suffered an injury, the charge would likely be elevated to "armed" or "aggravated" robbery.

United States law regarding robbery has its roots in the common law that we inherited from the English legal system. While most states have codified their robbery laws in their penal codes, in the absence of such a statute the common law definition would still apply.

The penal codes of each state define robbery in different ways, but the definitions contain the same basic elements. Robbery generally consists of:

- The taking, with the intent to steal, of;
- The personal property of another;
- From his or her person or in their presence;
- Against his or her will;
- By violence, intimidation or the threat of force.

Arson

Arson is defined as the willful and malicious burning or charring of property. There are many types of arson crimes, including setting fire to one's property with fraudulent intent — such as to collect insurance money. While the majority of arson crimes involve damage to buildings, arson can also be committed by a person who sets fire to forest land or a boat. Arson statutes typically classify arson as a felony due to the potential to cause injuries or death.

Many states recognize differing degrees of arson, based on such factors as whether the building was occupied and whether insurance fraud was intended. Less serious arson cases may result in minor punishments, while other arson cases may result in the death penalty. Arson is handled in various courts throughout the U.S. in many different ways.

Many states classify arson crimes into different categories or degrees. More serious categories or degrees of arson will result in stricter punishments. Setting fire to an occupied building, for instance, can result in a more severe arson charge than setting fire to an abandoned barn in the countryside.

Arson is investigated by elite law enforcement units using the most advanced chemical analyses to locate the point of origin of a fire. Law enforcement can take months or years to fully investigate before a case is charged. Law enforcement looks at the motivation behind the crime of arson. Arson occurs in domestic violence cases, to hide another crime including murder and for financial gain.

Vandalism

Vandalism is an offense that occurs when a person destroys or defaces someone else's property without permission. Effects of vandalism can include broken windows, graffiti, damage to vehicles, and even damage or destruction of a person's website. The results of vandalism may be found on billboards, street signs, and building structures, as well as near bus stops, tunnels, cemeteries, and many other public spaces.

While vandalism may be considered "art" by some, it is nonetheless a crime against property that is punishable by jail time, monetary fines, or both.

Shoplifting

"Shoplifting" generally refers to the theft of merchandise from a store or place of business. Shoplifting is a type of larceny, which simply means taking the property of someone else without their permission, and with the intent to permanently deprive the owner of the property taken.

Though states may punish shoplifting under their general larceny or theft statutes, many states have enacted statutes to specifically address shoplifting. States may refer to the crime by different names, including "retail theft" and "concealment of merchandise".

These state laws vary widely, but generally, shoplifting offenses includes two elements:

1. willfully concealing or taking possession of items being offered for sale; and

2. the intent to deprive the items' rightful owner (typically the store) of possession of the items, without paying the purchase price.

Chapter 11
Criminal Law

Alcohol Crimes

The relationship between alcohol and crime is complex. The misuse of legal substances can be connected to crime. Alcohol, while legal for adults, may be used in a manner that constitutes a crime or status offense (i.e., while operating a vehicle (DUI) or possession by a minor). Alcohol also impacts crime indirectly via the effects they have on users' behavior and by their association with violence and other illegal activity in connection with their manufacture, distribution, acquisition or consumption.

Sex Crimes

Sex crimes refer to criminal offenses of a sexual nature. Every state has laws against prohibiting the various types of sex crimes, such as rape and sexual assault, and each state has its own time limit (or "statute of limitations") in which victims of sex crimes may file a lawsuit against the alleged offender.

Commonly known sex crimes include, rape, child molestation, sexual battery, lewd conduct, possession and distribution of child pornography, possession and distribution of obscene material, prostitution, solicitation of prostitution, pimping, pandering, indecent exposure, lewd act with a child, and penetration of the genital or anal region by a foreign object.

Cyber Crimes

Cyber crimes are criminal offenses committed via the Internet or otherwise aided by various forms of computer technology, such as the use of online social networks to bully others or sending sexually explicit digital photos with a smart phone. But while cyber crime is a relatively new phenomenon, many of the same offenses that can be committed with a computer or smart phone, including theft or child pornography, were committed in person prior to the computer age.

Online Scams

The Internet offers a global marketplace for consumers and businesses. But thieves also recognize the potentials of cyberspace. The same scams that have been conducted by mail and phone can now be found on the World Wide Web and in email, and new cyberscams are emerging. Types of internet fraud include internet auction fraud, credit card fraud, investment fraud, and even what is know as "Nigerian letter or '419' fraud". Named for the violation of Section 419 of the Nigerian Criminal Code, it combines the threat of impersonation fraud with a variation of an advance fee scheme in which a letter, e-mail, or fax is received by the victim.

Phishing Scam

Phishing is an email fraud method in which the fraudster sends out a legitimate-looking email in an attempt to gather personal and financial information from recipients. Typically, the messages appear to come from well known and trustworthy websites including PayPal, eBay, MSN, or Google. A phishing scam, like the fishing expedition it's named for, is a speculative venture: the phisher puts the lure hoping to fool at least a few of the prey that encounter the bait.

Selling Fake Pharmaceuticals

The Food and Drug Administration (FDA) is responsible for ensuring that all the food, beverages, and drugs on the marketplace are safe and, in the case of drugs, effective treatments. Counterfeit medicine is fake medicine. It may be contaminated or contain the wrong or no active ingredient. They could have the right active ingredient but at the wrong dose. Drug counterfeiting occurs less frequently in the U.S. than in other countries due to the strict regulatory framework that governs the production of drug products and the distribution chain, and enforcement against violators. However, counterfeit drugs are illegal and may be harmful to your health.

Fraud and Financial Crimes

Fraud and financial crimes are a form of theft/larceny that occur when a person or entity takes money or property, or uses them in an illicit manner, with the intent to gain a benefit from it. These crimes typically involve some form of deceit, subterfuge or the abuse of a position of trust, which distinguishes them from common theft or robbery. In today's complex economy, fraud and financial crimes can take many forms.

Debit/Credit Card Fraud

Debit and credit card fraud also occurs when an individual has an intent to fraudulently obtain money, goods, or services by using the access card of a cardholder who has not authorized its use. Common examples of credit or debit card fraud include using someone else's credit or debit card without that person's consent, using your own credit or debit card knowing that it has been revoked or expired or that your available balance is less than the purchase price, and using a stolen or fraudulent credit or debit card to receive money, goods or services.

Forgery

The crime of forgery occurs when, with the intent to defraud, a person executes, alters or publishes a writing without the owner's knowledge or consent. This can also happen if s/he fraudulently makes a writing and holds it out to be the work of another. A "writing" can include money, coins, credit cards, checks, bank drafts, stock certificates, bonds, wills and deeds.

Wire Fraud

The crime of wire fraud occurs when someone voluntarily and intentionally uses an interstate communications device (such as a telephone or the internet) as a part of any scheme to defraud another of property, or anything else of value. For example, if you try to sell property you do not own, and in your attempt you use a your smartphone to send an email to someone trying to convince that person to purchase the land, you commit wire fraud. Wire fraud is a federal crime with serious potential consequences.

Types of Insurance Fraud

Insurance fraud is stealing. Simply put, insurance fraud is lying for the purpose of getting more money from an insurance company, whether it is auto insurance, life insurance, or any other kind of insurance. There are two types of insurance fraud: soft and hard fraud. An example of soft fraud is getting into a motorcycle accident and claiming your injuries are worse than they really are for financial gain. An example of hard fraud would be getting into that same motorcycle accident on purpose so that you can claim the insurance money. Both are crimes.

Public Safety Violations

Certain state and local laws prohibit behavior that could be considered disruptive or threatening to public safety or the general peace of a public area, such playing loud music in front of a restaurant or inciting violence in a public park. Public safety violations include disorderly conduct and disturbing the peace, which are considered "catch-all" violations for actions or words that compromise the safety or overall peace of public places, varying from state to state.

Disturbing the Peace and Fighting Words

In order to get convicted of provoking another person using "fighting words" the district attorney must prove, beyond a reasonable doubt, that you used offensive words which were inherently likely to provoke an immediate violent reaction, and those words were directed at one or more persons and spoken in a public place. What about the First Amendment? This offense is essentially an exception to the right of free speech that is otherwise guaranteed by the First Amendment to the United States Constitution because courts have held that the types of "offensive words" that this subdivision prohibits "necessarily invite a breach of the peace."

Disorderly Conduct and Assaulting a Police Officer

Sometimes disorderly conduct can be elevated to the more severe crime of assaulting a police officer. In many states, to be guilty you must, with the intent of preventing the officer from performing his or her duties, cause physical injury to the officer. Remember it's the intent to interfere with the officer's performance of his or her duties, not the intent to injure the officer. Some statutes also include firefighters, EMS / EMT personnel, emergency room doctors and nurses, investigators and social workers, Department of Corrections officers; Motor Vehicle inspectors, and probation officers.

Disturbing the Peace

One of the most aggravating problems between neighbors is noise. If your neighbor is seriously bothering you with noise, the neighbor is probably violating a local noise law.

Chapter 11
Criminal Law

Typical laws regulate the times, types and loudness of the noise you need not tolerate in the interests of being neighborly. Keep in mind, noise can legally exceed the limit in emergencies, such as road repair. Also, some cities issue permits for certain activities, such as a construction project or street fair.

Exercises

I. Multiple-choice Questions:

1. The state of Ames has a statute that defines criminal assault as occurring when one person "causes bodily injury to another". The case law of Ames defines criminal assault as a "general-intent crime".

George and Kramer are drivers searching for a parking spot at a mall in the state of Ames. Both drivers approach an empty spot at about the same time. They begin to argue over who is entitled to the spot. During the argument, Kramer, intending to scare George away, walks over to George's car and touches George's throat with a screwdriver. Unfortunately, when George twists his head to look at Kramer, he cuts his throat against the screwdriver point and is seriously injured.

Based on these facts, if Kramer is prosecuted for criminal assault, it is most likely that:

    A. Kramer is culpable because he intended to place the screwdriver against George's throat.

    B. Kramer is culpable because he created an inherently dangerous situation.

    C. Kramer is not culpable because he could not reasonably foresee George's actions.

    D. Kramer is not culpable because he lacked the intent to physically injure George.

2. Responding to a recent trend in gang violence, the California legislature enacted a statute that makes it a capital offense for any motorist to "knowingly" kill another

motorist with an explosive device. (Assume that California law follows the Model Penal Code's definition of "knowingly".)

One day, Freddy, a member of a gang called the Hooters, pulls alongside a car driven by Richie, a member of the Rockers gang. Richie makes a derogatory finger gesture toward Freddy. Enraged, Freddy lights a stick of dynamite, throws the stick into Richie's car, and then races away. Richie is killed when the dynamite explodes. Jack, who was sleeping in the back seat of Richie's car, is also killed. Freddy had no way of knowing that Jack was in Richie's car.

Based on these facts, can Freddy be successfully prosecuted under the statute for Jack's death?

  A. Yes, because he knowingly threw the dynamite into Richie's Car.

  B. Yes, because Jack was clearly within the zone of danger created by Freddy's conduct.

  C. No, because Freddy did not know Jack was in the Car.

  D. No, because Richie's conduct constituted "provocation".

3. Joe, desperately needing money for his drug habit, steals a television from a friend's house. (Assume that, under applicable law, no burglary has occurred.) Three days later, Joe holds a garage sale and offers to sell the TV to Molly for $50. When Molly asks Joe how he could sell the item for "such a bargain", Joe replies that he needs the money "quickly" to relocate to another city. Molly pays Joe $50 and takes the television without ever getting proof of title for the item.

Based on these facts, it is most likely that Joe could be successfully prosecuted for:

  A. False pretenses because Joe implicitly represented to Molly that he owned the television.

  B. Larceny by trick because Joe received $50 for the television, but gave no instrument of title to Molly.

  C. No crime because Joe made no express representations of ownership to Molly.

Chapter 11
Criminal Law

D. No crime because purchasers assume the risk of defective titles at events such as garage sales.

4. After Jethro was fired from his job, he decided to "get even" with his ex-employer. So, one night, Jethro broke into Farmer John's barn and set fire to John's favorite tractor. The barn was located approximately 100 feet from the main house.

One of Farmer John's neighbors, Leroy, saw smoke coming from the barn. Leroy ran over and put out the fire before any part of the barn was destroyed. There was, however, extensive charring to the barn. Also, several of the items in the barn were burned. (Assume that the common law view of arson is adhered to in this jurisdiction.)

Based on these facts, if Jethro is prosecuted for arson, it is most likely:

A. Jethro is not guilty because the barn was only charred.

B. Jethro is guilty because the fire caused damage to a structure adjacent to the main house.

C. Jethro is not guilty because he did not specifically intend to damage any structure (only Farmer John's tractor).

D. Jethro is not guilty because the barn isn't part of Farmer John's house.

5. Mr. Barnes, a senior partner at the We Sue For You law firm, gave a fax machine to Andrew, a file room clerk, to deliver to a repair shop. Andrew, who felt slighted because he was not given a Christmas bonus by Mr. Barnes, took the fax machine to a local pawnshop and obtained $200 for it. He then told Mr. Barnes that a thug had taken the fax machine from him at gunpoint. Two days later, Mr. Barnes happened to see the fax machine in the pawnshop window and called the police.

Andrew was subsequently arrested. (Assume that common law principles are applicable in this jurisdiction.)

Based on these facts, if Andrew is prosecuted for larceny, it is most likely that:

A. Andrew is guilty because he pawned Barnes's fax machine.

B. Andrew is guilty because he lied to Barnes when he said the fax machine was taken from him.

C. Andrew is not guilty because Barnes voluntarily gave him the fax machine.

D. Andrew is not guilty if he intended to redeem the fax machine from the pawnshop when he was arrested.

6. Anita Badcheck decides that she simply has to have a new Mercedes convertible. She goes to the local Mercedes dealer and writes a check for the price of the car from her personal account. She knows that she only has $50 in her account. Before the salesperson can verify that the check is good, he has a heart attack. After the manager calls for an ambulance, he tells Anita to "take the car" and gives her the car's title documents. Three days after Anita drives off in the new Mercedes, her check is returned to the dealership, marked "insufficient funds".

Based on these facts, if Anita is prosecuted for the crime of false pretenses, it is most likely that:

A. Anita is guilty because she took possession of the vehicle.

B. Anita is guilty because she took title to the vehicle.

C. Anita is not guilty because she only received possession of the vehicle.

D. Anita is not guilty because the vehicle and attendant documents of title were turned over voluntarily by the dealer.

7. Erica offered to sell her computer to Jamie for $1,000. Erica told Jamie that the computer worth at least $2,000. However, just the day before, Jamie had been told by an expert appraiser that the computer was worth "$500, at most". Jamie, believing that the computer was worth $2,000, gave Erica a money order for $1,000. Erica, however, lost the money order before she could cash it.

Based on these facts, if Erica is prosecuted for the crime of false pretenses, it is most likely that:

A. Erica is guilty because she fraudulently obtained Jamie's money order.

B. Erica is guilty because Jamie took possession of the computer.

C. Erica is not guilty because she never cashed the money order.

D. Erica is not guilty because her comment about the computer's value was merely her opinion, not a factual statement.

8. Allison was shopping at Bruno Magli, when she spotted an extraordinary pair of loafers. Allison checked the price tag and saw the shoes were marked at $350. She had only $200 in her pocketbook. Undaunted by her shortage of funds, Allison calmly took a $200 price tag from another pair of shoes and switched it with the price tag on the loafers she wanted to buy. The teenage cashier failed to notice the change in price tags. Allison happily took her new pair of shoes home.

Two days later, she was arrested when the store manager's inventory check revealed the tag switch.

Based on these facts, if Allison is prosecuted for larceny by trick, it is most likely that:

    A. Allison is guilty because she acquired the shoes by deceit.

    B. Allison is guilty because she fraudulently switched price tags

    C. Allison is not guilty because she acquired the legal title of the shoes.

    D. Allison is not guilty because she altered no digits on either of the price tags.

9. Mary asked Brian Beagal if she could borrow his new Toyota. She told Brian that she needed the car to go to a party at a professor's house. When she made the statement, she had no other purpose in mind. Brian gave her the keys and told Mary to have a good time. At the professor's party, Mary had a violent argument with her fiancé and decided that she had to get as far away from him as possible. Mary drove back to her house, put her most valuable possessions in Brian's car, and started on a trip out West. Mary was arrested one week later when a custom's official checked the car's license plate at the U.S.-Mexico border.

Based on these facts, it is most likely that Mary could be successfully prosecuted for:

    A. Larceny.

    B. False pretenses.

    C. Larceny by trick.

    D. Embezzlement.

10. Sid was the manager of the local Domino's Pizza. One night, while he was

working at Domino's, he opened the safe in the back office with the key the owner had given to him. Sid was given the key in order to pay for any unexpected expenditures that might arise while the owner was away. Sid took $250 from the safe. He did not use this money to pay for any business expenses. Rather, he used the money to buy an expensive watch for his girlfriend. Sid was arrested a few days later when the manager discovered the money was missing.

Based on these facts, it is most likely that Sid could be successfully prosecuted for:

A. Larceny.

B. False pretenses.

C. Larceny by trick.

D. Embezzlement.

II. Essay Question:

David broke into the home of Arnold. No one was at home. After taking several expensive items, David attempted to escape from Arnold's house.

Arnold, however, arrived home from a hunting trip just as David was climbing out a side window. Arnold yelled at David to stop, but David began to run down the street. Arnold grabbed his hunting rifle and attempted to shoot David in the leg. The bullet missed David, but fatally shot Bill, who was driving a car down David's street. Edith, Bill's wife, was also in the car and suffered a stroke after seeing her husband shot.

The car rolled into a tree and came to a stop Fred, a passerby, opened the driver's door with the intention of assisting the occupants. However, when he saw the bullet wound in Bill's chest, Fred decided there was nothing he could do. Fred noticed that Bill wore an expensive watch and began to remove it. Bill opened one eye and faintly motioned Fred away. Fred, however, took the watch off Bill's hand, saying, "You won't need this where you're going, my friend." Moments later, Bill died. Subsequently, Arnold, David, and Fred were apprehended by the police.

What crimes were committed and by whom?

Chapter 12
Criminal Procedure

Many people's first introduction to the legal system occurs during a criminal case. Each criminal case is different, but there are some steps that are common to most, if not all, criminal cases. In this section you will find information on what to expect at each stage of a typical criminal case — including tips on the arrest process, plea bargains, sentencing options, and more.

Arrest, Booking and Bail

Getting arrested can be a frightening experience no matter who you are. When someone is arrested by the police, a specific series of events follows. The police must follow legal procedures during the actual arrest process, and at many other stages along the way to actually placing a suspect in jail.

When someone is arrested and taken to jail their first concern is how they can get out. Several things must happen before the authorities release an individual from jail. The process typically involves a "booking" process and a bail hearing that determines whether the person arrested may be released pending trial and set the bail amount. Once the accused has "posted bail" themselves or through a bail bond agent they are released. This section provides articles describing the arrest, booking, and bail process, with helpful information describing how bail bonds work, how amounts are determined, and how they can help to secure a person's release from jail.

Arrest

An arrest occurs when a person has been taken into police custody and is no longer free to leave or move about. When and how an arrest takes place is very important.

Obviously, someone who has been handcuffed and read their rights knows they have been arrested, but not everyone who is arrested is handcuffed or explicitly told that they are under arrest. Whether or not the proper procedure is followed may determine the admissibility of evidence or even result in the case being dropped. Learn more about the arrest process, the basis for a legal arrest, challenges to unlawful arrests, the rights of those arrested and other relevant issues.

Booking

After an arrest a police officer will begin the "booking" process. This is an administrative process in which the police collect the suspect's personal information and organize evidence relating to the alleged crime. The officer will record evidence, observations and statements about the alleged crime, fingerprint and photograph the suspect, conduct a criminal background check, collect the suspect's personal property for storage until release, and place the suspect in a holding cell.

Bail Hearings

The purpose of bail is to ensure that an individual accused of a crime that is released into the community will willingly return for future court hearings and not commit new crimes, intimidate victims and witnesses, or flee to another jurisdiction. Those accused of minor crimes may simply be cited and released, but all others arrested and charged with crimes will have an opportunity to argue for their release at a bail hearing.

At the bail hearing a judge or magistrate examines the alleged crime, the accused's criminal background, connections within the community, financial resources, and length of residence in order to determine whether releasing the suspect would pose a threat to the safety of the community and whether the suspect is likely to appear at future hearings. Someone who poses a threat to the community may be held without bail. Likewise, someone who is a flight risk may be held without bail. Concerns about these and other factors also impact the amount of bail required.

More serious crimes typically result in a higher bail amount. Wealthy individuals may also face higher bail amounts to ensure that the bond represents a significant amount to the party paying. On the other hand, if the alleged crime is not serious, the accused can show evidence that they pose no risk to the community, and are likely to appear at future court hearings they may be released "on personal recognizance" without having to post bail.

Other conditions may be placed upon release including limits on travel, court ordered drug and alcohol abstinence or testing, periodic checks by an authority and restrictions on contact with victims or witnesses. Learn more about bail, factors considered in determining bail, and the conditions under which bail may be denied.

Pretrial Hearings and Motions

In the criminal justice system, a case is often decided before the actual trial. Prosecutors and defense attorneys can file any number of pre-trial motions that exclude evidence or otherwise shape the proceedings. Oftentimes, the outcome of a case hinges on the results of these motions and the hearings that accompany them.

Preliminary Hearing

A preliminary hearing takes place after arrest, booking, and a bail hearing have taken place. At the preliminary hearing the charges against the accused are read. The accused is asked whether they have an attorney or need one appointed by the court. They then answer the charges and "plead" guilty, not guilty, or no contest. Bail may be revisited and amended at this point, the prosecutor provides documents relevant to the case and a calendar is set for future activity on the case, including setting a schedule for pre-trial motions and the trial itself.

Criminal Charges

There are several different ways that criminal charges are brought against the accused. For relatively minor criminal charges a police officer can charge a crime by issuing a citation, commonly called a "ticket". Citations are only issued for infractions; crimes that are not punishable by prison. Someone cited with an infraction may simply pay the ticket to avoid going to court, or can appear in court to argue their case.

Criminal charges are brought in more serious cases with either an "indictment" or "information". An indictment issues after a grand jury proceeding. A prosecutor reviews the evidence gathered by the police and submits it to a jury. The jury then decides whether the accused should go to trial. This system is sometimes chosen when the prosecutor is uncertain about the evidence and may use the grand jury to test the strength of their evidence against the accused.

The other method of filing charges, an "information", takes place when the prosecutor files a document with the court alleging the specific crimes that the person has been accused of and providing statements that indicate why the person is accused of the crimes.

Discovery

Before a trial takes place both sides have an opportunity to exchange information about the facts of the case. Discovery takes place in both civil and criminal trials. Witnesses are questioned under oath in "depositions" or in written "interrogatories". Parties may also present written "requests to admit"; statements to which the other party can only answer by admitting or denying. This helps determine which facts are agreed upon by both sides and do not need to be argued at trial.

"Disclosures" are required when one party intends to take a particular action such as introduce an expert witness or raise certain unusual defenses, such as an insanity defense. Mandatory disclosures vary between states. Finally, "document production requests" are demands between the parties to produce certain documents. In criminal cases the prosecution must provide certain documents such as police reports even if no specific request is made. Decisions made during the discovery phase of a trial can have a serious impact on the outcome and in some cases whether a trial is even necessary.

Pre-Trial Motions

Pre-trial motions take place after the preliminary hearing and before trial. There may be many pre-trial motions in a single case and either side may make pre-trial motions. The outcome of these motions helps determine what evidence will be permitted at trial, what legal arguments are likely to be made, and whether a trial is even necessary. Pre-trial defense motions typically seek to exclude evidence that was improperly acquired and address legal and procedural questions more commonly than factual questions.

Plea Bargain

Many criminal cases are resolved through a plea bargain, usually well before trial. In a plea bargain, the defendant agrees to plead guilty to one or more charges (often to a lesser charge than one for which the defendant could stand trial) in exchange for a more lenient sentence (and/or so that certain related charges are dismissed).

A plea bargain is an agreement in a criminal case between the prosecutor and defendant that typically involves the defendant's agreement to plead guilty, often to a lesser offense or to a reduced sentence that has been agreed upon in advance. These agreements allow for the swift resolution of cases where there is little disagreement or where the evidence of guilt is overwhelming. Plea bargains increase efficiency for the courts and reduce expense and time for the defendant. Critics of plea bargaining complain that this efficiency comes at the expense of justice.

Plea Bargain Pros and Cons

Defendants frequently accept plea bargains to avoid a more serious charge, to have fewer charges brought against them, or to avoid the expense and stress of a trial. Plea bargains provide some security because they allow the defendant to negotiate the terms of sentencing, which under other circumstances may remain mysterious until after the trial is finished.

On the other hand, defendants who take a plea miss the opportunity to be found not-guilty; something that can happen for a variety of reasons, even in very strong cases. A defendant who takes a plea bargain waives many objections and opportunities to examine or challenge evidence against them. Appealing a plea bargain is much more difficult than appealing a decision at trail because pleas are voluntarily entered into and generally require that the defendant admit to the charges for which they are ultimately convicted.

Ultimately, a defendant should carefully consider the merits of their case and the possible outcomes at trial against the plea offered by the prosecution. The assistance of an attorney familiar with the jurisdiction and area of law can be very helpful, both in determining whether to take a plea and in negotiating a plea that is most favorable to the defendant.

Types of Plea Bargains

There are three basic kinds of plea bargains. Charge bargaining is an agreement where the defendant pleads guilty to a lesser charge so that greater charges will be dropped. Sentence bargaining is when the defendant agrees to plead guilty in return for a lighter sentence. Since the judge determines sentencing, not the prosecutor, this type of bargaining is not always successful. The judge may reject the plea because they disagree with the sentence, the jurisdiction may have punishments that are required by law and cannot be altered by an agreement, or the jurisdiction may have disallowed sentence bargaining altogether.

Finally, fact bargaining is the least common form of plea bargaining. The defendant agrees to stipulate to certain facts in order to prevent other facts from being brought into evidence. Most attorneys don't like fact bargaining and many courts don't allow it, which is why fact bargaining is uncommon.

Criminal Trial

After a defendant is formally charged with a crime, the case proceeds to the criminal trial phase (unless the defendant pleads guilty). This begins with jury selection, in which the prosecuting attorney and defense counsel select a jury from the randomly selected jury pool through the process of elimination. Once the jury is set, counsel for the prosecution and defense make their opening statements; present evidence, call witnesses to the stand for testimony and cross-examination, and then make their closing arguments. The jury then deliberates for as long as it takes to reach a verdict.

Criminal Rights

The criminal justice system is intimidating, but that doesn't mean that criminal defendants don't have rights. Through each stage of the criminal justice system, there are important rights that the government must uphold. This section provides information on the rights of those in the criminal justice system, including Miranda rights such as the right to remain silence, "search and seizure" rights, key rights of criminal defendants, and the various prisoner rights guaranteed by the U.S. Constitution.

Search and Seizure

Search and seizure is the legal term used to describe a police officer's examination of a person's home, vehicle, or business to find evidence that a crime has been committed. If evidence is found, the agent may then "seize" it. Search and seizure also includes placing an individual under arrest.

The Fourth Amendment of the United States Constitution protects our right to privacy by prohibiting unreasonable intrusions into our personal property. In order to uphold these rights, the legislature and the courts created legal safeguards to allow officers to interfere with a person's Fourth Amendment rights only under specific conditions.

Miranda Rights

If you have ever watched Law and Order, you have probably seen a police officer advise the suspect of his or her Miranda Rights. This warning is read after an arrest has been made and before police questioning is conducted.

The warning, which is intended to inform you of your rights regarding police questioning, does not have to be read to you if you are not placed under arrest. Why? Because if you are not arrested for committing a crime, you are not going to trial, so you don't need to be warned that what you say can be used against you during trial.

If you have been read your Miranda Rights and waive your right to remain silent or to have an attorney present, you can later change your mind by saying "I plead the Fifth."

Trial Rights

At a criminal trial, a defendant has several very important rights. The most crucial being that a person is presumed innocent until proven guilty. Defendants also have the right to face their accusers, the right to refuse to incriminate themselves, and the right to avoid being prosecuted twice for the same offense, among others.

Keep in mind, the right to a fair and public hearing does not always apply to cases involving immigration law; extradition, tax or voting rights.

The Right to Counsel

The right to counsel is provided by the Sixth Amendment of the Constitution, though it was decades before this was interpreted to mean that the court should provide counsel to the indigent. Learn more about who may be entitled to a court-appointed attorney, the kinds of proceedings that trigger the right to counsel, and situations in which invoking the right to counsel can help protect your rights before, during and after a criminal trial.

The Right Against Self-Incrimination

The phrase "pleading the Fifth" will be familiar if you have watched many movies or television shows that take place in a courtroom. This refers to the Fifth Amendment of the Constitution, which says that no person can be compelled to testify against themselves. In practice the right is a little more complicated than it is depicted on TV though. Learn about the Fifth Amendment's history, how it is used in a legal proceedings and other situations in which the Fifth Amendment Right might be applicable.

The Right to Trial by a Jury of Peers

Although there is no part of the Constitution that provides for a trial by a "jury of peers" the notion is older than the United States and well established in our legal system. Unfortunately for some it doesn't mean exactly what it sounds like. A jury of peers does not imply that the jury will include even a single member that resembles the accused. Jurors are selected randomly from the community and if the resulting jury is made up entirely of a different gender, race or social class this is not generally a violation of the right. "Peers" in this context more accurately means "fellow citizens." Learn more about the history of trials by jury, the process for selection, permitted and forbidden jury challenges and other issues that impact jury selection.

The Insanity Defense

Nearly every crime has, as part of the elements for conviction, a state of mind that the person committing the crime must be shown to have had; these range from intentional to negligent or reckless. Someone with mental issues may commit acts involuntarily, without understanding the import of their actions, or laboring under the mistaken belief that something else is happening. The insanity defense is infrequently used, but has still generated a wide range of tests and rules that are applied differently from state-to-state. Learn more about the insanity defense, its treatment in various states, and the logic and application of the many tests and rules for legal insanity.

Sentencing

After a criminal defendant is convicted or pleads guilty, a judge will decide on the appropriate punishment during the sentencing phase of a criminal case. In some circumstances, the judge is able to enhance or reduce a sentence based upon factors specific to the crime and the defendant. A sentence may include fines, incarceration, probation, suspended sentence, restitution, community service, and participation in rehabilitation programs.

Mandatory Sentences and "Three Strikes" Laws

Some states and all federal criminal statutes include mandatory sentencing guidelines that require judges to impose sentences uniformly. Mandatory sentencing schemes are intended to eliminate inconsistency in sentencing practices and often address a public perception of judicial leniency. "Three Strikes" laws are another sort of mandatory sentencing that has been put in place in the federal laws and about half of the states.

These laws provide for mandatory life imprisonment of felons convicted of three crimes where at least one was a serious violent felony. Mandatory sentencing systems and "Three Strikes" laws especially have been the subject of extensive debate. Questions have been raised about the effectiveness and fairness of these laws and challenges to their constitutionality have been brought, though to date none have been successful.

Probation and Suspended Sentence

A judge may opt to sentence the defendant to probation or issue a suspended sentence. Probation is usually only available to first-time or low-risk offenders. The defendant is released into the community but must satisfy certain conditions and abide by certain rules. If the defendant fails to comply with the terms of probation the judge may then revoke the probation and send the defendant to jail instead.

Similarly, with a suspended sentence a judge may postpone the imposition or execution of a sentence. If the suspended sentence is conditional this is dependent upon the defendant's fulfilling certain conditions, often enrollment in a substance abuse program. Learn more about probation, suspended sentences, the rights of those accused of violating the terms of the programs, and other issues that commonly arise in diversionary or alternative sentencing programs.

Fines and Restitution

Another alternative to incarceration involves the defendant paying their debt to society a little more literally. Fines are payments made to the court. A criminal fine serves to punish the offender, help compensate the state for the costs of prosecution, and deter future criminal acts. Sometimes fines are given in place of jail time, particularly for minor crimes and first offenses.

At other times they may be ordered in addition to a jail term. Restitution is another kind of money payment made by the convicted, but in this case the money is paid to a victim in order to compensate for the damage they suffered. For example, a speeding ticket results in a fine collected by the court, while a graffiti artist is ordered to pay restitution to the owner of the building they defaced so that it can be repainted.

Death Penalty

Some serious criminal offenses are punishable by death, most often violent homicides where it is determined by the jury that the convicted offender lacks remorse. Capital punishment, commonly referred to as the death penalty, remains controversial and has been outlawed in some states.

Historical Background

The death penalty was commonly used in Europe and the early days of the territories

Chapter 12
Criminal Procedure

in the Americas, even for minor crimes of theft and for acts that wouldn't be criminal today, such as blasphemy. There was considerable variation in death penalty laws from colony to colony. Cesare Beccaria's 1767 essay On Crimes and Punishment led to the abolition of the death penalty in Austria and Tuscany. While there was no abolition in the United States, the essay's influence did result in the use commonly being restricted to very serious crimes.

In the 1800s some states took executions out of the public eye and use was restricted or eliminated in other states. Previously mandatory death penalty crimes were replaced with discretionary death penalty punishments.

Then in the 1900s several states outlawed the death penalty, but panic in the wake of the Russian Revolution led to its reinstatement in some jurisdictions. Throughout the Depression and Prohibition the death penalty was used more frequently.

Temporary Abolition

The popularity of the death penalty began to decline in the 1950's as many allied nations outlawed its use. Furman v. Georgia is a 1972 Supreme Court case that (along with two others) found that a Georgia death penalty statute providing the jury full discretion in sentencing could result in arbitrary sentencing. The court, in a deeply split decision, found that the statute was cruel and unusual, violating the Eighth Amendment. With this decision the Supreme Court voided 40 death penalty statutes and suspended the death penalty since the statutes were no longer valid.

Reinstated Death Penalty

Following the Furman decision Florida rewrote its death penalty statutes, shortly after which 34 other states enacted their own revised death penalty laws. These laws avoided the arbitrariness complained of in Furman by mandating capital punishment for those convicted of capital crimes. This method was later found unconstitutional by the Supreme Court in Woodson v. North Carolina. Other states issued guidelines to judges and juries. The Supreme Court upheld this system in Gregg v. Georgia and several other cases, leading to the reinstatement of the death penalty under the new sentencing guidelines and also finding the death penalty itself constitutional under the Eighth Amendment.

Since this time subsequent decisions have found that the execution of the mentally retarded is prohibited under the Eighth Amendment (Atkins v. Virginia) as is the execution of persons who were under the age of 18 when committing capital crimes (Roper v. Simmons.)

Criminal Appeals

A person who has been convicted of a crime has a number of options for seeking additional relief from the criminal justice system — including filing an appeal to have a criminal conviction overturned or sentence reduced.

An appeal is the review of the trial court's activities for legal error. The appellate court only reviews the "record" of the lower court proceedings and will not consider new evidence. The record consists of the court reporter's transcripts of statements by the judge, attorneys, and witnesses. Any documents or objects entered into evidence also become part of the record.

The appealing party files a "brief"; a written explanation of the errors claimed on appeal. The opposition frequently files a brief rebutting the appeal and asking for the conviction and sentence to be upheld. A response brief is typically permitted and in some cases the court will permit oral arguments from the two sides before rendering a decision.

Winning an Appeal

Winning an appeal can be very difficult. At trial the prosecution must prove their case beyond a reasonable doubt. On appeal the burden is on the defendant to prove that an error was made and that the error was serious. Errors that don't affect substantial rights are disregarded as harmless. In addition to having the burden of proof the defendant must also contend with the fact that appeals courts are highly deferential to findings in the lower court. They reason that the judge and jury were present for the actual trial and testimony and as a result grant their opinions authority except where errors or misjudgments are egregious.

Chapter 12
Criminal Procedure

If an appeal is successful one possible outcome is the reversal of the conviction. These are relatively rare, however some kinds of errors are so egregious that they are presumed harmful, such as coerced confessions, and if they can be proven may result in a reversal. Appeals courts are even more reluctant to overturn sentencing decisions. One significant exception is in cases where the sentence falls outside of legal guidelines. In such instances the appellate court may send the case back to trial court for resentencing within the correct parameters.

Writs and Habeas Corpus

A writ is a document or order from a higher court that directs a lower court or official to take a specified action. A defendant can typically only appeal a decision to a higher authority once, but can file multiple writs arising from the same trial, or several different kinds of writs for the same matter. A writ is seen as an extraordinary remedy and isn't typically granted where there is another means of address, such as appeal, available. Writs help defendants contest an issue that could not be raised on appeal.

Habeas Corpus is a writ used to challenge the legal basis of the convict's imprisonment or the conditions in which they are held. Habeas Corpus is seen as a great defense against being held indefinitely without charges and is meant to check the government's power and provide prisoners a legal method to protest their imprisonment.

Exercises

I. Multiple-choice Questions:

1. Sub lived in a residential neighborhood over which planes often flew. Sub liked his privacy, so he erected a tall fence that completely enclosed his backyard. One reason he liked his privacy was that he grew marijuana in his yard. Unbeknownst to Sub, the police had received a tip as to his activities. They rented a plane, flew overhead, used binoculars, and took pictures of the marijuana. The police accurately submitted this information to a judge, who then issued a search warrant. Executing the warrant, the

police seized Sub's marijuana, which was used at trial against him; Sub's pretrial motion to suppress the marijuana was denied.

Under the U.S. Constitution, the trial court's ruling was:

 A. Incorrect, because individuals have a reasonable expectation of privacy with respect to items contained within the home.

 B. Incorrect, because the marijuana was within the curtilage of Sub's home.

 C. Incorrect, if the marijuana was not observable from ground level.

 D. Correct, because Sub had no reasonable expectation of privacy in his backyard with respect to aerial surveillance.

2. Two police officers in a squad car received a radio message from headquarters to be on the lookout for a large green sedan occupied by two women who had just committed a bank robbery. An hour later they saw a car answering this description travelling down a main boulevard leading out of town. They pulled the car over the side of the road and walked over to it. One of the police officers told the occupants that they were under arrested for bank robbery. Doreen, the driver, suddenly put the car into gear and drove off. The officers, unable to overtake the car and afraid they would lose sight of it in heavy traffic, shot at the car. A bullet struck Valerie, the passenger sitting next to Doreen.

Doreen was caught five minutes later. Valerie died from loss of blood. Doreen was taken to the police station.

The bank robbers had hand the teller a handwritten note demanding money. Doreen was asked to write out the words of the note and had her fingerprints taken. Doreen complied. She was then, for the first time, allowed to telephone a lawyer, who thereafter represented her.

Doreen was charged with the bank robbery and the murder of Valerie. At trial, the prosecution, after introducing the robber's note to the teller, also offered into evidence Doreen's exemplar of the words of the note written at the demand of the police. On appropriate objection, the court should rule that this evidence is:

Chapter 12
Criminal Procedure

A. Admissible.

B. Inadmissible, if Doreen was not advised that her handwriting sample could be admitted into evidence against her.

C. Inadmissible, if Doreen was not advised that she could refuse to give a handwriting sample.

D. Inadmissible, if Doreen had not been informed that she had a right to have counsel present.

3. Jack and Paul planned to hold up a bank. They agreed that Paul would drive the car (owned by Jack) during the gateway. Jack entered the bank while Paul remained as lookout in Jack's car. After a few moments, Paul panicked and drove off.

Soon after leaving the scene, Paul was stopped by the police for speeding. Noting his nervous condition, the police asked Paul if they could search the car. Paul reluctantly agreed. While Paul looked on, one of the police reached into the ignition and removed the keys. These keys were used to open the trunk, where heroin was found.

In the trial against Jack for bank robbery, the prosecution's BEST argument to sustain the validity of the search of Jack's car would be that:

A. The search was reasonable in light of Paul's nervous condition.

B. The search was incident to a valid arrest.

C. Paul consented to the search.

D. Exigent circumstances, including the inherent mobility of a car, justified the search.

4. A grand jury was investigating a murder. The only information kown to the prosecutor was a rumor that Suspect might have been involved. The grand jury subpoenaed Suspect. Without specifying why, suspect refused to answer questions about the murder. Suspect was found in contempt and had appealed this determination. The finding of contempt will be:

A. Affirmed, because a subpoenaed grand jury witness must answer all questions.

B. Affirmed, because Suspect did not specifically invoke the Fifth Amendment privilege against self-incrimination.

C. Reversed, because grand jury witness are not legally obliged to answer questions.

D. Reversed, if Suspect's answer might have implicated him in a crime.

5. Dillon held up a gasoline station. During the robbery he shot and killed a customer who attempted to apprehend him. Dillon was prosecuted for deliberate, premeditated murder, but was acquitted. Thereafter, he was indicted for armed robbery of station. Dillon's attorney moved to dismiss the indictment on the ground that further proceedings were unconstitutional because of Dillon's prior trial.

The motion to dismiss should be:

A. Granted, because once Dillon was acquitted on any charge arising out of the robbery, the prosecution was constitutionally estopped from proceeding against Dillon on any other charge resulting from the same transaction.

B. Granted, because the Double Jeopardy Clause prohibits a subsequent trial on a lesser included offense.

C. Denied, because there is no constitutional requirement that all known charges against Dillon be brought in the same prosecution.

D. Denied, because estoppel never applies when the defendant is charged with committing two different crimes.

Questions 6-7 are based on the following fact situation:

Nancy was a developmentally disabled adult who was serving a two-year sentence for burglary when police detectives received an anonymous tip implicating her in the unsolved killing of a police officer during a traffic stop several years earlier. Investigators pursued their suspicion and soon had collected a varied body of evidence linking her to the crime.

Two detectives arranged for Nancy to be brought from her cell at the state correctional facility and into a small interview room. There, she was questioned over a period of six hours about her suspected involvement in the unsolved murder. Her questioners did not advise her of her *Miranda* rights or otherwise indicate that she was

Chapter 12
Criminal Procedure

not obligated to answer them, but they did tell her that she could choose to leave and return to her cell.

After indicating on a number of occasions that she was "done talking," but without ever asking to be brought back to her cell, Nancy began to make incriminating statements in a misguided effort to deny responsibility. Once officers confronted her with the accumulating inconsistencies in her answers, Nancy became confused and eventually provided a detailed confession describing her role in the (formerly) unsolved killing.

Based on the forensic and testimonial evidence gathered by homicide detectives, including her confession at the correctional facility, Nancy is indicted for and convicted of first-degree murder under aggravated circumstances for causing the death of a peace officer in the performance of their official duty. She is ultimately sentenced to death.

6. Defense counsel's effort to have Nancy's confession thrown out will likely:

    A. Fail, because she was not in custody for purposes of *Miranda* during the prison interrogation.

    B. Succeed, because being incarcerated is the quintessential custodial condition.

    C. Fail, because she never invoked her right to silence.

    D. Succeed, because her statement that she was "done talking" was an unambiguous invocation of her right to silence.

7. If Nancy cannot invalidate her conviction, the best argument in seeking to overturn her sentence would be:

    A. That there is an emerging international consensus that the death penalty violates standards of human decency.

    B. That the death penalty has been shown to be ineffective as a deterrent and disproportionately applied to certain groups of offenders.

    C. That imposing the death penalty on developmentally disabled or "mentally retarded" offenders is cruel and unusual punishment.

    D. That litigation over capital sentences ultimately impose excessive costs on taxpayers, and that cases often languish for years while the expenses accumulate.

Questions 8–10 are based on the following fact situation:

After a series of muggings within a foursquare-block vicinity, police conducted a comprehensive sweep of the area. The mugger was described as a white male, about six feet tall, with blond hair and a goatee. While on patrol in this area, uniformed Officer O'Leary noticed Byron walking nervously down the street with his hands in his pockets. O'Leary could tell that Byron was white, about six feet tall, and had blond hair, but could not, from her angle of view, determine if he had a goatee. When O'Leary attempted to approach Byron for the purpose of determining if he had a goatee, Byron (having spotted O'Leary) hurriedly entered the apartment building that was closest to him. O'Leary followed him. When she saw Byron on the lighted stairway, O'Leary noticed that Byron did have a goatee and arrested him on the spot. After handcuffing and putting him in the squad car, but before reading Byron his *Miranda* rights, O'Leary asked Byron where he'd been at 9:00 P.M. on the preceding night (the date and time of the most recent mugging). Byron broke down and confessed to that mugging and several others.

O'Leary then searched Byron's pockets and found a diamond ring, which was later identified as the one taken from a recent mugging victim.

At the station, Byron initially claimed his innocence. However, when he considered his earlier confession and the ring, he agreed to plead guilty, based on a promise prosecutor of a reduced sentence. Soon afterward, however, Byron made a motion to permit withdrawal of the guilty plea and the entry of a not guilty plea. The court granted Byron's motion.

At his trial, Byron took the stand and was asked just one question by his attorney, "Did you commit the robberies with which you are charged?" Byron answered, "No." The prosecution then attempted to cross-examine Byron. However, the prosecution was prevented from doing so by the court when Byron's attorney asserted the Fifth Amendment privilege against self-incrimination. The court also prevented the prosecution's attempt to introduce evidence of Byron's confession to O'Leary for the purpose of impeachment.

8. Which of the following statements describes most accurately Byron's standing to object to the introduction into evidence of the diamond ring?

    A. Byron has standing, because he was inside a residential structure when the ring was seized.

    B. Byron has standing, because the ring was in his pocket.

    C. Byron does not have standing, because he was unlawfully on the premises of the apartment house.

    D. Byron does not have standing, because he did not own the ring.

9. If Byron contends that the search that produced the ring violated his Fourth Amendment rights, the most accurate statement is:

    A. Byron is correct, because exigent circumstances did not exist.

    B. Byron is correct, because there was no probable cause to arrest him.

    C. Byron is correct, because there was no probable cause to believe Byron had the ring on his person.

    D. Byron is incorrect, because O'Leary had probable cause to make the arrest.

10. Assume, for the purpose of this question only, that Byron's confession and the ring were inadmissible. On which of the following grounds, if factually true, could the court properly allow Byron to withdraw his plea of guilty prior to sentencing?

    I. A criminal defendant is permitted to withdraw a guilty plea at any time.

    II. Byron was under the mistaken impression that the confession was admissible when he pleaded guilty.

    III. The guilty plea was "involuntary" because it was induced by the promise of a lighter sentence.

    A. I only.

    B. II and III only.

    C. II only.

    D. None of the above.

II. Essay Question:

Donald and his brother Ronald were small-time crooks whose business had suffered a downturn. They devised a plan to increase their income by responding to Internet ads offering valuable items for sale and then robbing the sellers at gunpoint. Wearing clever disguises and taking turns as the gunman, all went well until one of their victims resisted their demands to hand over his goods and was shot in the struggle. While recovering from his injuries, the victim was able to give investigators enough information to identify Donald and Ronald as suspects. Donald and Ronald were subsequently arrested outside of a grocery store near their home. At the time of their arrest, a police officer told each, "Anything you say can and will be used against you in court; and if you are unable to afford counsel, a lawyer will be appointed for you." Neither made any statement when they were arrested.

Later, at the police station, Ronald was interrogated by detectives from the Major Crimes Unit over a three-hour period. Before they began questioning, they repeated the warnings recited above. For the first two hours and 45minutes, he sat silent and refused to answer any questions. However, at that point in the interrogation Ronald suddenly blurted out, "We just wanted the money—we never meant to hurt anybody!" and then began to sob uncontrollably.

Donald and Ronald were charged with robbery, attempted robbery, and assault with a deadly weapon. The two were tried together after the court denied a motion by each for severance. Ronald's statement to the robbery detectives was admitted at trial over the objection of each defendant, and both were convicted as charged.

Did the court err in admitting Ronald's statement?

    1. against Ronald? Discuss.

    2. against Donald? Discuss.

Chapter 13
Criminal Evidence

The law of evidence governs how parties, judges, and juries offer and then evaluate the various forms of proof at trial. In some ways, evidence is an extension of civil and criminal procedure. Generally, evidence law establishes a group of limitations that courts enforce against attorneys in an attempt to control the various events that the trial process presents in an adversarial setting.

There are many arguments in favor of evidence law; here are five of the most common ones:

To ameliorate pervasive mistrust of juries;

To further legal or social policies relating to a matter being litigated;

To further substantive policies unrelated to the matter in suit;

To create conditions to receive the most accurate facts in trials;

To manage the scope and duration of trials.

Federal Rules of Evidence: Overview

In the United States, the federal courts must follow the Federal Rules of Evidence (FRE); state courts generally follow their own rules, which are generally imposed by the various state legislatures upon their respective state courts. The FRE is the most influential body of American evidence law. The FRE encompasses the majority of the laws of evidence in 68 brief sections. Its language is accessible, easy to read, and mostly free of technical jargon and complicated cross-referencing. The FRE has been enormously influential in the development of U. S. evidence law. This influence in part is a result of its brevity and simplicity.

Before 1975, U.S. evidence law was mostly a creature of the common law tradition. The FRE was drafted and proposed by a distinguished advisory committee composed of practitioners, judges, and law professors appointed by the United States Supreme Court. Just 20 years after the FRE was adopted in the federal system, almost three-quarters of the states had adopted codes that closely resemble the FRE.

The FRE applies in all federal courts in both criminal and civil cases. Understanding some of the basic provisions of the FRE will enable most people to figure out what is going on at trial, even if there are deviations between the FRE and applicable state laws of evidence.

Rules of Evidence

- Circumstantial Evidence: This is not what you would call "smoking gun" evidence, but rather some piece of information that strongly infers a set of circumstances. For instance, video surveillance showing that the defendant was on the same city block where a crime was committed at around the same time would be circumstantial evidence.
- Corroborating Evidence: Evidence that strengthens another piece of evidence, even if it is not directly related to the crime. For example, a witness claims John was at the scene of the crime at a particular time. If another witness has proof that John failed to show up to work at that same time, then it could be considered corroborating evidence.
- Hearsay: This is not given under oath or offered as official evidence, but merely stated. For example, Fred says he heard that John was in a street gang; but without any evidence, Fred's statement is merely hearsay (and not admissible).
- Exclusionary Rule: This rule of evidence applies to that which was obtained in violation of the defendant's constitutional rights. Seizing property without a warrant often is considered a violation and thereby subject to the exclusionary rule.

Hearsay Evidence

The rule against hearsay is deceptively simple and full of exceptions. Hearsay is an out of court statement, made in court, to prove the truth of the matter asserted. In other words, hearsay is evidence of a statement that was made other than by a witness while testifying at the hearing in question and that is offered to prove the truth of the matter stated. For example, Witness A in a murder trial claimed on the stand: "Witness B (the "declarant") told me that the defendant killed the victim." The definition of hearsay is not too difficult to understand. But the matter can become very confusing when one considers all of the many exceptions to the general rule against hearsay.

Even if a statement meets the requirements for hearsay, the statement may yet be admissible under one of the exceptions to the hearsay rule. The Federal Rules of Evidence (FRE) contains nearly thirty of these exceptions. Most of them are generally available, although a few of them are limited to times when the declarant is unavailable.

There are twenty-four exceptions in the federal rules that do not require proof that the person who made the statement is unavailable. These are:

1. Business records, including those of a public agency
2. Certain public records and reports
3. Evidence of a judgment of conviction for certain purposes
4. Evidence of the absence of a business record or entry
5. Excited utterances or spontaneous statements
6. Family records concerning family history
7. Judgments of a court concerning personal history, family history, general history, or boundaries, where those matters were essential to the judgment
8. Learned treatises used to question an expert witness
9. Market reports, commercial publications, and the like
10. Marriage, baptismal, and similar certificates
11. Past recollections recorded
12. Recorded documents purporting to affect interests in land

13. Records of religious organizations concerning personal or family history

14. Records of vital statistics

15. Reputation concerning boundaries or general history

16. Reputation concerning family history

17. Reputation of a person's character

18. Statements about the declarant's present sense impressions

19. Statements about the declarant's then existing mental, emotional, or physical condition

20. Statements in authentic ancient documents (at least 20 years old)

21. Statements in other documents purporting to affect interests in land and relevant to the purpose of the document

22. Statements made by the declarant for the purpose of medical diagnosis or treatment

23. Statements of the absence of a public record or entry

24. The "catchall" rule

The last exception, the so-called "catchall" rule, bears some explanation. This rule does not require that the declarant be unavailable to testify. It does say that evidence of a hearsay statement not included in one of the other exceptions may nevertheless be admitted if it meets these following conditions:

- It has sound guarantees of trustworthiness.
- It is offered to help prove a material fact.
- It is more probative than other equivalent and reasonably obtainable evidence.
- Its admission would forward the cause of justice.
- The other parties have been notified that it will be offered into evidence.

Character Evidence

Character is a general quality usually attributed to a person. Under criminal law, character evidence cannot be used in court to show that the person acted on a particular occasion in conformity with a particular character trait. For example, a defendant's tendency to over exaggerate or lie to friends and family cannot be used as evidence that he defrauded others out of money or property.

Sentencing Stage

While character evidence generally isn't allowed during the trial phase to show a person acted a certain way, it's frequently introduced during the sentencing stage. Prosecutors often introduce evidence of past misconduct or personality flaws to show that a convicted defendant merits a greater sentence. Alternatively, defense attorneys often introduce character witnesses during the sentencing phase to attest to defendants' positive traits and deeds.

Character vs. Habit

Habit, on the other hand, can be used as evidence in certain circumstances. A habit is a behavior that's specific, regular, and consistently repeated. It doesn't describe a personality or character trait of the person, but something he or she does habitually, or regularly. For instance, if the defendant visited a certain coffee shop every morning for years, that fact could be used as evidence that he was probably at the coffee shop on the morning it was robbed. Occasionally, some character traits can be linked with a habit, so the distinction between the two can be hard to make at times.

Character Evidence in Civil Suits

In civil suits, similar to criminal cases, evidence that a person has a certain character trait generally cannot be used to prove that the person acted in conformity with that character trait on a particular occasion. Character evidence may be proved where it's an integral issue in a dispute, as in defamation cases, or where a party puts character in issue.

Documentary Evidence

Evidence contained in or on documents can be a form of real evidence. For example, a contract offered to prove the terms it contains is both documentary and real evidence. When a party offers a document into evidence, the party must authenticate it the same way as any other real evidence, either by a witness who can identify the document or by witnesses who can establish a chain of custody for the document.

Ways to Challenge Documentary Evidence

When people deal with documentary evidence, it is a good idea to consider these four potential pitfalls, which could be used to challenge a document's admissibility in court:

1. Parol evidence

2. Authentication

3. Best evidence

4. Hearsay

Parol Evidence

The parol evidence rule prohibits the admission of certain evidence concerning the terms of a written agreement. It operates on the assumption that whatever is included in a signed agreement contains the final and complete agreement of the parties. It therefore could bar evidence of any agreements made before or at the same time as the actual written agreement, which were not included in the final written agreement. There are exceptions to the parol evidence rule and it is usually considered an issue of substantive law, rather than a pure evidentiary matter. However, it can come into play to bar documentary evidence indicating the presence of additional agreements.

Authentication

Authentication is essentially showing the court that a piece of evidence is what it claims to be and documentary evidence can be authenticated similar to other real evidence. However, the failure to properly authenticate a document could result in the court denying its admissibility. A document can be authenticated when a party admits in the record to its existence or when a witness with personal knowledge confirms that the document is what it claims to be or confirms handwriting or other aspects of the document.

Some kinds of documents are essentially self-authenticating under the Federal Rules of Evidence (FRE). These include:

- Acknowledged documents to prove the acknowledgment

- Certain commercial paper and related documents
- Certificates of the custodians of business records
- Certified copies of public records
- Newspapers
- Official documents
- Periodicals
- Trade inscriptions

Best Evidence

The best evidence rule can be used to deny the admissibility of copies or replications of certain documents. Under this rule, when the contents of a written document are offered in evidence, the court will not accept a copy or other proof of the document's content in place of the original document unless an adequate explanation is offered for the absence of the original. The FRE permits the use of mechanically reproduced documents unless one of the parties has raised a genuine question about the accuracy of the copy or can somehow show that its use would be unfair. Also under the FRE, summaries or compilations of lengthy documents may be received into evidence as long as the other parties have made the originals available for examination.

Hearsay

Documents can be considered hearsay if they contain statements made out of court (and not under oath) and where they are being used in court to prove the truth of those statements. While there are many exceptions to the general rule prohibiting hearsay, if a document does not meet an exception, the court can prevent its admission as evidence.

Scientific and Forensic Evidence

There are many types of evidence that are commonly used at trial. Scientific and forensic types of evidence can be extremely helpful in proving your case, but there are rules and standards that these types of evidence must meet before they can be submitted during a trial.

You may be wondering what on earth scientific evidence could mean in regards to a trial. In general, scientific evidence is based off of knowledge that has been developed by using the scientific method. This means that the basis for the evidence has been hypothesized and tested and is generally accepted within the scientific community. This could mean that the theory on which the scientific evidence is based has been published in scientific journals and has been subjected to peer review within the scientific community.

Generally, many types of forensic evidence are often considered scientific evidence, like DNA matching, fingerprint identification, and hair/fiber evidence. The methods used to develop these types of evidence are generally beyond the scope of knowledge that judges and juries possess and are therefore normally introduced as scientific evidence.

However, this is not to say that scientific evidence cannot be excluded from a courtroom or trial. There are often many steps that must be taken before a piece of scientific evidence can be put forth in a courtroom as factual evidence. In general, a scientific theory must have established itself in the scientific community and become generally accepted as the truth before it will be asserted as evidence at trial.

For example, because it has been around for so long and because it has proven to be reliable, evidence regarding fingerprint matching is generally admissible as forensic evidence in trial. In addition, things like radar and laser speed guns are generally accepted as being a valid method to tell the speed of a car at a given time and can be admitted as evidence. But keep in mind that there will often be new types of scientific evidence that parties will attempt to submit at trial — science that may not have a solid foundation within the scientific community.

If one side of a trial wishes to submit scientific evidence that is not yet generally accepted within the scientific community, it often happens that the court orders a mini-trial to be held in order to determine the validity of the scientific theory on which the evidence is based. As an example, DNA evidence had to go through many mini-trials before it became generally accepted as valid evidence at trail.

In the future, we may see more mini-trials as more types of forensic evidence are introduced in court. As another example, many scientists are currently working on using functional Magnetic Resonance Imaging (fMRI) as a new type of lie detection machine (this works by imaging, in real time, the flow of blood around the brain). If, during a mini-trial, a judge can be convinced that a new, as-of-yet unproven, type of scientific evidence should be introduced at trial, then the judge will allow it to be presented.

Admissibility

Evidence comes in four basic forms:

1. Demonstrative evidence
2. Documentary evidence
3. Real evidence
4. Testimonial evidence

Some rules of evidence apply to all four types and some rules apply to one or two of them. All of these forms of evidence must be admissible, though, before they can be considered as probative of an issue in a trial.

Basically, if evidence is to be admitted at court, it must be relevant, material, and competent. To be considered relevant, it must have some reasonable tendency to help prove or disprove some fact. It need not make the fact certain, but at least it must tend to increase or decrease the likelihood of some fact.

Once admitted as relevant evidence, the finder of fact (judge or jury) will determine the appropriate weight to give a particular piece of evidence. A given piece of evidence is considered material if it is offered to prove a fact that is in dispute in a case. Competent evidence is that evidence that accords with certain traditional notions of reliability. Courts are gradually diminishing the competency rules of evidence by making them issues related to the weight of evidence.

Certain Admissibility Issues with Testimonial Evidence

Testimonial evidence is usually the more common form of evidence, where someone takes the stand and is asked questions about a case. Because this evidence involves the statements of other people regarding certain facts, which can be tainted by poor memories or bias, there are a number of admissibility rules that apply.

For example, while witnesses may testify as to what they observed or perceived during an event, in some situations they may also testify about statements they heard outside of court (and not under oath). Such statements often constitute hearsay evidence and are generally not admissible because they are not as reliable as statements made in court and under oath. However, there are many exceptions to the hearsay rule allowing for the admission of statements made outside of court.

There are also times when a witness may seek to provide testimony about a person's character, often to make the point that the person is the "type" of person who would or would not say or do what is at issue in a case. This type of evidence also has reliability problems as it does not directly show whether the person actually did or said what is at issue. Because of this, character evidence is generally not admissible, but there are exceptions.

In addition, there are times when certain evidence is so complicated, like DNA evidence, that it requires an expert to interpret and explain. This type of expert testimony is only admissible once the expertise of the witness is established and his or her testimony is found to be based on reliable methods and acknowledged within the scientific community.

Suppressing Inadmissible Evidence

When one side of a case tries to introduce evidence that is not relevant, material or competent, the other side can ask, before or during trial, to have the evidence suppressed on admissibility grounds. One area where a motion to suppress is commonly raised is with chain of custody issues where a piece of evidence is not properly secured from its collection to trial.

So, for example, if one side can show that a blood sample was not properly labeled or a weapon was not properly locked in an evidence room, there is no way to trust the results of any subsequent blood test or a fingerprint analysis. While this evidence may be relevant and material, it would not be competent because of intervening custody problems that could have led to inaccurate test results.

Suppress Evidence

If you've been charged with a crime but have doubts about a key piece of evidence, you may be able to get it thrown out at trial. Your guilt or innocence isn't the issue here, but rather the admissibility of police evidence. An experienced defense attorney knows how to suppress evidence that is collected illegally or which is otherwise inadmissible. But in order to have evidence thrown out, no matter how illegitimate you think it is, you must first file a motion to suppress evidence with the court. A judge will then make a ruling on the admissibility of the evidence.

Evidence used in a criminal case must be both "relevant" and "competent", meaning it needs to be directly related to the charges and collected/handled in accordance with the law. Knowing how to suppress evidence in a legal proceeding is an important step in any criminal defense. See FindLaw's Criminal Evidence section for related resources.

The Exclusionary Rule

The exclusionary rule prevents the government from using most evidence gathered illegally. It usually comes into play when evidence is obtained in violation of a suspect's Fourth Amendment rights against unlawful search and seizure. For example, a murder weapon cannot be used at trial if police illegally searched a defendant's home to recover it. An officer generally must obtain a valid search warrant and follow proper procedures for a piece of evidence to be admissible at trial. The rule may also be triggered by police violations of the Fifth or Sixth Amendment.

Additionally, the "fruit of the poisonous tree" doctrine holds that otherwise admissible evidence, testimony, or even confessions may be excluded from trial if they resulted from an illegal search or some other constitutional violation. For example, a suspect is arrested and tells police where to find the gun used to commit the crime. But if he was not read his Miranda Rights or police ignored his pleas to speak to his lawyer, the gun may later be deemed inadmissible in court.

Reasons a Court May Suppress Evidence

Your attorney should know how to suppress evidence against you if your constitutional rights have been violated. Here are some common reasons a court may suppress evidence:

- Unlawful Search and Seizure: The Fourth Amendment protection against unlawful search and seizure applies to many situations involving police officers, including routine traffic stops and visits to your home. With some important exceptions, police must have a valid search warrant, a valid arrest warrant, or probable cause that a crime has been committed in order to search for and gather evidence.
- Failure to Read Miranda Rights: The law requires that officers read "Miranda rights" to a suspect in custody prior to their questioning or interrogation. These rights inform the suspect that she has the right to remain silent, that anything she says may be used against her in court, and that she has the right to an attorney. If the suspect has not been "read his rights", confessions or statements made after the arrest may not be admissible. See "Miranda" Rights and the Fifth Amendment for specific details on how this right works.
- Chain of Custody Errors: The "chain of custody" refers to the documentation and proper care of evidence, from its seizure by police to its presentation at trial. If the chain of custody is broken, the evidence may lack credibility and could be deemed inadmissible. For example, a woman involved in a car crash has her blood drawn (with a warrant) to see if she was intoxicated while driving. But the police mislabel or mix up the blood evidence with others at the lab. This evidence may be suppressed because the chain of custody was improper.

Exceptions to the Rule

There are certain instances where evidence may still be admissible even when police overstep the boundaries or fail to follow protocol, including the following exceptions:

- Inevitable Discovery: If the judge rules that an illegally seized piece of evidence eventually would have been discovered through legal means, it may be admitted. For instance, an officer illegally enters a suspect's home and finds a cocaine lab. The occupant already was a suspect and police were about to request a search warrant for his home. If a judge concludes that a normal police investigation would have likely uncovered that same evidence without the illegal entry, the evidence may be admissible.

- Good Faith: If an officer has every reason to believe he is acting within the limits of the law, then some procedural errors may be overlooked. For example, police search a suspect's home based on what they honestly and reasonably believed to be a valid search warrant. Unfortunately, the warrant suffered from a technical legal defect that police were unaware of. Since the police acted in good faith, the evidence derived from the search warrant may not necessarily be excluded in court. If police had known about the defect (or should have known), then the evidence may still be excluded.

- Independent Source: If a source (other than the officer who illegally seized evidence) would have provided that same evidence, a court may rule it admissible. This is similar to the inevitable discovery exception. For example, police illegally search a suspect's home and find documents showing that she is the mastermind of a large-scale Internet scam. But later that day, an informant sends the same documents to the police. The evidence may be admissible, since an independent source provided the same evidence.

Leading Questions

As indicated by its name, a leading question is one that leads a witness to an answer, by either suggesting the answer or by substituting the words of the questioning attorney for those of the witness. Many leading questions call for answers of either "yes" or "no". But not all questions that call for an answer of "yes" or "no" are leading questions. As an example, consider the following hypothetical courtroom exchange:

Questioning Attorney: The defendant owned the firearm that is an exhibit in this case, correct?

Witness: Yes.

Questioning Attorney: And this is the firearm that was used in the murder, correct?

Witness: Yes.

As you can see, a sophisticated attorney can use leading questions to get a witness to validate the attorney's words. In effect, this allows the attorney to indirectly testify through the witness, which can be quite effective. Leading questions can also be used to create perceptions by not allowing a witness to qualify their answer. For example, in the exchange above, the witness may want to testify that the gun was stolen from the defendant before the murder, but since that question was not asked, the witness could not provide that specific answer, leaving certain perceptions in the minds of a jury.

When Are Leading Questions Allowed? Because of their potential to lead to misleading testimonial evidence, these types of questions are not allowed on direct examination, that is, when a party's attorney is questioning their own witnesses. In those instances, attorneys must normally use open-ended questions such as, "On the day in question, what did you observe?" However, these questions sometimes call for narratives that can produce long speeches on irrelevant matters, wasting the time of the court and the parties. Open-ended narrative questions are unpopular with courts and should be avoided.

Judges do have the discretion to allow leading questions during the direct examination of a witness in matters that:

- Deal with simple or uncontested background issues in order to save the court's time;
- Will help to elicit the testimony of a witness who, due to age, incapacity, or limited intelligence, is having difficulty communicating her evidence; or
- Involve adverse or hostile witnesses (witnesses are considered adverse or hostile when their interests or sympathies may lead them to resist testifying truthfully and in most cases, an adverse party or a witness associated with an adverse party is

considered hostile).

Leading questions are also allowed during a cross-examination when an attorney is questioning the other party's witnesses. This is because one of the purposes of cross-examination is to test the credibility of statements that a witness made on direct examination. It's also due to the fact that witnesses for one party may not be as forthcoming or helpful when questioned by the other party's attorney.

Exercises

I. Multiple-choice Questions:

Questions 1–4 are based on the following fact situation:

Kathy was employed as an auto mechanic by the Arrow Body Shop. She often test-drove cars she repaired. During one routine test-drive, Kathy was exceeding the posted speed limit when she collided with Elmer's vehicle at an intersection. Elmer had failed to stop at the stop sign preceding the intersection. Elmer was thrown out of his car into a ditch and his car was totaled. When she saw that Elmer had been seriously injured, Kathy ran to the ditch to help him. She told him, "I'm really sorry. I guess I didn't fix the brakes as well as I thought." Later, Kathy readjusted the brakes of the vehicle she had been driving at the time of the accident. Elmer brought an action against Arrow Body Shop for personal injuries and property damage.

1. At trial, Elmer called Bystander to testify to Kathy's statement about the brakes after the accident. Arrow's objection to Bystander's testimony should be:

   A. Sustained, because Kathy's statement is inadmissible against Arrow.

   B. Sustained, because Elmer did not stop at the stop sign.

   C. Overruled, because it is a declaration against interest.

   D. Overruled, because it is an admission of a party-opponent.

2. Elmer offered evidence proving that Kathy had readjusted the brakes of her vehicle after the accident. Arrow's objection to the evidence should be:

A. Overruled, because it tends to prove Kathy's negligence.

B. Overruled, because it is relevant to Kathy's state of mind.

C. Sustained, because it constitutes assertive conduct.

D. Sustained, for public policy reasons.

3. Kathy sought to introduce evidence proving that she had a good driving record. The evidence is:

A. Inadmissible, because it is character evidence.

B. Inadmissible, because it is self-serving.

C. Admissible, because it is character evidence.

D. Admissible, because it is habit evidence.

4. Kathy brought a counterclaim against Elmer, contending that his negligence caused the accident. She calls Allen, Elmer's friend, to testify to the fact that Elmer never stops at the stop sign at the accident intersection and invariably "runs" every stop sign. Elmer's objection to Allen's testimony should be:

A. Sustained, because it is not the best evidence.

B. Sustained, because character evidence is inadmissible in a civil case.

C. Overruled, because it is evidence of habit.

D. Overruled, because it is self-serving.

5. Violet, a pedestrian, was struck by a car in a hit-and-run accident. Pamela, a police officer, arrived half an hour after the accident. Violet was in shock and came in and out of consciousness. As Pamela applied first aid, Violet muttered, "I know I'm going to die. Oh God, he ran the light!" Violet fell back into unconsciousness, but he revived again and muttered, "Why didn't he stop?" Pamela heard Violet's comments clearly and made a note of them. Good police work by Pamela and others led to the discovery that Daft was driving the car that struck Violet. Almost miraculously, Violet survived, although her injuries would leave her with some severe disabilities. Violet filed a tort action against Daft. Before the case came to trial, Violet died of a heart of a heart attack. The causes of the heart attack were totally unrelated to the accident. The laws

of the jurisdiction allow for survival of personal injury actions. Thus, Violet's estate is substituted for Violet as plaintiff.

Plaintiff's attorney seeks to have Pamela testify to Violet's statements at the time of the accident. How will the court rule?

    A. Inadmissible, because Violet did not die as a result of the accident.

    B. Inadmissible, because this is a civil case and not a criminal matter.

    C. Admissible, because Violet's statements were present sense impressions.

    D. Admissible, because the statements were made at a time when Violet feared impending death.

6. Pye's and Delta's cars collided at an intersection. The impact of the collision was sufficient to cause both cars to overturn. Immediately after the accident occurred, Wrench came upon the scene. Wrench noted that the wheels of both cars were still spinning, and the wheels of Delta's car were spinning faster that the wheels of Pye's car.

At the trial that arises out of the collision, Pye's attorney calls Wrench to the stand. Wrench testifies that he is an automobile mechanic with 12 years' experience. Wrench also testifies that he arrived at the scene immediately after the accident and saw the wheels on both cars still spinning. Pye's attorney asks Wrench to testify as to what speed the respective cars were traveling at the time of the accident based upon his observations of the spinning wheels. Delta's attorney objects.

Should Wrench's testimony regarding the speed of the cars be admitted?

    A. Yes, as Wrench's personal opinion.

    B. Yes, as a matter based upon personal observation.

    C. No, unless Wrench has been qualified as an expert in auident reconstruction.

    D. No, unless there is another witness to corroborate Wrench's presence at the accident scene.

7. Laura, a pedestrian, heard a horn sounding. She looked up and saw two cars (driven by Porter and Davidson) enter an intersection and collide. Porter sued Davidson, and Porter's attorney calls Laura to the stand as a witness. On direct examination, she

is asked to describe the accident scene, position of the cars in the intersection, etc. On cross-examination, Davidson's attorney goes over the same ground with the witness. He asks her whether there was any broken glass on the pavement, to which she responds, "Yes, lots of it," and before Davidson's lawyer can ask his next question, Laura blurts out, "They had to be going over 50!" Davidson's attorney moves to strike the statement.

How should the court rule?

  A. Strike it, as unresponsive to any question asked.

  B. Strike it, because Laura had no way of knowing how fast the cars were traveling.

  C. Not to strike, because Davidson's attorney "opened the door" to anything Laura might say about the accident.

  D. Not to strike, because the statement accuses both cars of going over 50, and is not prejudicial to only one side

8. A state court is **least** likely to take judicial notice of which of the following?

  A. The blood type that occurs with greatest frequency in the population is O-positive.

  B. Main street, upon which the courthouse is situated, runs north and south.

  C. The sun rose at 6:52 a.m. on Friday, December 12, of last year.

  D. In Australian law, there is no private action for environment issues.

9. In its lead editorial in the Sunday edition, *The Daily Bugle*, a suburban daily newspaper, printed the following: "There is only one expression that accurately describes the activities of businessman — real estate developer Rodney Richman in our community. That expression is 'common thief,' and Richman knows it." Rodney Richman promptly filed suit against *The Daily Bugle* for defamation.

During the course of the presentation of Richman's case, Richman sought to put Sarge on the stand. Sarge is prepared to testify that Richman once saved the life of a fellow soldier in Vietnam.

If the newspaper's lawyer objects, the court should rule that Sarge's testimony is:

A. Admissible, because the plaintiff has a right to introduce evidence of his good character.

B. Admissible, because Richman's character has been brought into question by the editorial.

C. Inadmissible, because Sarge's testimony is not probative of any material issue.

D. Inadmissible, because specific instances of conduct are not admissible to prove character.

10. Pat files suit against Don, asserting that "Goering", a German shepherd dog belonging to Don, had bitten her without provocation. Don denied that his dog bit Pat. At the trial, Porter, Pat's attorney, called Pat to the stand. After asking Pat's name and address, he asked only one further question, namely: "Were you bitten by a German shepherd dog with a white forepaw?" Pat replied in the affirmative and was dismissed from the stand.

Porter then called Don to the stand as a adverse witness. After ascertaining Don's name and address, Porter asked Don only one question: "Do you own a German shepherd dog with a white forepaw?" Upon receiving Don's affirmative answer, Porter said, "No further questions, Your Honor."

Don's attorney, Debra, rose to cross-examine Don. Her first question to Don was, "Has your German shepherd dog ever displayed anything other than a gentle disposition?" Porter immediately objected to the question.

What should be the most likely ruling of the court on Porter's objection?

A. Sustained, because Debra is improperly attempting to introduce character evidence when character had not been called into question.

B. Sustained, because Debra's question goes beyond the proper scope of cross-examination.

C. Overruled, because the plaintiff brought up the dog in direct examination.

D. Overruled, because the testimony sought is relevant and is otherwise admissible.

II. Essay Question:

P received injuries in an automobile accident involving two vehicles driven by D and X. The cars collided at an intersection, causing the vehicle driven by D to strike P, a pedestrian. P brings suit against D for $15,000.

1. At the trial, P called Dr. Jones, who testified that P was brought to his office by D shortly after the accident, and that D said: "I'll pay this man's bill."

2. P testified that prior to trial there had been extensive settlement negotiations between the parties and that D had offered to pay $5,000 in full settlement of P's claim. P also testified that during these negotiations, D had said to him on one occasion: "I might have gone through the light a little late."

3. Mrs. D, D's wife, was called as a witness by P. She testified that one evening during dinner, and while the butler was present, D said to her: "I'm afraid that I'm at fault in that collision with X."

4. Bystander is called as a witness for D. Bystander testifies that, shortly after the accident, he heard X say: "I'm dying, I'm dying. The accident was all my fault. I'm glad I have insurance." Other evidence disclosed that X, although injured, was not in a serious condition. However, X died shortly thereafter en route to the hospital when the ambulance into which he had been placed struck a tree.

Discuss the admissibility of the above items of evidence, assuming that all appropriate objections have been made.

Part III
WTO Law & Legal Translation and Writing

Chapter 14

Understanding the WTO: Basics

What Is the World Trade Organization?

Is It a Bird, Is It a Plane?

There are a number of ways of looking at the WTO. It's an organization for liberalizing trade. It's a forum for governments to negotiate trade agreements. It's a place for them to settle trade disputes. It operates a system of trade rules. (But it's not Superman, just in case anyone thought it could solve — or cause — all the world's problems!)

Above all, it's a negotiating forum … Essentially, the WTO is a place where member governments go, to try to sort out the trade problems they face with each other. The first step is to talk. The WTO was born out of negotiations, and everything the WTO does is the result of negotiations. The bulk of the WTO's current work comes from the 1986–1994 negotiations called the Uruguay Round and earlier negotiations under the General Agreement on Tariffs and Trade (GATT). The WTO is currently the host to new negotiations, under the "Doha Development Agenda" launched in 2001.

Where countries have faced trade barriers and wanted them lowered, the negotiations have helped to liberalize trade. But the WTO is not just about liberalizing trade, and in some circumstances its rules support maintaining trade barriers — for example to protect consumers or prevent the spread of disease.

It's a set of rules … At its heart are the WTO agreements, negotiated and signed by the bulk of the world's trading nations. These documents provide the legal ground-rules for international commerce. They are essentially contracts, binding governments to keep their trade policies within agreed limits. Although negotiated and signed by governments, the goal is to help producers of goods and services, exporters, and importers conduct their business, while allowing governments to meet social and environmental objectives.

The system's overriding purpose is to help trade flow as freely as possible — so long as there are no undesirable side-effects — because this is important for economic development and well-being. That partly means removing obstacles. It also means ensuring that individuals, companies and governments know what the trade rules are around the world, and giving them the confidence that there will be no sudden changes of policy. In other words, the rules have to be "transparent" and predictable.

And it helps to settle disputes ... This is a third important side to the WTO's work. Trade relations often involve conflicting interests. Agreements, including those painstakingly negotiated in the WTO system, often need interpreting. The most harmonious way to settle these differences is through some neutral procedure based on an agreed legal foundation. That is the purpose behind the dispute settlement process written into the WTO agreements.

Born in 1995, But Not So Young

The WTO began life on 1 January 1995, but its trading system is half a century older. Since 1948, the General Agreement on Tariffs and Trade (GATT) had provided the rules for the system. (The second WTO ministerial meeting, held in Geneva in May 1998, included a celebration of the 50th anniversary of the system.)

It did not take long for the General Agreement to give birth to an unofficial, de facto international organization, also known informally as GATT. Over the years GATT evolved through several rounds of negotiations.

The last and largest GATT round, was the Uruguay Round which lasted from 1986 to 1994 and led to the WTO's creation. Whereas GATT had mainly dealt with trade in goods, the WTO and its agreements now cover trade in services, and in traded inventions, creations and designs (intellectual property).

Principles of the Trading System

The WTO agreements are lengthy and complex because they are legal texts covering

Chapter 14
Understanding the WTO: Basics

a wide range of activities. They deal with: agriculture, textiles and clothing, banking, telecommunications, government purchases, industrial standards and product safety, food sanitation regulations, intellectual property, and much more. But a number of simple, fundamental principles run throughout all of these documents. These principles are the foundation of the multilateral trading system.

A Closer Look at These Principles:

Trade without discrimination

1. Most-favoured-nation (MFN): treating other people equally Under the WTO agreements, countries cannot normally discriminate between their trading partners. Grant someone a special favour (such as a lower customs duty rate for one of their products) and you have to do the same for all other WTO members.

This principle is known as most-favoured-nation (MFN) treatment. It is so important that it is the first article of the General Agreement on Tariffs and Trade (GATT), which governs trade in goods. MFN is also a priority in the General Agreement on Trade in Services (GATS) (Article 2) and the Agreement on Trade-Related Aspects of Intellectual Property Rights (TRIPS) (Article 4), although in each agreement the principle is handled slightly differently. Together, those three agreements cover all three main areas of trade handled by the WTO.

Some exceptions are allowed. For example, countries can set up a free trade agreement that applies only to goods traded within the group — discriminating against goods from outside. Or they can give developing countries special access to their markets. Or a country can raise barriers against products that are considered to be traded unfairly from specific countries. And in services, countries are allowed, in limited circumstances, to discriminate. But the agreements only permit these exceptions under strict conditions. In general, MFN means that every time a country lowers a trade barrier or opens up a market, it has to do so for the same goods or services from all its trading partners — whether rich or poor, weak or strong.

2. National treatment: Treating foreigners and locals equally. Imported and locally-

produced goods should be treated equally — at least after the foreign goods have entered the market. The same should apply to foreign and domestic services, and to foreign and local trademarks, copyrights and patents. This principle of "national treatment" (giving others the same treatment as one's own nationals) is also found in all the three main WTO agreements (Article 3 of GATT, Article 17 of GATS and Article 3 of TRIPS), although once again the principle is handled slightly differently in each of these.

National treatment only applies once a product, service or item of intellectual property has entered the market. Therefore, charging customs duty on an import is not a violation of national treatment even if locally-produced products are not charged an equivalent tax.

Freer Trade: Gradually, Through Negotiation

Lowering trade barriers is one of the most obvious means of encouraging trade. The barriers concerned include customs duties (or tariffs) and measures such as import bans or quotas that restrict quantities selectively. From time to time other issues such as red tape and exchange rate policies have also been discussed.

Since GATT's creation in 1947–1948 there have been eight rounds of trade negotiations. A ninth round, under the Doha Development Agenda, is now underway. At first these focused on lowering tariffs (customs duties) on imported goods. As a result of the negotiations, by the mid-1990s industrial countries' tariff rates on industrial goods had fallen steadily to less than 4%.

But by the 1980s, the negotiations had expanded to cover non-tariff barriers on goods, and to the new areas such as services and intellectual property.

Opening markets can be beneficial, but it also requires adjustment. The WTO agreements allow countries to introduce changes gradually, through "progressive liberalization". Developing countries are usually given longer to fulfil their obligations.

Predictability: Through Binding and Transparency

Sometimes, promising not to raise a trade barrier can be as important as lowering one, because the promise gives businesses a clearer view of their future opportunities. With stability and predictability, investment is encouraged, jobs are created and consumers

Chapter 14
Understanding the WTO: Basics

can fully enjoy the benefits of competition — choice and lower prices. The multilateral trading system is an attempt by governments to make the business environment stable and predictable.

The Uruguay Round increased bindings

Percentages of tariffs bound before and after the 1986–1994 talks

	Before	After
Developed countries	78	99
Developing countries	21	73
Transition economies	73	98

(These are tariff lines, so percentages are not weighted according to trade volume or value)

In the WTO, when countries agree to open their markets for goods or services, they "bind" their commitments. For goods, these bindings amount to ceilings on customs tariff rates. Sometimes countries tax imports at rates that are lower than the bound rates. Frequently this is the case in developing countries. In developed countries the rates actually charged and the bound rates tend to be the same.

A country can change its bindings, but only after negotiating with its trading partners, which could mean compensating them for loss of trade. One of the achievements of the Uruguay Round of multilateral trade talks was to increase the amount of trade under binding commitments (see table). In agriculture, 100% of products now have bound tariffs. The result of all this: a substantially higher degree of market security for traders and investors.

The system tries to improve predictability and stability in other ways as well. One way is to discourage the use of quotas and other measures used to set limits on quantities of imports — administering quotas can lead to more red-tape and accusations of unfair play. Another is to make countries' trade rules as clear and public ("transparent") as possible. Many WTO agreements require governments to disclose their policies and practices publicly within the country or by notifying the WTO. The regular surveillance of national trade policies through the Trade Policy Review Mechanism provides a further means of encouraging transparency both domestically and at the multilateral level.

Promoting Fair Competition

The WTO is sometimes described as a "free trade" institution, but that is not entirely accurate. The system does allow tariffs and, in limited circumstances, other forms of protection. More accurately, it is a system of rules dedicated to open, fair and undistorted competition.

The rules on non-discrimination — MFN and national treatment — are designed to secure fair conditions of trade. So too are those on dumping (exporting at below cost to gain market share) and subsidies. The issues are complex, and the rules try to establish what is fair or unfair, and how governments can respond, in particular by charging additional import duties calculated to compensate for damage caused by unfair trade.

Many of the other WTO agreements aim to support fair competition: in agriculture, intellectual property, services, for example. The agreement on government procurement (a "plurilateral" agreement because it is signed by only a few WTO members) extends competition rules to purchases by thousands of government entities in many countries. And so on.

Encouraging Development and Economic Reform

The WTO system contributes to development. On the other hand, developing countries need flexibility in the time they take to implement the system's agreements. And the agreements themselves inherit the earlier provisions of GATT that allow for special assistance and trade concessions for developing countries.

Over three quarters of WTO members are developing countries and countries in transition to market economies. During the seven and a half years of the Uruguay Round, over 60 of these countries implemented trade liberalization programmes autonomously. At the same time, developing countries and transition economies were much more active and influential in the Uruguay Round negotiations than in any previous round, and they are even more so in the current Doha Development Agenda.

Chapter 14
Understanding the WTO: Basics

At the end of the Uruguay Round, developing countries were prepared to take on most of the obligations that are required of developed countries. But the agreements did give them transition periods to adjust to the more unfamiliar and, perhaps, difficult WTO provisions — particularly so for the poorest, "least-developed" countries. A ministerial decision adopted at the end of the round says better-off countries should accelerate implementing market access commitments on goods exported by the least-developed countries, and it seeks increased technical assistance for them. More recently, developed countries have started to allow duty-free and quota-free imports for almost all products from least-developed countries. On all of this, the WTO and its members are still going through a learning process. The current Doha Development Agenda includes developing countries' concerns about the difficulties they face in implementing the Uruguay Round agreements.

The Case for Open Trade

The economic case for an open trading system based on multilaterally agreed rules is simple enough and rests largely on commercial common sense. But it is also supported by evidence: the experience of world trade and economic growth since the Second World War. Tariffs on industrial products have fallen steeply and now average less than 5% in industrial countries. During the first 25 years after the war, world economic growth averaged about 5% per year, a high rate that was partly the result of lower trade barriers. World trade grew even faster, averaging about 8% during the period.

The data show a definite statistical link between freer trade and economic growth. Economic theory points to strong reasons for the link. All countries, including the poorest, have assets — human, industrial, natural, financial — which they can employ to produce goods and services for their domestic markets or to compete overseas. Economics tells us that we can benefit when these goods and services are traded. Simply put, the principle of "comparative advantage" says that countries prosper first by taking advantage of their assets in order to concentrate on what they can produce best, and then by trading these products for products that other countries produce best.

In other words, liberal trade policies — policies that allow the unrestricted flow of goods and services — sharpen competition, motivate innovation and breed success. They multiply the rewards that result from producing the best products, with the best design, at the best price.

But success in trade is not static. The ability to compete well in particular products can shift from company to company when the market changes or new technologies make cheaper and better products possible. Producers are encouraged to adapt gradually and in a relatively painless way. They can focus on new products, find a new "niche" in their current area or expand into new areas.

Experience shows that competitiveness can also shift between whole countries. A country that may have enjoyed an advantage because of lower labour costs or because it had good supplies of some natural resources, could also become uncompetitive in some goods or services as its economy develops. However, with the stimulus of an open economy, the country can move on to become competitive in some other goods or services. This is normally a gradual process.

Nevertheless, the temptation to ward off the challenge of competitive imports is always present. And richer governments are more likely to yield to the siren call of protectionism, for short term political gain — through subsidies, complicated red tape, and hiding behind legitimate policy objectives such as environmental preservation or consumer protection as an excuse to protect producers.

Protection ultimately leads to bloated, inefficient producers supplying consumers with outdated, unattractive products. In the end, factories close and jobs are lost despite the protection and subsidies. If other governments around the world pursue the same policies, markets contract and world economic activity is reduced. One of the objectives that governments bring to WTO negotiations is to prevent such a self-defeating and destructive drift into protectionism.

Comparative Advantage

This is arguably the single most powerful insight into economics.

Chapter 14
Understanding the WTO: Basics

Suppose country A is better than country B at making automobiles, and country B is better than country A at making bread. It is obvious (the academics would say "trivial") that both would benefit if A specialized in automobiles, B specialized in bread and they traded their products. That is a case of absolute advantage.

But what if a country is bad at making everything? Will trade drive all producers out of business? The answer, according to Ricardo, is no. The reason is the principle of comparative advantage.

It says, countries A and B still stand to benefit from trading with each other even if A is better than B at making everything. If A is much more superior at making automobiles and only slightly superior at making bread, then A should still invest resources in what it does best — producing automobiles — and export the product to B. B should still invest in what it does best — making bread — and export that product to A, even if it is not as efficient as A. Both would still benefit from the trade. A country does not have to be best at anything to gain from trade. That is comparative advantage.

The theory dates back to classical economist David Ricardo. It is one of the most widely accepted among economists. It is also one of the most misunderstood among non-economists because it is confused with absolute advantage.

It is often claimed, for example, that some countries have no comparative advantage in anything. That is virtually impossible.

The GATT Years: From Havana to Marrakesh

The WTO's creation on 1 January 1995 marked the biggest reform of international trade since after the Second World War. It also brought to reality — in an updated form — the failed attempt in 1948 to create an International Trade Organization.

Much of the history of those 47 years was written in Geneva. But it also traces a journey that spanned the continents, from that hesitant start in 1948 in Havana (Cuba), via Annecy (France), Torquay (UK), Tokyo (Japan), Punta del Este (Uruguay), Montreal (Canada), Brussels (Belgium) and finally to Marrakesh (Morocco) in 1994. During that period, the trading system came under GATT, salvaged from the aborted attempt to create the ITO. GATT helped establish a strong and prosperous multilateral trading system that became more and more liberal through rounds of trade negotiations. But by the 1980s the system needed a thorough overhaul. This led to the Uruguay Round, and ultimately to the WTO.

GATT: "Provisional" for Almost Half a Century

From 1948 to 1994, the General Agreement on Tariffs and Trade (GATT) provided the rules for much of world trade and presided over periods that saw some of the highest growth rates in international commerce. It seemed well-established, but throughout those 47 years, it was a provisional agreement and organization.

The original intention was to create a third institution to handle the trade side of international economic cooperation, joining the two "Bretton Woods" institutions, the World Bank and the International Monetary Fund. Over 50 countries participated in negotiations to create an International Trade Organization (ITO) as a specialized agency of the United Nations. The draft ITO Charter was ambitious. It extended beyond world trade disciplines, to include rules on employment, commodity agreements, restrictive business practices, international investment, and services. The aim was to create the ITO at a UN Conference on Trade and Employment in Havana, Cuba in 1947.

Meanwhile, 15 countries had begun talks in December 1945 to reduce and bind customs tariffs. With the Second World War only recently ended, they wanted to give an early boost to trade liberalization, and to begin to correct the legacy of protectionist measures which remained in place from the early 1930s.

This first round of negotiations resulted in a package of trade rules and 45,000 tariff concessions affecting $10 billion of trade, about one fifth of the world's total. The group had expanded to 23 by the time the deal was signed on 30 October 1947. The tariff concessions came into effect by 30 June 1948 through a "Protocol of Provisional Application". And so the new General Agreement on Tariffs and Trade was born, with 23 founding members (officially "contracting parties").

Chapter 14
Understanding the WTO: Basics

The 23 were also part of the larger group negotiating the ITO Charter. One of the provisions of GATT says that they should accept some of the trade rules of the draft. This, they believed, should be done swiftly and "provisionally" in order to protect the value of the tariff concessions they had negotiated. They spelt out how they envisaged the relationship between GATT and the ITO Charter, but they also allowed for the possibility that the ITO might not be created. They were right.

The Havana conference began on 21 November 1947, less than a month after GATT was signed. The ITO Charter was finally agreed in Havana in March 1948, but ratification in some national legislatures proved impossible. The most serious opposition was in the US Congress, even though the US government had been one of the driving forces. In 1950, the United States government announced that it would not seek Congressional ratification of the Havana Charter, and the ITO was effectively dead. So, the GATT became the only multilateral instrument governing international trade from 1948 until the WTO was established in 1995.

For almost half a century, the GATT's basic legal principles remained much as they were in 1948. There were additions in the form of a section on development added in the 1960s and "plurilateral" agreements (i.e. with voluntary membership) in the 1970s, and efforts to reduce tariffs further continued. Much of this was achieved through a series of multilateral negotiations known as "trade rounds" — the biggest leaps forward in international trade liberalization have come through these rounds which were held under GATT's auspices.

In the early years, the GATT trade rounds concentrated on further reducing tariffs. Then, the Kennedy Round in the mid-sixties brought about a GATT Anti-Dumping Agreement and a section on development. The Tokyo Round during the seventies was the first major attempt to tackle trade barriers that do not take the form of tariffs, and to improve the system. The eighth, the Uruguay Round of 1986–1994, was the last and most extensive of all. It led to the WTO and a new set of agreements.

The Tokyo Round: A First Try to Reform the System

The Tokyo Round lasted from 1973 to 1979, with 102 countries participating. It continued GATT's efforts to progressively reduce tariffs. The results included an average one-third cut in customs duties in the world's nine major industrial markets, bringing the average tariff on industrial products down to 4.7%. The tariff reductions, phased in over a period of eight years, involved an element of "harmonization" — the higher the tariff, the larger the cut, proportionally.

In other issues, the Tokyo Round had mixed results. It failed to come to grips with the fundamental problems affecting farm trade and also stopped short of providing a modified agreement on "safeguards" (emergency import measures). Nevertheless, a series of agreements on non-tariff barriers did emerge from the negotiations, in some cases interpreting existing GATT rules, in others breaking entirely new ground. In most cases, only a relatively small number of (mainly industrialized) GATT members subscribed to these agreements and arrangements. Because they were not accepted by the full GATT membership, they were often informally called "codes".

They were not multilateral, but they were a beginning. Several codes were eventually amended in the Uruguay Round and turned into multilateral commitments accepted by all WTO members. Only four remained "plurilateral" — those on government procurement, bovine meat, civil aircraft and dairy products. In 1997 WTO members agreed to terminate the bovine meat and dairy agreements, leaving only two.

Did GATT Succeed?

GATT was provisional with a limited field of action, but its success over 47 years in promoting and securing the liberalization of much of world trade is incontestable. Continual reductions in tariffs alone helped spur very high rates of world trade growth during the 1950s and 1960s — around 8% a year on average. And the momentum of trade liberalization helped ensure that trade growth consistently out-paced production growth throughout the GATT era, a measure of countries' increasing ability to trade with each other and to reap the benefits of trade. The rush of new members during the Uruguay

Chapter 14
Understanding the WTO: Basics

Round demonstrated that the multilateral trading system was recognized as an anchor for development and an instrument of economic and trade reform.

But all was not well. As time passed new problems arose. The Tokyo Round in the 1970s was an attempt to tackle some of these but its achievements were limited. This was a sign of difficult times to come.

GATT's success in reducing tariffs to such a low level, combined with a series of economic recessions in the 1970s and early 1980s, drove governments to devise other forms of protection for sectors facing increased foreign competition. High rates of unemployment and constant factory closures led governments in Western Europe and North America to seek bilateral market-sharing arrangements with competitors and to embark on a subsidies race to maintain their holds on agricultural trade. Both these changes undermined GATT's credibility and effectiveness.

The problem was not just a deteriorating trade policy environment. By the early 1980s the General Agreement was clearly no longer as relevant to the realities of world trade as it had been in the 1940s. For a start, world trade had become far more complex and important than 40 years before: the globalization of the world economy was underway, trade in services — not covered by GATT rules — was of major interest to more and more countries, and international investment had expanded. The expansion of services trade was also closely tied to further increases in world merchandise trade. In other respects, GATT had been found wanting. For instance, in agriculture, loopholes in the multilateral system were heavily exploited, and efforts at liberalizing agricultural trade met with little success. In the textiles and clothing sector, an exception to GATT's normal disciplines was negotiated in the 1960s and early 1970s, leading to the Multifibre Arrangement. Even GATT's institutional structure and its dispute settlement system were causing concern.

These and other factors convinced GATT members that a new effort to reinforce and extend the multilateral system should be attempted. That effort resulted in the Uruguay Round, the Marrakesh Declaration, and the creation of the WTO.

The Uruguay Round

It took seven and a half years, almost twice the original schedule. By the end, 123 countries were taking part. It covered almost all trade, from toothbrushes to pleasure boats, from banking to telecommunications, from the genes of wild rice to AIDS treatments. It was quite simply the largest trade negotiation ever, and most probably the largest negotiation of any kind in history.

At times it seemed doomed to fail. But in the end, the Uruguay Round brought about the biggest reform of the world's trading system since GATT was created at the end of the Second World War. And yet, despite its troubled progress, the Uruguay Round did see some early results. Within only two years, participants had agreed on a package of cuts in import duties on tropical products — which are mainly exported by developing countries. They had also revised the rules for settling disputes, with some measures implemented on the spot. And they called for regular reports on GATT members' trade policies, a move considered important for making trade regimes transparent around the world.

A Round to End All Rounds?

The seeds of the Uruguay Round were sown in November 1982 at a ministerial meeting of GATT members in Geneva. Although the ministers intended to launch a major new negotiation, the conference stalled on agriculture and was widely regarded as a failure. In fact, the work programme that the ministers agreed formed the basis for what was to become the Uruguay Round negotiating agenda.

Nevertheless, it took four more years of exploring, clarifying issues and painstaking consensus-building, before ministers agreed to launch the new round. They did so in September 1986, in Punta del Este, Uruguay. They eventually accepted a negotiating agenda that covered virtually every outstanding trade policy issue. The talks were going to extend the trading system into several new areas, notably trade in services and intellectual property, and to reform trade in the sensitive sectors of agriculture and textiles. All the original GATT articles were up for review. It was the biggest negotiating mandate on trade ever agreed, and the ministers gave themselves four years to complete it.

Chapter 14
Understanding the WTO: Basics

Two years later, in December 1988, ministers met again in Montreal, Canada, for what was supposed to be an assessment of progress at the round's half-way point. The purpose was to clarify the agenda for the remaining two years, but the talks ended in a deadlock that was not resolved until officials met more quietly in Geneva the following April.

Despite the difficulty, during the Montreal meeting, ministers did agree a package of early results. These included some concessions on market access for tropical products — aimed at assisting developing countries — as well as a streamlined dispute settlement system, and the Trade Policy Review Mechanism which provided for the first comprehensive, systematic and regular reviews of national trade policies and practices of GATT members. The round was supposed to end when ministers met once more in Brussels, in December 1990. But they disagreed on how to reform agricultural trade and decided to extend the talks. The Uruguay Round entered its bleakest period.

Despite the poor political outlook, a considerable amount of technical work continued, leading to the first draft of a final legal agreement. This draft "Final Act" was compiled by the then GATT director-general, Arthur Dunkel, who chaired the negotiations at officials' level. It was put on the table in Geneva in December 1991. The text fulfilled every part of the Punta del Este mandate, with one exception — it did not contain the participating countries' lists of commitments for cutting import duties and opening their services markets. The draft became the basis for the final agreement.

Over the following two years, the negotiations lurched between impending failure, to predictions of imminent success. Several deadlines came and went. New points of major conflict emerged to join agriculture: services, market access, anti-dumping rules, and the proposed creation of a new institution. Differences between the United States and European Union became central to hopes for a final, successful conclusion.

In November 1992, the US and EU settled most of their differences on agriculture in a deal known informally as the "Blair House accord". By July 1993 the "Quad" (US, EU, Japan and Canada) announced significant progress in negotiations on tariffs and related subjects ("market access"). It took until 15 December 1993 for every issue to be finally resolved and for negotiations on market access for goods and services to be concluded (although some final touches were completed in talks on market access a few weeks later). On 15 April 1994, the deal was signed by ministers from most of the 123 participating governments at a meeting in Marrakesh, Morocco.

The delay had some merits. It allowed some negotiations to progress further than would have been possible in 1990: for example some aspects of services and intellectual property, and the creation of the WTO itself. But the task had been immense, and negotiation-fatigue was felt in trade bureaucracies around the world. The difficulty of reaching agreement on a complete package containing almost the entire range of current trade issues led some to conclude that a negotiation on this scale would never again be possible. Yet, the Uruguay Round agreements contain timetables for new negotiations on a number of topics. And by 1996, some countries were openly calling for a new round early in the next century. The response was mixed; but the Marrakesh agreement did already include commitments to reopen negotiations on agriculture and services at the turn of the century. These began in early 2000 and were incorporated into the Doha Development Agenda in late 2001.

What Happened to GATT?

The WTO replaced GATT as an international organization, but the General Agreement still exists as the WTO's umbrella treaty for trade in goods, updated as a result of the Uruguay Round negotiations. Trade lawyers distinguish between GATT 1994, the updated parts of GATT, and GATT 1947, the original agreement which is still the heart of GATT 1994. Confusing? For most of us, it's enough to refer simply to "GATT".

The Post-Uruguay Round Built-in Agenda

Many of the Uruguay Round agreements set timetables for future work. Part of this "built-in agenda" started almost immediately. In some areas, it included new or further negotiations. In other areas, it included assessments or reviews of the situation at specified times. Some negotiations were quickly completed, notably in basic telecommunications,

Chapter 14
Understanding the WTO: Basics

financial services. (Member governments also swiftly agreed a deal for freer trade in information technology products, an issue outside the "built-in agenda".)

The agenda originally built into the Uruguay Round agreements has seen additions and modifications. A number of items are now part of the Doha Agenda, some of them updated.

There were well over 30 items in the original built-in agenda. This is a selection of highlights:

1996

- Maritime services: market access negotiations to end (30 June 1996, suspended to 2000, now part of Doha Development Agenda)
- Services and environment: deadline for working party report (ministerial conference, December 1996)
- Government procurement of services: negotiations start

1997

- Basic telecoms: negotiations end (15 February)
- Financial services: negotiations end (30 December)
- Intellectual property, creating a multilateral system of notification and registration of geographical indications for wines: negotiations start, now part of Doha Development Agenda

1998

- Textiles and clothing: new phase begins 1 January
- Services (emergency safeguards): results of negotiations on emergency safeguards to take effect (by 1 January 1998, deadline now March 2004)
- Rules of origin: Work programme on harmonization of rules of origin to be completed (20 July 1998)
- Government procurement: further negotiations start, for improving rules and procedures (by end of 1998)
- Dispute settlement: full review of rules and procedures (to start by end of 1998)

1999

- Intellectual property: certain exceptions to patentability and protection of plant varieties: review starts

2000

- Agriculture: negotiations start, now part of Doha Development Agenda
- Services: new round of negotiations start, now part of Doha Development Agenda
- Tariff bindings: review of definition of "principle supplier" having negotiating rights under GATT Art 28 on modifying bindings
- Intellectual property: first of two-yearly reviews of the implementation of the agreement

2002

- Textiles and clothing: new phase begins 1 January

2005

- Textiles and clothing: full integration into GATT and agreement expires 1 January

I. Multiple-choice Questions:

1. The following are the correct ways of looking at the WTO EXCEPT:

   A. It's an organization for liberalizing trade.

   B. It's a forum for governments to negotiate trade agreements.

   C. It operates a system of trade rules.

   D. It is a Superman to solve all the world's problems.

2. WTO is a place where member governments go, to try to sort out the _____ problems they face with each other.

   A. politics   B. trade   C. education   D. all the above

3. Which of the following statements is NOT true?

   A. WTO is just about liberalizing trade, and in some circumstances its rules support

Chapter 14
Understanding the WTO: Basics

maintaining trade barriers .

B. The WTO was born out of negotiations, and everything the WTO does is the result of negotiations.

C. The WTO system's overriding purpose is to help trade flow as freely as possible.

D. And it helps to settle disputes , this is a third important side to the WTO's work.

4. The WTO began life on 1 January 1995, but its trading system is half a century older. Since 1948, the _____ had provided the rules for the system.

   A. ABA   B. GATT   C. NATO   D. WHO

5. The last and largest GATT round, was the _____ which lasted from 1986 to 1994 and led to the WTO's creation.

   A. Uruguay Round   B. Geneva Round
   C. Tokyo Round   D. Sweden Round

6. Whereas GATT had mainly dealt with trade in goods, the WTO and its agreements now cover trade in _____ and intellectual property.

   A. services   B. traded inventions
   C. trade designs   D. all of the above

7. The regular surveillance of national trade policies through the Trade Policy Review Mechanism provides a further means of encouraging _____ both domestically and at the multilateral level.

   A. punishment   B. transparency
   C. immigration   D. engagement

8. Suppose country A is better than country B at making automobiles, and country B is better than country A at making bread. It is obvious (the academics would say "trivial") that both would benefit if A specialized in automobiles, B specialized in bread and they traded their products. That is a case of _____ .

   A. Absolute advantage   B. Punitive damage
   C. Comparative advantage D. Comparative damage

9. In November 1992, the US and _____ settled most of their differences on agriculture in a deal known informally as the "Blair House accord".

   A. EU
   B. UK
   C. France
   D. Germany

10. The WTO replaced GATT as an international organization, but the _____ still exists as the WTO's umbrella treaty for trade in goods, updated as a result of the Uruguay Round negotiations.

    A. Blair House Accord
    B. TRIPS
    C. ADR
    D. General Agreement

II. Essay Question:

What is your comment on the WTO?

Chapter 15
Legal Translation

Overview

Legal translation is the translation of texts within the field of law. As law is a culture-dependent subject field, the work of legal translation and its products are not necessarily linguistically transparent.

As the mistranslation of a passage in a contract, for example, could lead to lawsuits and loss of money, translation is often considered to be preferably handled by professional translators specialising in legal translation should translate legal documents and scholarly writings.

When translating a text within the field of law, the translator should keep the following in mind. The legal system of the source text (ST) is structured in a way that suits that culture and this is reflected in the legal language; similarly, the target text (TT) is to be read by someone who is familiar with the other legal system (corresponding to the jurisdiction for which TT is prepared) and its language. Most forms of legal writing, and contracts in particular, seek to establish clearly defined rights and duties for certain individuals. It is essential to ensure precise correspondence of these rights and duties in the source text and in the translation. Legal translation may also involve, certificates of accuracy, witness statements, depositions, trusts, wills, articles of incorporation, litigation documents, immigration documents, property/exhibit labels and in some cases attendance in court by the translator(s).

Apart from terminological lacunae, or lexical gaps, the translator may focus on the following aspects. Textual conventions in the source language are often culture-dependent and may not correspond to conventions in the target culture. Linguistic structures that are often found in the source language may have no direct equivalent structures in the target language. The translator therefore has to be guided by certain standards of linguistic, social and cultural equivalence between the language used in the source text (ST) to produce a text (TT) in the target language. Those standards correspond to a variety of different principles defined as different approaches to translation in translation theory. Each of the standards sets a certain priority among the elements of ST to be preserved in TT. For example, following the functional approach, translators try to find target language structures with the same functions as those in the source language thus value the functionality of a text fragment in ST more than, say, the meanings of specific words in ST and the order in which they appear there.

Different approaches to translation should not be confused with different approaches to translation theory. The former are the standards used by translators in their trade while the latter are just different paradigms used in developing translation theory.

There is a confusion between the names of some of the translation standards used in legal practice. Not many lawyers and judges are familiar with the terminology used in translation theory, and they often ask court interpreters and translators to provide verbatim translation. They often view this term as a clear standard of quality that they desire in TT. However, usually it does not mean to provide verbatim translation in the meaning of the standard described in translation theory with which they are not familiar. Their use of this term is based on a layperson's misconception that an accurate translation is achieved simply when "the correct" words of the target language are substituted for the corresponding words of ST. In reality, they just want to have a faithful and fluent translation of ST having no doubt that a good translator will provide it. They do not realize that word-by-word translations could sound as complete nonsense in the target language, and usually have no idea of different professional translation standards. Many translators would probably choose to adhere to the standard that they themselves find more appropriate in a given situation based on their experience rather than to attempt to educate the court personnel.

Translators of legal texts often consult law dictionaries, especially bilingual law dictionaries. Care should be taken, as some bilingual law dictionaries are of poor quality and their use may lead to mistranslation.

What Is Legal Translation?

By Richard Brooks

The term legal translation refers to the translation of any text used within the legal system. As documents used for legal purposes are generally required to be submitted in the official language of a relevant jurisdiction the term can encompass a wide variety of texts including, but not limited to, witness statements, legal rulings and precedents, filed patents, transcripts, official reports, financial documents and identity documentation. A wide variety of other sources of information can also be subject to legal translation depending on their contextualised relationship to legal proceedings. For example the Will and testament of an expatriate may be subject to translation into the language of the jurisdiction in which they have died in order for a probate lawyer to begin the process of executing the instructions contained therein. Generally legal translation services are only undertaken by those with specialist knowledge as mistranslations, especially of contracts, can carry significant financial and legal consequences.

The means of regulating legal translators vary from country to country. In many countries specific degrees are offered in Legal and Business Translation. Some states (such as Argentina and Brazil) require the use of state-certified public translators whilst a majority of states, including Spain, Sweden and The Netherlands stipulate that legal translators swear legal oaths and are centrally regulated and examined in order to ensure proficiency and good practice (this is also known as a sworn translation). Furthermore other legislations (such as Italy) require legal translations to be notarised (i.e. certified) by a relevant legal professional.

On the other hand sometimes the United States and the United Kingdom do not strictly require accreditation in order for an individual to carry out a translation intended for usage in a legal context, this does depend on case to case and our company does provide certificates of accuracy on request. In countries such as these the lack of central regulation is offset by independent bodies (or trade associations) that offer their own qualifications and membership as a means of accreditation that serves as a benchmark of quality. Other certifications that should be mentioned include our own certification (A Certificate of Accuracy) and Apostille which is a stamp acknowledging that the notarisation has been completed by a registered Notary Public.

Find a Legal Translator

It is important that those looking to employ a legal translator ensure that candidates have demonstrable legal and linguistic understanding of the languages used in both the original document (the source text) and the finished article (the target text). The abilities of a prospective translator can be ascertained by considering their certification, their qualifications, their membership of the aforementioned trade associations and their relative experience with the languages involved. The U.S. Consortium of Language Access in the Courts advises that "In general the best result is obtained if the chosen translator's mother tongue is in the target language (the language that the material will be translated into)".

High profile or sensitive cases may need the translator to be security cleared. Different levels of security exist in each country and where NDA is not considered to be high enough additional audit trails and security measures can be applied to projects. Translators have been known to work on secondment within client premises/networks if security teams deem it necessary.

It is also often a requirement to transcribe material. This is when the source "text" is contained within audio format (mp3, CD, tape etc.). This does sometimes include translation (as the original might not be in the language you need) and so will therefore follow the same process as legal translation, this service is referred to as multilingual transcription.

Legal translations present particular problems to translators because of the relationship between the source text and the particular legal and cultural conventions of the jurisdiction in which it originated. As such providing literal translations of source texts can result in

Chapter 15
Legal Translation

target texts failing to convey the precise rights and duties set out by the source. This lack of comparability can have important legal ramifications, as outlined above. Therefore the translator has to consider a number of factors when undertaking their work. As well as contending with accidental linguistic gaps and structural differences between the source and target languages the translator must consider culturally dependent textual variations. As such it is necessary for the translator to work according to a variety of standards of cultural and social equivalence rather than providing a simple verbatim linguistic translation in order to avoid losing important legal context and consequence from the source text. Thus the legal translator will often choose to maintain the functionality and overarching meaning of the source text rather than focusing on the relative comparability of individual terms or words within the text.

Legal Translation Terminology

Often legal professionals (many of whom are unfamiliar with the terminology specific to translation theory) will request a verbatim translation from a professional legal translator or interpreter. Whilst this term generally implies complete accuracy it is not necessarily entirely applicable to legal translation. A literal word-for-word translation could lack the cultural and legal context of the target language and therefore fail to convey the aforementioned rights and duties laid out in the source text.

In order to achieve appropriate translations the translator will often utilise a reputable bilingual legal dictionary. Whilst relevant reference books are plentiful and there are now legal dictionaries online it is important that the translator ensures the veracity of these tools as many are of questionable quality and it is of the utmost importance that translation mistakes are avoided.

The Qualities and Skills of A Legal Translator

Legal translators work on some of the most sensitive and important documents to be found in any given organisation and are tasked with delivering exceptional results in line with some exacting demands.

As a whole, they have to ensure that the meaning of one piece of text is accurately conveyed as much in a new language. Moreover, every nuance of the original document has to be captured and repurposed — without any loss of integrity — so that it is understood, legally speaking, in the target language. It's a serious job that is challenging but extremely rewarding.

In this piece, we take a closer look at some of the qualities and skills legal translators need to possess.

The Profile of a Legal Translator

Legal translators, more often than not, are commissioned to translate technical and complex documents into their native language. This is an important point to be aware of because native speakers of a language tend to have a better understanding and knowledge of their primary vernacular than those for whom it is a second language.

Though a graduate degree or masters in law or a language is not a prerequisite qualification for a legal translator, it does carry authority. That said, a background and expertise in the two areas cited above is essential because, simply put, legal translation is not a vocation you can casually fall into. Accordingly, a passion and genuine interest in these subjects is a welcome asset.

Core Attributes Expected of a Legal Translator

Legal translators need to possess an ability to quickly absorb, comprehend and engage with complex texts and effectively deliver accurate solutions in line with criteria.

They also need to work well under pressure, as a lot of assignments that come through can be last minute with clients keen on a quick turnaround. As we noted in our feature on the challenges of legal translation, this is, by no means, easy going.

There is a lot of risk associated, after all, with mistranslating legal documents, even those that have been, in the original text, written out in as clear a manner as possible and with full consideration of the law. There can never be any room for ambiguity.

Specific Skills That Legal Translators Have

Legal translators possess a commanding knowledge of their native tongue and

Chapter 15
Legal Translation

an equally robust level of authority with a second language. This you can attribute as being a language specific skill-set (and implied in all of this is the ability to write clear, grammatically correct text).

In terms of thematic skills, a high level of expertise in legal matters is, as a rule, required, especially in the legal systems of at least two countries. While there are many overlaps between nations in terms of their respective bodies of law, there are significant differences too.

Specialist knowledge of certain branches of the legal system is also helpful, as this ensures an even greater level of expertise with regards to certain areas of law. By its very nature, it's an expansive discipline and thus, the more legal translators know about a particular area, the more confident clients can be in the quality and accuracy of the final document.

Additionally, being able to contextualise legalese between the two systems is suggestive of a knowledge base that is extensive and up-to-date. It is this richness that allows meaning to be properly passed from one language to another, with no loss in translation.

An Invaluable Resource

It should be clear from the above that legal translators have a distinct skill-set that reinforces why they are such an asset. Consider, for example, that they have to be excellent writers in at least two languages, possess an understanding of two legal systems and be able to act as a bridge between the two and you can appreciate the value they offer all types of organisations. In an increasingly globalised world, they're going to be increasingly important.

Top 5 Reasons an Expert Translator Is a Necessity in the Legal Sector

In the modern world of business, nothing is as static geographically as it once was. Companies are increasingly working in new markets in new countries and dealing with countless contacts across the world for any number of reasons — The International Labor Organization (ILO) estimates as many 50,000 companies are now multinational. But as much as this can be a rewarding business strategy to employ, it can also be a challenging one for companies.

Legal disputes happen in the business world, but in the modern world, where business are in contact with other countries more than ever, these are more common cross-border than they have ever been, with millions taking place every year. It's, therefore, vital that all companies can call on the expertise of a legal translation expert when they need to.

This is important not just in terms of reacting to things that have happened, but also throughout any stage of the business process, be it when dealing with procurement, services or contracts. A legal translation expert is priceless for most companies. Here, we take a look at a few reasons.

Speed to Market

Perhaps one of the most important issues in the legal translation sector is speed. Business deals are won and lost in the blink of an eye, and companies need to know that they can rely on someone who cannot only translate something accurately and legally soundly, but also quickly, so that contracts, deals and cases are not being held up unnecessarily.

Fluidity of Law

It's also vital that your legal translator is able to keep up with the ever-changing world of business law, both in the target and origin languages' nations. The law is rarely ever static, and if someone is going to be translating documents, it's important that they are not only well versed on the laws of the countries they need to know about, but that they never cease to learn, always keeping abreast of the changes they need to know about.

Legal Language

Translation in the legal word is about more than simply switching words and phrases to make everything make sense. In legal terminology, there are words and phrases that would mean nothing on their own, but everything in legal terms, so having a translator on board who has a knowledge of how legal terms work is very important.

Chapter 15
Legal Translation

Legal Diversity

As much as the world of business is more global than it's ever been, no two countries are legally identical. If someone is going to be translating documents from one language to another, it's important that they, therefore, have some knowledge of the nuances that exist, and the difference between laws in each of the nations, to make sure documents remain as relevant and useful as possible.

Accurate Translation

As with any sector, the accuracy of a translated document in the legal market is absolutely vital. In a sector where one word can make all the difference to the meaning, tone or gravity of a document, having an expert translator who is fluent in the legal language of the target country is vital to finding legal success.

When it comes to translating legal documentation, getting it right can be a minefield, with the potential for so much to go wrong, but with the right translator bringing the right skills to the table, companies can rest assured that they are on firm legal ground.

How to Become a Court Interpreter in 5 Steps

Court interpreters are called upon for special judicial cases that require translating oral speech into another language. This way, if any witnesses have been called to the stand who don't speak English, they have a reliable way of expressing themselves. The job may also require interpreters to read aloud documents in a language other than that in which they were written. To obtain a position as a court interpreter, graduates are required to earn a bachelor's degree in translation studies or court interpreting and must demonstrate an exceptional understanding of English and another language. They must also have a strong grasp of legal terminology and the legal process. On-the-job training will occur after graduation.

Discover the qualifications for this career, and review the typical salary for court interpreters using the table below.

Degree Required	Bachelor's degree; postsecondary certificate programs in the field may be helpful to those with a bachelor's degree
Education Field of Study	Translation studies, court interpreting
Key Skills	Speaking, writing, listening, interpersonal, fluency in English and a second language
Certification	Certification is optional
Job Growth (2014—2024)	29% increase *(for all interpreters and translators)* *
Median Salary (2015)	$44,190 *(for all interpreters and translators)* *

Source: *U.S. Bureau of Labor Statistics

What Is a Court Interpreter?

As a court interpreter, you are responsible for helping non-English speaking individuals communicate in a judicial environment. You must be fluent in a foreign language, and should also be well versed in both U.S. and international legal systems. You might be responsible for interpreting in depositions, arraignments, trials, legal meetings or preliminary hearings. No specific degree is required; however, most court interpreters have a bachelor's degree.

Step 1: Earn a High School Diploma

Several different educational paths can set you on your goal towards becoming a court interpreter. However, most employers will require you to have at least a high school diploma. High school courses that can prepare you for the career include those relating to English, communication and reading comprehension skills. If you were not raised in a bilingual household, you should also consider taking foreign language courses in high school.

Step 2: Obtain a Bachelor's Degree

According to the U.S. Bureau of Labor Statistics (BLS), most court interpreters hold at least a bachelor's degree. One undergraduate program you can enroll in is a bachelor's degree in translation studies. Such a program should allow you to concentrate on one foreign language, such as Spanish, French or German. Additional courses might cover diction, phonetics, composition and translation processes.

Step 3: Complete a Certificate Program

If you are already fluent in a foreign language, or have already completed a bachelor's degree program in translation studies, you may want to consider enrolling in a professional court interpreter certificate program. Such programs are designed to provide you with an understanding of U.S. law and the judicial system. They are often offered through four-year universities, community colleges and professional organizations. Courses covered include simultaneous translating skills, court procedures, court interpreting and the penal code.

Step 4: Work as a Translator or Interpreter

Many employers only hire those translators who have a degree, 3–5 years of experience or both, according to the BLS. You can gain the requisite experience by working for a translation company. You might also complete an internship or do volunteer interpreter work for a community organization.

Step 5: Become a Court interpreter

Although it is not a requirement, you can become certified as a translator or interpreter through the American Translators Association or the Translators and Interpreters Guild. According to the BLS, translators and interpreters held roughly 49,650 jobs in 2015. The median wage in the field during that year was about $44,190.

What Are Some Related Alternative Careers?

If you don't think becoming a court interpreter is right for you but are interested in pursuing a similar career, you may want to consider becoming a court reporter or a general interpreter. Court reporters are only required to earn a postsecondary non-degree award prior to employment and work to create accurate transcriptions of each trial. General interpreters specialize in converting one language to another and can work in a multitude of industries. They're required to earn a bachelor's degree in translation studies before seeking employment.

Exercises

I. Translate the following paragraphs into English:

民主法治建设迈出重大步伐。积极发展社会主义民主政治，推进全面依法治国，党的领导、人民当家做主、依法治国有机统一的制度建设全面加强，党的领导体制机制不断完善，社会主义民主不断发展，党内民主更加广泛，社会主义协商民主全面展开，爱国统一战线巩固发展，民族宗教工作创新推进。科学立法、严格执法、公正司法、全民守法深入推进，法治国家、法治政府、法治社会建设相互促进，中国特色社会主义法治体系日益完善，全社会法治观念明显增强。国家监察体制改革试点取得实效，行政体制改革、司法体制改革、权力运行制约和监督体系建设有效实施。

把纪律挺在前面，着力解决人民群众反映最强烈、对党的执政基础威胁最大的突出问题。出台中央八项规定，严厉整治形式主义、官僚主义、享乐主义和奢靡之风，坚决反对特权。巡视利剑作用彰显，实现中央和省级党委巡视全覆盖。坚持反腐败无禁区、全覆盖、零容忍，坚定不移"打虎""拍蝇""猎狐"，不敢腐的目标初步实现，不能腐的笼子越扎越牢，不想腐的堤坝正在构筑，反腐败斗争压倒性态势已经形成并巩固发展。

中国特色社会主义进入新时代，我国社会主要矛盾已经转化为人民日益增长的美好生活需要和不平衡不充分的发展之间的矛盾。我国稳定解决了十几亿人的温饱问题，总体上实现小康，不久将全面建成小康社会，人民美好生活需要日益广泛，不仅对物质文化生活提出了更高要求，而且在民主、法治、公平、正义、安全、环境等方面的要求日益增长。同时，我国社会生产力水平总体上显著提高，社会生产能力在很多方面进入世界前列，更加突出的问题是发展不平衡不充分，这已经成为满足人民日益增长的美好生活需要的主要制约因素。

II. Translate the following English into Chinese:

Welcome to the 21st Century. Where practicing law requires us to don the garb of computers and the Internet. And where litigation is as costly as ever. Lawyer bills running $10,000 a month are not unusual in a hotly contested breach of contract lawsuit. With every word, phrase and sentence carrying the potential for winning or losing, the stakes are high. Simple logic, therefore, directs us to cautious and thoughtful drafting.

Drafting contracts is actually one of the simple pleasures of practicing law. Just 3 years ago at this Convention I presented 50 tips for contract writing. This article updates those tips in the context of our new tools and abilities. Following these tips could result in your writing a contract so clear no one will want to litigate it, saving your client from the trials and tribulations of litigation, truly a good reason to write the contract that stays out of court.

These tips apply to writing all kinds of agreements: office leases, real estate contracts, sales agreements, employment contracts, equipment leases, prenuptial agreements. They even apply to stipulations and settlements in litigation, where you want an agreement so clear that it avoids future litigation. Wherever clarity and simplicity are important, these tips will guide you there. The Appendix provides a few sample forms to illustrate these tips.

Chapter 16
Legal Writing

Overview

In many legal settings specialized forms of written communication are required. In many others, writing is the medium in which a lawyer must express their analysis of an issue and seek to persuade others on their clients' behalf. Any legal document must be concise, clear, and conform to the objective standards that have evolved in the legal profession.

There are generally two types of legal writing. The first type requires a balanced analysis of a legal problem or issue. Examples of the first type are inter-office memoranda and letters to clients. To be effective in this form of writing, the lawyer must be sensitive to the needs, level of interest and background of the parties to whom it is addressed. A memorandum to a partner in the same firm that details definitions of basic legal concepts would be inefficient and an annoyance. In contrast, their absence from a letter to a client with no legal background could serve to confuse and complicate a simple situation.

The second type of legal writing is persuasive. Examples of this type are appellate briefs and negotiation letters written on a clients behalf. The lawyer must persuade his or her audience without provoking a hostile response through disrespect or by wasting the recipient's time with unnecessary information. In presenting documents to a court or administrative agency he or she must conform to the required document style.

The drafting of legal documents, such as contracts and wills, is yet another type of legal writing. Guides are available to aid a lawyer in preparing the documents but a unique application of the "form" to the facts of the situation is often required. Poor drafting can lead to unnecessary litigation and otherwise injure the interests of a client.

The legal profession has its own unique system of citation. While it serves to provide the experienced reader with enough information to evaluate and retrieve the cited authorities, it may, at first, seem daunting to the lay reader. Court rules generally specify the citation format required of all memoranda or briefs filed with the court. These rules have not kept up with the changing technology of legal research. Within recent years, online and disk-based law collections have become primary research tools for many lawyers and judges. Because of these changes, there has been growing pressure on those ultimately responsible for citation norms, namely the courts, to establish new rules that no longer presuppose that a publisher's print volume (created over a year after a decision is handed down) is the key reference. (See the reports of the Wisconsin Bar and the AALL.) Several jurisdictions have responded and many more are sure to follow.

Learn the Fundamentals of Writing First—Experiment Later

*By Bryan A. Garner**

It's often said that you must know the rules before you break them. But why is that, exactly? It's a question worth pondering.

I recently flew coast to coast sitting beside a young filmmaker with an MFA from New York University. He's a finalist this year at the Cannes Film Festival. I asked him whether he's ever met someone who wanted to do something with the camera that nobody had ever thought of doing before—something boldly original.

"I think you're describing me before I got serious!" he said.

"That's funny," I said. "What would you think if you handed a violin to someone who said, 'I am going to do something with this instrument that nobody has done before.' Or what if you handed a set of golf clubs to someone who said, 'I am going to play the game with these clubs in a way never before imagined!'"

"It would be foolish," he said.

---

* Bryan A. Garner is the president of LawProse Inc. He is the author of many books and the editor-in-chief of all current editions of *Black's Law Dictionary*.

Naturally, I agreed.

Mastery of any discipline begins with imitation. You must know what's been done before, and you must know about technique. You must know the rules of the discipline so that you can produce consistently strong results. Otherwise, you're just acting in ignorance, and the quality of your results will be wildly variable—and generally poor.

So great pianists play in very much the same way, and their individual virtuosity comes through only in subtle ways. Professional golfers may look very different from one another, but they're very much alike in the fundamentals—especially how the clubface, shoulders, feet and body look at the moment of impact with the ball. If there's variation among true experts, it's at the fringes. And all true experts have begun by imitating their great predecessors.

Sensible Rules for Writers

The same is true of writers. You have to know certain rules. I can think of eight offhand:

You must fervently want to be understood, and therefore you must see things from the readers' point of view—and it's best to think of your readers in the broadest possible way.

Sentences need to be linked to one another, fore and aft.

The same is true of paragraphs.

The first paragraph or two are the most valuable real estate you have, so you must make the most of them.

The closing paragraph is the second most valuable real estate, so you mustn't squander it—but instead cinch the deal (you're selling your ideas).

Because the primary position of emphasis in an English sentence is the end, you must try to end sentences emphatically if you want to keep your readers from dozing.

Once you've written a draft, you must ruthlessly cut every unnecessary word (not being too hard on the word).

You must be attentive to the fine points of phrasing, word choice and punctuation—

not for the sake of pedantry but for the sake of making comprehension effortless for your readers.

Those are good rules.

Kick These Edicts

But many of us, at an impressionable age, picked up lots of bad rules that no reputable authority countenances. Unlike the eight just listed, they're all simple prohibitions:

You mustn't begin a sentence with a conjunction, such as And, But or Nor.

You should never begin a sentence with Because.

You mustn't write a one-sentence paragraph.

You should never use first person.

You mustn't end a sentence with a preposition.

You mustn't split an infinitive (those who believe this often don't know what an infinitive is).

You should never use Since as a softer equivalent to Because, and you should never use While to mean Although.

You must never use contractions.

Those aren't really rules. They're the stylistic equivalent of hearsay upon hearsay. Reputable writing authorities repudiate them, one and all. So part of the problem is to figure out what the real rules are—and then figure out when it makes sense to break them.

Notice that the simple-Simon prohibitions above are probably intended for young children. An analogous rule would be that of the Suzuki method of violin instruction, in which children are taught that before playing, they must begin with a zip-and-step (parting their feet [zip] and then moving the right foot forward [step]). But imagine the reaction you'd get from a virtuoso violinist if you accused them of violating a "rule" by not zipping and stepping at the beginning of a performance. It would be absolute nonsense.

When it comes to supposed rules of writing, it's good to know what's at their foundation. Some are aimed at curing young schoolchildren of elementary blunders. We teach kids not to begin with And or But precisely because they tend to begin all their sentences that way (especially And), and they need to be weaned off the habit. We teach them not to begin a sentence with Because just to keep them from perpetrating sentence fragments by mistakenly putting a period rather than a comma after the Because clause.

We teach them not to write one-sentence paragraphs so they'll learn how to compose well-developed paragraphs. We teach them to write without I and me because beginners easily become addicted to mentioning themselves excessively — and need to learn to write with a more objective tone. All the while, we ignore the fact that they'll ultimately need some sentence-starting conjunctions, some Because sentences, some one-sentence paragraphs and some uses of first person.

Other "prohibitions" are mostly nonsense and always have been: the idea that you mustn't end with a preposition or must never split an infinitive. The great H.W. Fowler demolished these false idols in his *1926 A Dictionary of Modern English Usage*. Nobody has successfully countered him. Most writing authorities, if they mention these bugaboos at all, take pains to eliminate them.

What about contractions? Again, it's arguably useful to teach children a type of formal prose style before they mature and learn to relax their style (relax, I said, not be lax). It's good that they learn you are, and later you're, so they're not hampered by a fundamental confusion between your and you're. The same could be said of their and they're (and there, for that matter). But contractions are an effective antidote to stuffiness, and they aid readability—demonstrably. Consider this sentence from The Law of Judicial Precedent (2016): "To say that a trial court or appellate court generally won't rethink a prior ruling isn't to say that it can't." An uncontracted style there will strike many as either stilted or downright laughable.

Learn First, Ignore as Needed

I should point out that my late co-author Justice Antonin Scalia disagreed with me about contractions. But he broke his own rule and allowed contractions throughout our first joint book, Making Your Case. And on occasion he broke his own rule, even in judicial opinions.

Chapter 16
Legal Writing

There are Bluebook rules worth breaking. One is the notion that explanatory parentheticals are "recommended" with many citations — a convention that spoils any product with in-line citations. Even proponents of in-line citations, such as Justice Scalia and Judge Richard Posner (no fan of the Bluebook), acknowledge that trailing parentheticals bastardize paragraphs when the citations are interlarded within the writing. Another is the idea that underlining is an acceptable practice in court documents.

Still, I would never say you shouldn't learn established citation form just because you can later decide to ignore certain elements of it.

When it comes to breaking rules, Paul J. Kiernan of Washington, D.C., cites the Harlem Globetrotters basketball team. They know how to play basketball, make passes, dunks and so on, but they're entertaining because they then break or bend those rules for comic effect. If they couldn't play a real game, their breaking the rules wouldn't work. Or consider the comic classical pianist Victor Borge, who followed the same pattern. Or if you appreciate fine couture, think of Alexander McQueen and what he did with clothing design.

Only after you can truly perform as the discipline requires can you break rules to good effect.

Ten Tips for Transitioning to Legal Writing

Perhaps before you came to law school you were a journalist. Or perhaps you've published scholarly works in the field of Economics or English. Maybe you wrote short stories or plays. Whatever kind of writing you did before, after writing your first legal memo you will notice that legal writing is different, and that transitioning to legal writing is difficult. Remember through this process that good critical writing "in a particular field does not simply happen as a result of a person's mind maturing, but is a consequence of experience gathered by working with others more experienced in some particular discourse community." In other words, think of learning the skill of legal writing in terms of being socialized into the community of legal readers and writers rather than simply as a small variation on something you've already been doing for years. Here are a few tips to make the transition to legal writing go more smoothly:

1. Be Prepared for Your Writing to Worsen Before It Improves

As students new to the legal community, and as you struggle to acquire new legal writing skills, expect temporarily to lose skills you once mastered. You may never have struggled with organizing a paper or writing a clear and coherent sentence before, but don't be frustrated when some of the feedback you receive on your legal writing reflects writing problems you've never had before. Legal writing imposes new demands on your mind. There are lots of new things that you are thinking about when you sit down to write your first memo, like how to follow the structure of a legal document, how to synthesize a rule, and how to write an effective case comparison. As you focus on mastering these new skills, it is often simply too much to focus simultaneously on sentence structure or effective paragraphs.

This should prepare you for two things. First, don't be dismayed when some of the feedback you receive reflects writing problems you thought you had overcome long ago. This is normal and is simply evidence that you're learning new things. Second, as you revise and edit your legal writing, read through your document several times to look for different issues. Dedicate at least one read-through to spotting ordinary writing issues that may exist apart from the new legal writing skills you're trying to master.

2. Read Great Examples of the Types of Documents You Are Learning to Write

The judicial opinions that constitute the meat of what you read as a law student are very different documents (that serve a very different purpose) from the memos and briefs you will write as a practitioner. Although not assigned for class, take the time to read a few examples of what constitutes an exemplary memo or brief in our field. Briefs in most federal cases are readily available on Lexis and Westlaw — try a court of appeals brief by a well-respected practitioner in a recent case. Ask a writing professor to see a few of the best objective memos he or she has received. Reading well-written documents of the type you are drafting will help you become a socialized member of the legal writing community.

3. Learn the Structure of Legal Writing Now So You Can Adapt It Later

When you learned to write a five-paragraph essay, you wrote five paragraphs, each with a designated function—an introduction, three main points, and a conclusion. When you wrote essays in college, you broke these rules to cover as many points as you needed to cover, without regard to the formula. The same goes for legal writing. It will seem formulaic and perhaps repetitive at first always to include a topic sentence immediately after a pointheading, or to roadmap your discussion. But stick to it. Once you learn the conventions of legal writing, you will be able to "break the rules", or perhaps more accurately, to adapt the formula to better serve your needs as a more advanced writer.

4. Use Your Writing Process as an Organizational Tool

Some writers have never written a document without an outline or other form of pre-writing, but some writers come to law school never having found pre-writing useful. As a legal writer, pre-writing strategies can both save you time and effort and improve your legal writing. For instance, most well-written legal documents are broken down into sections and subsections that help guide your reader through your analysis by including signposts for what will come ahead. Developing these signposts first during your pre-writing process can help you determine if you have organized your document in the most reader-friendly way.

You can begin thinking about organization before you write in many ways. You may find it useful to organize the product of your research in particular piles or folders that will correspond to sections in your final document. A "brain-dump" on paper before you actually begin writing can also help you begin to see where ideas and organizational structure are beginning to coalesce. Outlines are also a great way to pre-write legal documents. In addition to encouraging you to think about organization before you begin to write, the pre-writing process can also give you an idea whether you've completed enough research to draft, or if there are sections of your analysis where your case law is thin and would benefit from a second round of searching. Whatever writing process works for

you, use your process to think about organization early.

5. Avoid the Temptation to Write in Legalese

As a first year law student, you are primarily assigned cases to read. Sometimes the judges who authored the opinions you are reading are great writers. Sometimes they are not. In any case, you will be reading many opinions that were written a century ago and which no longer represent the writing conventions of the profession. Today, concise and readable legal writing is expected from lawyers, and you should be cautious of emulating the writing style of judges from times past. It is tempting to dress up your writing in legalese like "heretofore" and "aforementioned" because as a writer new to the legal profession you may confuse the jargon of the profession of yore with the expected conventions of the current legal community.

You will learn to distinguish between words and phrases that are simply jargon and can be re-phrased or omitted, and words and phrases that have a special legal meaning, or are "terms of art". You should use terms of art in your writing and use them consistently across a document. The ability to distinguish between the two will come with time and exposure to legal writing. In general try to avoid the temptation to write in legalese and instead stick to plain and readable English.

6. Do Not Over-quote Cases

As a novice in the legal community, there is an overwhelming sense that "the law is the law, and you can't paraphrase the language of the law". Novice legal writers will always prefer to quote language from a judicial opinion to serve as a "rule statement", for example, rather than synthesize various judicial opinions to construct what might be a better rule more appropriate to the facts of their case. This is a normal tendency. After all, judges are well-respected experts in our field and novice writers feel under-qualified to say what the law is. Be conscious of your tendency to stick to the authority of the concrete, and strive to be comfortable enough in the law and in your research to paraphrase and synthesize rather than quote from a case for every proposition. Both your legal analysis and your legal

Chapter 16
Legal Writing

writing will improve with the effort.

7. Learn to Be a Critical Reader of Your Own Writing

You already know how to revise and edit certain types of writing. But learning how to be a critical reader of your own legal writing is also a skill you must master. In addition to spotting ordinary writing issues, you must also learn to look for issues in legal structure and analysis. These can be difficult for you to spot in your own writing because you as the researcher and writer know the case law so well that you may assume things that your reader doesn't know, and also because you often will thoroughly convince yourself of your position by the time you've written a draft (particularly with regard to persuasive writing). Ask your professors and your peers for their tips on becoming your own best editor.

Some people prefer to compose a reader-based outline. In one version of this technique, you write one word next to each paragraph of your document that sums up what that paragraph is about and what function it serves. Another way to construct a reader-based outline is to copy and paste the topic sentence (or topic and concluding sentences) of each paragraph into a separate document. This can help you see organizational issues when you look at the interrelationship of those summary words or sentences to determine whether your paragraphs make sense in the order you've placed them.

Some people prefer a checklist approach that focuses on structure—did I include a topic sentence? Did I follow that sentence with a rule? Does my case comparison follow the structure I was taught? Making yourself slow down as an editor and check off that all the component parts of your document are present and in order can also help you spot places where your analysis may be spotty or doesn't logically follow. Whatever technique works for you, be sure that you test yourself on the solidity of your analysis as you edit your own work.

8. Expect to Re-write, Not Just Proofread

Many students come to law school never having substantially revised or re-written a document. These writers are accustomed to writing a document in one go, then proofreading it for grammatical and spelling errors and submitting it for review. If this is you, expect substantially to alter your writing process. Legal documents are the product of a lot of research and a lot of thinking. Most of that research and thinking doesn't happen in one go. Instead, after initial research and drafting, you'll always find that there are important sections of your document for which you have little to no information, or that the way you structured the document isn't actually the most logical way to present the information. You will very rarely, if ever, write a legal document in one sitting, proofread it, and send it on its way. Instead, build enough time into your writing process to research, pre-write, draft, research again, think, re-organize, re-write, revise, and then proofread — and then to do it all over again after you have received feedback.

9. *Talk About Legal Writing with Professors, Fellows, and Peers*

You have many resources at your disposal—fellow students and teachers who are ready and willing to talk about your writing with you. Talking about your legal writing with socialized members of the legal writing community is one of the best ways to improve it. It is difficult to write for a new discourse community, and it can be even more difficult for a novice legal writer to spot deficiencies in his or her own writing and reasoning. Use the resources available to you to get feedback on your legal writing that you can use to help incorporate the conventions of the profession into your writing. Not only will your writing improve, but you'll simultaneously be learning another skill expected of attorneys. In practice, you will be expected to discuss and defend your work orally. Attorneys rarely just write a document alone in their office and submit it to a superior or to a court. Instead, in practice, you will receive multiple rounds of feedback from superiors and peers both on the legal substance of your document and the conventions and style of the piece. You must be able to accept and utilize this feedback in re-drafting. Practice that skill early by talking about your legal writing with your professors, fellows, and peers.

10. *Invest the Time Now, Reap the Benefits Later*

You are busy as a first-year student. But remember that Legal Research & Writing is the only class you take as a first-year student that really teaches you a skill marketable to employers. Invest the time now to focus on becoming a socialized member of the

Chapter 16
Legal Writing

legal discourse community, and you will reap the benefits of becoming an excellent legal writer as you enter the job market for summer employment and post-graduation positions. Everyone anticipates that you will forget most of what you learned in law school — except they will expect you to remember, and to have mastered, legal writing.

Ten Tips for Better Legal Writing

Throughout your career as a lawyer, you'll be judged professionally on two main things: your interpersonal skills and your writing. Although the requirements of writing assignments will vary depending on your organization, your supervisor and your clients, here are 10 pointers that will improve your work product.

1. Be sure you understand the client's problem. When given an assignment, ask plenty of questions. Read the relevant documents and take good notes. Learn all you can about the client's situation. If you're a junior asked to write a memo or a motion but you aren't told anything about the client's actual problem, ask what it is in some detail. You must be adequately briefed—and that's partly your responsibility. There's almost no way to write a good research memo in the abstract. As you're reading cases and examining statutes, you'll be in a much better position to apply your findings if you know the relevant specifics.

2. Don't rely exclusively on computer research. Combine book research with computer research. Don't overlook such obvious resources as Corpus Juris Secundum and American Jurisprudence. Look at indexes, digests and treatises to round out your understanding of the subject matter. And when it comes to computer research, don't forget Google Books (especially the advanced-search function): It can open up a great variety of fresh resources in addition to what you find with Westlaw or Lexis.

3. Never turn in a preliminary version of a work in progress. A common shortcoming of green or hurried researchers, especially when a project is slightly overdue, is to turn in an interim draft in the hope of getting preliminary feedback. That can be ruinous. What busy supervisor wants to read serial drafts? Besides, you should never turn in tentative work—it's better to be a little late than wrong. That goes for turning in projects to impatient clients

as well. But keep your supervisor (and, if warranted, your client) updated on the status of your work.

4. Summarize your conclusions up front. Whether you're writing a research memo, an opinion letter or a brief, you'll need an up-front summary. That typically consists of three things: the principal questions, the answers to those questions and the reasons for those answers. If you're drafting a motion or brief, try to state on page one the main issue and why your client should win—and put it in a way that your friends and relatives could understand. That's your biggest challenge.

If you're writing a research memo, put the question, the answer and the reason up front. Don't delay the conclusion until the end, as unthinking writers do, naively assuming that the reader will slog all the way through the memo as if it were a mystery novel. And never open with a full-blown statement of facts—despite what you may have learned elsewhere. Why? Because facts are useless to a reader who doesn't yet understand what the issue is. Instead, integrate a few key facts into your issue statement.

5. Make your summary understandable to outsiders. It's not enough to summarize. You must summarize in a way that every conceivable reader—not just the assigning lawyer—can understand. So don't write your issue this way: "Whether Goliad can take a tax deduction on the rent-free space granted to Davidoff under I.R.C. 170(f)(3)?" That's incomprehensible to most readers because it's too abstract and it assumes insider knowledge. Also, it doesn't show any mastery of the problem.

You'd be better off setting up the problem in separate sentences totaling no more than 75 words: "Goliad Enterprises, a for-profit corporation, has granted the Davidoff Foundation, a tax-exempt charity, the use of office space in Goliad's building free of charge. Will the Internal Revenue Service allow Goliad to claim a charitable deduction for the value of the rent-free lease?"

Then provide the brief answer: "No. Section 170(f)(3) of the Internal Revenue Code disallows charitable deductions for grants of partial interests in property such as leases."

Front-loading the information, with a comprehensible question before the answer, is

Chapter 16
Legal Writing

more helpful to your senior colleagues because it achieves greater clarity. Don't presume that your colleagues will (or can) translate your obscurity.

6. Don't be too tentative in your conclusions, but don't be too cocksure, either. Law school exams encourage students to use the one-hand-other-hand approach: The outcome could be this, or it could be that. Even experienced lawyers sometimes hedge needlessly. This approach can look wishy-washy. What's wanted is your best thought about how a court will come down on an issue.

7. Strike the right professional tone: natural but not chatty. Some lawyers, especially less experienced ones being encouraged to avoid legalese, end up turning blithely informal and flouting the norms of standard English, especially in email messages. For example, they might write "u" instead of "you" and "cd" instead of "could". Some even use emotions. Even if you find yourself working for a firm where some people do these things, exercise restraint. Use conventional punctuation and capitalization in your email messages. Your colleagues won't think any less of you, and your supervisors will appreciate your professionalism.

8. Master the approved citation form. Find out what the standards are for citing authority in your jurisdiction. In California, lawyers follow the California Style Manual. In New York, they should (but frequently don't) follow the New York Law Reports Style Manual. In Texas, every knowledgeable practitioner follows the Texas Rules of Form. Other states have their own guides. And, of course, The Bluebook and the ALWD Guide to Legal Citation are widely used as defaults (and sometimes required by court rules). Even if you're not inclined to care much about these things, you'd better learn to obsess over them. Otherwise, you'll look unschooled.

9. Cut every unnecessary sentence; then go back through and cut every unnecessary word. Verbosity makes your writing seem cluttered and underthought. Learn to delete every surplus word. For example, general consensus of opinion is doubly redundant: A consensus relates only to opinions, and a consensus is general by its very nature. You can replace the phrase a number of with several or many. And in order to typically has two

words too many — to can do the work alone. So instead of in order to determine damages, write to determine damages.

The late Judge David Bazelon of the U.S. Court of Appeals for the District of Columbia Circuit was a stickler for super-tight prose. Once, when his student clerk, Eugene Gelernter (now a New York City litigator), brought him a draft opinion, the great judge said: "Nice draft, Gene. Now go back and read it again. Take out every paragraph you don't need, then every sentence you don't need. Then go back and take out every word you don't need. Then, when you're done with that, go back and start the whole process all over again." We should all have such a mentor.

10. Proofread one more time than you think necessary. If you ever find yourself getting sick of looking at your work product and starting to do something rash such as throwing your hands up and just turning it in at that moment, pull yourself up short. Give it a good dramatic reading. Out loud. You'll still find some slips and rough patches—and you'll be glad you did. Better that you find the problems than your readers do. Learn the lesson that mutilating and reworking your own first drafts actually builds your ego as a writer and editor.

Let's say you're a 30-year lawyer, like me — not a new lawyer. These same pointers hold true. It's a good reminder: Don't take shortcuts.

Exercises

I. Delete at least four consecutive words in the following sentences, replace those words with just one word. You may rephrase ideas and rearrange sentences, but don't change the meaning.

- Even assuming that the fog caused injury to Roelke, Amskills had no duty to prevent that injury because it was idiosyncratic and Amskills could not have been expected to foresee such injury.
- At no time prior to the initial public offering did the underwriters or any officers,

directors, or employees have knowledge of any facts that would suggest that "Palm Harbor" could not be completed on schedule and in accordance with specifications.

- Beale has wholly failed to allege facts that, if true, would establish that competition among the nation's law schools would be reduced or that the public has been in any way injured, and this failure to allege facts that would establish an injury to competition warrants the dismissal of her restraint-of-trade claim.
- The Business Corporation Law does not address the ability of a New York corporation to indemnify individuals who are not its employees.
- The court examined a number of cases and stated that there appeared to be only a limited number of instances in which there would exist a duty to disclose the illegal conduct of persons who, through political campaigns, seek election to a public office.

II. Lease Terminology

Black's Law Dictionary, 6th edition, defines a contract as an "agreement between two or more persons which creates an obligation to do or not to do a particular thing." A lease is a contract in which a property owner (landlord or lessor) gives the rights of possession of that property to another (tenant or lessee) for a specified rent and a specified period of time. The lease covers the rights and responsibilities of each of the parties. A lease may also specify under what circumstances one party has no specific obligation to the other.

MODEL LEASE

This lease is made and entered into this _____ day of _____ 20 _____ between the Landlord _____ whose principal place of business is _____ phone _____ and the Tenant _____ .

1. DESCRIPTION OF THE PREISES

The Landlord leases to the Tenant the dwelling unit located at _____ , Apt. , City of _____ Champaign County, Illinois. The dwelling unit is _____ unfurnished _____ furnished only with oven/range and refrigerator _____ furnished by landlord with the appliances and furnishings listed on the attached addendum which is incorporated by reference as part of this lease.

2. TERM OF THE LEASE

This lease shall begin on the _____ day of _____ 20 _____ and shall end on the _____ day of _____ 20 _____ . It is agreed that on the starting date of this lease, Landlord will deliver to the Tenant possession of the dwelling unit in clean condition and good repair.

3. AMOUNT AND DUE DATE OF RENTAL PAYMENTS

Tenant shall pay to Landlord the sum of $ _____ as rent for the full terms of the lease , payable in monthly installments of $ _____ due on the _____ day of each month. The first payment of $ _____ shall be due on _____ and the final payment of $ _____ shall be due on _____ . Rent shall be mailed or delivered in person to _____ .

4. SECURITY AND DAMAGE DEPOSIT

Tenant shall pay to Landlord a security and damage deposit of $ _____ on or before _____ 20 _____ .

Within 5 days after Tenant moves in, Tenant shall complete a written report of any deficiencies in the condition of the dwelling unit, appliance and furnishings and will provide Landlord with a copy of said report. Upon moving out, Tenant shall be liable for Landlord's actual costs to restore the dwelling unit to the same condition as it was when Tenant first moved in NORMAL WEAR AND TEAR EXCEPTED.

Landlord may not withhold any money from the deposit for said costs unless Landlord provides to Tenant an itemized statement of such costs, attaching copies of paid receipts for actual work done, within 30 days of date the Tenant vacates and mailed to the Tenant's last known address. The security and damage deposit, plus bank interest, minus any charges for damages and unpaid rent, shall be paid to the Tenant by the

Landlord within 30 days of the date the Tenant vacates the premises.

5. JOINT AND SEVERAL LIABILITY

Unless otherwise stated herein, all persons signing this lease as Tenant shall be held jointly and severally liable for all terms of this lease. This means any one tenant may be held responsible to Landlord for payment of rent or charges for damages owed by roommates.

6. PARKING

Parking space number _____ is leased by Landlord to Tenant for the full term of this lease for _____ no additional charge; _____ a monthly rental fee of $ _____ .

7. SUBLETTING

Tenant shall not assign this lease nor sublet the dwelling unit without first obtaining the written consent of the Landlord. Landlord agrees said consent will not be withheld unless the proposed replacement tenant is found to be unsuitable, based on the same criteria used to evaluate the original Tenant.

8. UTILITIES AND SERVICES

Landlord and Tenant agree that the parties indicated below shall be responsible for the payment of all bills for provision of utilities and services. Whenever the Tenant is required to reimburse the Landlord for a share of common-metered utilities or common services, Landlord shall state herein or on an addendum, the formula for calculating Tenant's share of the actual bill.

Electricity bills will be paid by _____ Landlord _____ Tenant/Heat bills will be paid by _____ Landlord _____ Tenant/Gas bills will be paid by _____ Landlord _____ Tenant/Water bills will be paid by _____ Landlord _____ Tenant.

Trash hauling will be paid by _____ Landlord _____ Tenant/Recycling tax will paid by _____ Landlord _____ Tenant/Lawn care will be provided by _____ Landlord _____ Tenant/Snow removal will be provided by _____ Landlord and Tenant. Other _____ .

9. TENANT RESPONSIBILITIES

To keep the dwelling unit in a clean and sanitary condition at all times.

To take reasonable precautions to avoid stopping up the drains.

To take reasonable precautions to prevent the freezing of water pipes by not turning the heat off during winter months.

To place trash in the appropriate receptacles provided by the Landlord.

To make no alterations to the premises without the Landlord's written consent.

To keep noise levels to a minimum and avoid disturbing the neighbors, especially between the hours of 11:00 PM and 7:00 AM.

To notify the Landlord in writing of any needed repairs.

To pay for any repairs needed as a result of the negligence of Tenant or Tenant's guests.

10. LANDLORD RESPONSIBILITIES

To provide pest extermination at Landlord's expense, to keep the premises free of vermin, rodents and pests.

To enter the dwelling unit only in case of emergency of after providing Tenant with 24 hours' notice of the date and time of the entry, and to enter only for the purposes of making needed repairs, to exhibit the premises to prospective renters or buyers of for pest control.

To maintain the premises in accordance with all property maintenance and housing codes and to promptly perform needed repairs, including but not limited to: repairs to plumbing, heating, hot water heater, electrical wiring, air-conditioning, roof, walls, floors, doors, windows, screens, locks, elevators, mailboxes, fixtures, appliances and furnishings, all at Landlord's sole expense, except when repair is needed as a result of Tenant's negligence. Landlord will perform repairs such as broken locks or lack of heat, water or other essential services shall be made immediately. If repairs cannot be completed within these time periods, Landlord shall notify Tenant of the reason for the delay and shall perform repairs within a reasonable amount of time thereafter. Landlord shall provide monetary compensation to Tenant for long delays in making needed repairs.

If Landlord fails to make needed repairs within 14 days after receiving written notice from Tenant, Tenant may contact an appropriate tradesperson to arrange to have repairs made and Landlord hereby agrees that Tenant may deduct the cost of said repairs from subsequent rent payments.

11. BREACH OF LEASE

If either the Landlord or Tenant breaches any provision of this lease, either party may pursue all remedies provided under the laws of the State of Illinois or the municipality, including suit for eviction as provided by state law.

12. RENEWAL

The renewal deadline is _____. Landlord agree that, prior to this date, s/he will not rent this unit for the subsequent lease term to anyone other than Tenant.

13. ADDENDUM

No oral agreements are binding on either Landlord or Tenant. Any additional agreements are contained on the attached addendum, which is _____ pages and is incorporated by reference as part of this lease. (Check here if no addendum is added to lease _____.)

Landlord _____ Date
Tenant _____ Date
Tenant _____ Date
Tenant _____ Date

Part 1

Read this model lease written by the Tenant Union at the University of Illinois at Urbana-Champaign, and then answer the questions.

1. Both the introduction and Section 4, paragraph 2, of the lease contain doublets. (See Vocabulary Development, Task 19.) What are they? What one-word synonym could be used in their place?

2. In Section 4, what modals are used to express the obligations of the tenant and landlord? (Modals are words like can, should, and ought to.) Which is the most frequent?

3. In Section 5, what does the modal may mean in the sentence "This means any one tenant may be held responsible to Landlord for payment of rent..."?

4. A group of words from Middle and Old English beginning with here- are found in order legal cases and legal documents. Examples include hereinabove, hereinafter, and heretofore. While some of these here-words are now being substituted for more modern expressions, others such as hereafter, hereby, and herein are still common today. What does herein mean in the following sentence? Or what expression could be substituted for herein?

"Whenever the Tenant is required to reimburse the Landlord for a share of common-metered utilities or common services, Landlord shall state herein or an addendum, the formula for calculating Tenant's share of the actual bill."

5. The term hereby is often used in the creation of a legal agreement. For example, in a wedding ceremony it is common to hear the words "I hereby pronounce you husband and wife." What does hereby in this utterance tell the listener?

6. In the following sentence from the lease, would it make a difference if hereby were removed?

"If Landlord fails to make needed repairs within 30 days after receiving written notice from Tenant, Tenant may contact an appropriate tradesperson to arrange to have repairs made and Landlord hereby agrees that Tenant may deduct the cost of said repairs from subsequent rent payment."

7. In section 10, paragraph 3, the lease states that the landlord will keep the property up to code "at the Landlord's sole expense." What does sole mean in this sentence? Does it mean the same thing in the following sentences? If not, what does it mean?

● The sole issue is whether the lease gives the TENANT the option to renew the

Chapter 16
Legal Writing

lease on the basis of the same rental rate as "for the original term".

- [S]ince the odor of marijuana was the sole factor to support the search, the Court finds that there was not sufficient probable cause for the warrantless search of Defendant's vehicle.

- A prenuptial agreement which specifies that certain property is the sole property of one spouse removes that separate property from the reach of a creditor of the other spouse.

8. Back references are words or phrases in English used to "refer back" or "make reference" to something that has been previously said. Back reference is also referred to as anaphoric reference. One simple example of a back reference is the word his, as in "The plaintiff brought his case to federal court." His refers back to the plaintiff.

Underline the back reference in each of the following sentences. What does it refer to? What synonyms could be used in its place?

- Within five days after Tenant moves in, Tenant shall complete a written report of any deficiencies in the condition of the dwelling unit, appliances and furnishings and will provide Landlord with a copy of said report.

- The damages issue must go to a jury trial if a party so requests.

- Petitioner established by clear and convincing evidence that respondent had no contact with either the child or petitioner during the six months prior to the filing of the abandonment petition..., and such lack of contact "evidence his intent to forego his parental rights."

Part 2 Conditions

Leases and other types of contracts often state conditions. Underline the conditions expressed in the following sentences. How would you explain to someone who doesn't speak English as a first language what each excerpt means. Sentence 4 has two conditions.

1. Defendant, who had already leased space on the 29th floor of One New York

Plaza, was interested in leasing the 33rd floor from plaintiff. Defendant would only lease that floor on the condition that the prime landlord would agree to a telephone communication linkage system between the 29th and 33rd floors.

2. [T]he lease will continue so long as the tenant is not in default on the lease.

3. [T]he common law rule [states] that the landlord, in the absence of an express covenant, is not obligated to repair or paint.

4. [T]he tenant shall have the right to sublet the premises with the prior permission and consent of the landlord, not to be unreasonably withheld, provided the tenant shall give at least ten days prior written notice by certified mail... Landlord shall have ten days from the time of the receipt of said notice to reply thereto and in the event landlord for any reason does not consent to the subletting the landlord must set forth the specific reasons why no consent is being given to the proposed subletting.

Part 3 Notwithstanding, Irrespective of

What is the meaning of notwithstanding and irrespective of in the following excerpts on landlord-tenant disputes? Given a synonym for each. Explain the difference in meaning between the two.

Notwithstanding

- By express provision of the Real Property Law, every residential lease or rental agreement, written or oral, contains an implied warranty of habitability... Notwithstanding the Landlord's argument to the contrary, a tenant can assert her rights under such warranty without need to give prior written.

- A tenant who continues to use a building which is dangerously out of repair, and when this dangerous condition is patent and known to the tenant, the tenant cannot recover for damages resulting from this dangerous condition. This is true notwithstanding the fact that the landlord or owner of the premises has had notice of and has inspected the dangerous condition of the premises, and has negligently failed to repair them.

Irrespective of

- [T]he Property Code not only permits the parties to contract over who will pay for repairs when the tenant causes damage, it specifically authorizes the parties to shift by contract costs of repairs for certain damages from the landlord to the tenant irrespective of whether the damage was caused by the tenant.
- The tenant has a right to possess the premises and can therefore maintain an action for trespass, irrespective of the landlord's consent.

Selected Readings

1. Entertainment & Sports Law
*By Kirk T. Schroder**

Entertainment & Sports Industries: Some Practice Considerations for Beginners

Despite the lack of a universally accepted definition of what entertainment lawyers do, a legal practice in this industry is distinct from other areas of law. No body of case law per se constitutes "entertainment law". An entertainment lawyer regularly counsels clients on issues involving a wide range of legal practice areas, including intellectual property, contracts, business, employment/labor, securities, international, taxation, immigration, and litigation. The legal practice areas on which the entertainment lawyer relies the most will depend on the nature of the client's work within the entertainment industry.

In addition to case law, certain states have specific statutes pertaining to the entertainment industry. The great majority of entertainment contracts negotiated today are entered into and performed in New York and California. Because the entertainment industries are so firmly entrenched in those states, extensive regulation of the entertainment industry exists in those jurisdictions.

The choice of law of either state can create significantly different outcomes with respect to the interpretation and enforceability of the contract. A working knowledge of the entertainment-related regulations in those two states is essential for this practice area even if the attorney does not intend to practice in New York or California. Likewise, the attorney should actively identify and learn the entertainment-related statutes and regulations affecting clients in his or her state.

Many different trade guilds and unions operate throughout the entertainment industry. Their

---

* Kirk T. Schroder practices entertainment and art law with the firm of LeClair Ryan, P.C., in Richmond, Virginia. This article is an abridged and edited version of one that originally appeared in The Entertainment & Sports Lawyer, Winter 1996 (13:4).

agreements cover basic fee arrangements and working conditions for essential creative and technical personnel. They control when the client is a "signatory" to a union/guild agreement of this type and/or when the production involves union members. Even if the state has right-to-work laws, these union rules still affect entertainment clients.

In traditional legal areas, knowledge of relevant cases, statutes, regulations, and collective bargaining agreements typically constitute sufficient competence for legal practitioners. However, this is not true for entertainment lawyers. An entertainment lawyer must also understand how the client does business within the industry.

The fact that entertainment is a document-intensive business further underscores the necessity for lawyers who represent entertainment clients to comprehend the business practices of the industry. This point cannot be overemphasized. In fact, entertainment lawyers have found that in today's entertainment environment it is not enough for them to understand the business practices of only one particular field within the industry. A lawyer's depth of knowledge of industry business practices almost always determines his or her degree of effectiveness.

One simple way to learn about the trends and developments within the entertainment industry is to read the industry trade publications faithfully. Also, many bar and legal education organizations sponsor seminars pertaining to the entertainment industry and provide great networking opportunities.

Sometimes lawyers beginning in the entertainment field improperly assess their market for available entertainment clients. The best way to understand the market for clients in the entertainment industry is to survey the local legal market for potential clients and compare that market to the overall level of entertainment industry activity in various geographic regions in the country.

Geography plays a role in the equation. The industry is primarily centered in New York, Los Angeles, and Nashville. If the entertainment attorney chooses to practice in one of these cities, he or she will face a different set of challenges to the practice of entertainment law than someone who wants to practice entertainment law in a market other than those three cities. However, general guidelines apply to both markets.

Any plan to develop an entertainment law practice initially should address how the entertainment lawyer gains the necessary competence. Remember that the entertainment industry thrives on relationships. Thus, the lawyer must take the time to meet people who work in the industry and learn about their business.

If the lawyer starts from scratch, typically he will have clients who can't pay the bills but will still give him an opportunity to obtain valuable experience. For example, most actors and actresses struggle to make ends meet with part-time jobs. However, the types of issues they confront (such as talent releases, independent contractor tax issues, union affiliation) are at the core of some basic entertainment legal and business principles.

Investing time and energy in developing legal and business competence always pays off. Entertainment clients can and do shop and compare lawyers. Perceived competence will distinguish the attorney from others within the market who also hold themselves out as entertainment lawyers.

More opportunity exists for entertainment lawyers in the three primary markets. Thus, the competition for clients and legal positions in these markets is very high. Although it is more difficult, a lawyer can develop an entertainment law practice and represent entertainment clients in a secondary market. But proper planning becomes a critical necessity. Those who accept this challenge must, at a minimum, (1) assess the market at different geographic levels, and (2) be aware of how the industry continues to expand into secondary markets.

Advancements in technology will continue to increase the opportunities for entertainment lawyers practicing outside the primary markets. As the economy expands, more avenues for programming open, especially through nontraditional channels.

Lawyers who begin to represent clients in the entertainment industry should not assume that their present professional liability insurance will cover claims made against them for entertainment-related legal work. It is critically important to engage an insurance broker early on to learn what guidelines he or she uses to provide coverage in this area.

Lawyers who are new at representing entertainment clients find themselves drawn in by their clients to perform other services. These nonlegal activities include serving as an agent, a manager, or an investment advisor for clients, and they may prove hazardous for lawyers. The problems associated with nonlegal activities can be avoided. When dealing with entertainment clients, the lawyer must make it clear what can and cannot be done for the client. This is best accomplished through an engagement letter that states the scope of the lawyer's activities for the client.

At the heart of the attorney-client relationship lie the fiduciary responsibilities the attorney owes to the client. Many contend that there is something special, unique, and extraordinary about the artist-fiduciary relationship in the entertainment industry. In any event, lawyers who begin to practice in the entertainment field must establish proper guidelines of conduct early in their careers.

All lawyers starting in the entertainment field are, at one time or another, faced with the dilemma of how to bill clients who cannot afford to pay their traditional fees. Unlike most traditional practice areas, lawyers in the entertainment industry can create varying fee arrangements with their clients. However, in some instances, certain nontraditional fee arrangements may present an entertainment lawyer with professional and ethical problems.

A growing practice by some entertainment lawyers is to take a percentage fee arrangement from their clients. Structuring fee arrangements, especially nontraditional arrangements, requires the careful attention of an entertainment lawyer. Lawyers starting out in the entertainment field should develop acceptable fee and billing practices from an ethical and practical perspective.

As the entertainment sector of the economy grows, the field of entertainment law will provide many new and exciting opportunities for lawyers who wish to practice in this area even if they are not practicing in New York, Los Angeles, or Nashville. The key to their successes will depend upon how well they respond to the important practical and ethical considerations presented above.

Practicing Entertainment Law

Not too long ago, practicing entertainment law was a dream job for many up-and-coming law students, as well as attorneys looking to lateral into their truly desired specialties. Dreams of a glamorous lifestyle were all too common: visions of the chance to hobnob with celebrities, to work on the most interesting cases in the profession, and many perks, such as concert tickets, attending movie premieres, and sporting events, danced in their heads. Along with the high salaries and potential to cross over into a highly desirable entertainment company as in-house counsel, the glamour and fame that many assumed came hand in hand with this job made this dream irresistible.

In reality, working as an entertainment lawyer is not as glamorous, and maybe this perception has finally reached the general lawyer population, since the number of applications to these firms has dropped in recent months. In truth, few entertainment law firms have the kinds of perks, desirable clients, and lifestyles people often associate with them. But entertainment law still remains a highly desirable profession, with many unsure what the practice actually entails aside from the myth.

What Is Entertainment Law?

Depending upon whom you ask, you will find a variety of answers to the question. While there is no agreed-upon definition per se, entertainment law is actually just a distinction based upon the type of clients rather than the type of work these lawyers practice. Entertainment lawyers typically counsel clients in business or intellectual property law, including accompanying contracts, copyright, litigation and licensing issues, and sometimes other concerns that pertain to employment, securities, international, taxation, and immigration practice areas. In actuality, an entertainment lawyer spends his time performing research, writing briefs, and filing motions just like any other contract, business litigation, or I.P. lawyer.

The reason behind the entertainment specialty is that the clients these lawyers provide services for happen to be in the entertainment business in some capacity. While firms who represent talent will deal with celebrities, those who represent management deal with companies. Often this means clients who are heads of Warner Bros., MTV, CBS, and many other high-profile corporations. And while you may get the chance to have a celebrity client, your everyday existence consists of tasks that most litigation lawyers deal with, such as writing briefs, taking depositions, researching topics, and filing motions. While perks such as tickets and premieres occasionally come with the territory, they are not an industry norm. The truth is, you still spend the majority of your time at the office doing research and writing, just like other lawyers. Attending high-profile events and getting whisked away by clients in limos to movie premieres, dinner events, and sporting arenas are infrequent perks that cannot be expected. If this is the life you think entertainment lawyers have, then this practice area will leave you very disappointed.

In addition, dealing with celebrities does not always live up to the reputation. You go to work and see a noted celebrity in the elevator, only to discover he is attending a deposition with a senior partner at your firm; and while there may be a rapport, oftentimes dealing with creative, high-profile entertainment industry types can be more frustrating. While you may get the occasional glimpse at a celebrity, the star-struck tendency quickly dissipates, and the deposition or meeting becomes like many others: addressing the facts of your client's case and their concerns. Furthermore, a lot of celebrities are difficult to deal with, showing up notoriously late to court appearances or missing them altogether, pulling fits about wearing suits, or simply being temperamental. Suddenly, you may find yourself yearning for the normal, non-entertainment client.

This is not to say that practicing entertainment law lacks excitement. On the contrary, the intellectual property issues that emerge, as well as defamation, contract, and copyright issues, are all interwoven into an interesting and appealing context. What may appear tedious and dry in an I.P. firm suddenly comes alive against the backdrop of the latest television show or may involve an interesting set of circumstances the average client just does not face. Quirky and humorous and often very appealing, the cases are interesting in nature. But again, the tasks are the same: research and writing, motions, and court dates that are required for other cases.

In addition, working with and for members of the creative industry creates an interesting merger of law and business and a context removed from typical intellectual property scenarios, which can be tedious and dry. Rather, working on high-profile or newsworthy cases that appeal to the public's sense of popular culture can be exciting. Because of this, your cases make for the best dinner conversation. They are the types of stories both colleagues and the general public will be interested in hearing. This makes the practice exciting. Despite the long hours and intense work schedule, the cases are interesting to work on and talk about, and this makes for a desirable aspect to the specialty.

Breaking in

Breaking into the entertainment field is difficult, whether you are a law student or whether you are a mid-level associate seeking a lateral position. The bottom line is you must have worked in the capacity that entertainment law requires: intellectual property cases, preferably complex, as well as business litigation for well-known clients related to the entertainment sector. In addition, networking and luck also play a large role in landing this type of position.

As a student, the ability to earn a position in the entertainment law field depends upon the combination of going to a top school or working at an IP or business litigation firm to have the crossover topics, as well as luck. As an associate, the competition continues to be fierce, and, again, working in a similar industry is key. Networking — having appropriate contacts — will be the important component to help secure a position in this ever-desirable specialty. This will be important again if you decide to consider the partner track, go solo, or seek an in-house position at an entertainment company.

You have to be able to show the firm that you can handle the caseload and the type of work, as well as to understand the true nature of entertainment law. This means that if you want to practice entertainment litigation, you must show your strength as a litigator for complex business cases with high-profile clients, just the type of work you will end up practicing at the entertainment law firm. In addition, you must show an eagerness to work on these types of cases and that you realize you will be a hard-working attorney who happens to work in the entertainment sector.

What It Takes to Succeed

As has often been noted, the world is a small place, and the legal world is no exception. The chances of your running into someone you know or once knew or someone removed by three degrees of separation is highly likely in this context. Networking is crucial to making your mark as an up-and-coming attorney. In the entertainment industry, this is even truer. The world of entertainment law is a small one, with the primary cities being New York, Los Angeles, and Nashville. Certainly you are bound to run into someone you know either as opposing counsel or in some other context. This means that keeping cordial relations with all parties and all attorneys on a particular case is particularly important if you seek longevity. Also, keeping contacts allows an attorney to stay abreast of the changes in the profession, which occur frequently, and all of this allows an attorney to consider options that are not readily available or advertised. This usually translates into in-house opportunities, which are considered to be the most desirable positions in the entertainment field.

Networking is also imperative in the entertainment industry to create business for your firm. You need the contacts and the name to learn about a potential client's business and to meet a potential client directly or indirectly as well. This is crucial because in this industry, reputation and visibility are often the most relied-upon factors clients use in determining whether to work with you. If you are seeking to become partner of an entertainment firm, you will have to network to gain a reputation and bring in business to show a firm your strengths and your irreplaceability.

Conclusion

While entertainment law does not coincide with the myth, it is still a highly desirable and extremely competitive specialty. Entertainment lawyers work on complex cases, spending the majority of their time in the same manners that other lawyers do, and yet they are seen as the more glamorous members of the profession. Regardless of the myth, these lawyers work on interesting cases that affect basic rights of members of the creative industry.

Whatever the choice, one must consider what the practice actually entails, going beyond the popular myth. It may just be that you are actually happy with the position that you have. Otherwise, a position in the entertainment field can achieve the sense of excitement and visibility that will leave you with a level of job satisfaction you have not yet experienced. If that's the case, entertainment law may just be your calling.

Selected Readings

2. Admiralty

Overview

Admiralty law or maritime law is the distinct body of law (both substantive and procedural) governing navigation and shipping. Topics associated with this field in legal reference works may include: shipping; navigation; waters; commerce; seamen; towage; wharves, piers, and docks; insurance; maritime liens; canals; and recreation. Piracy (ship hijacking) is also an aspect of admiralty.

The courts and Congress seek to create a uniform body of admiralty law both nationally and internationally in order to facilitate commerce. The federal courts derive their exclusive jurisdiction over this field from the Judiciary Act of 1789 and from Article III, 2 of the U.S. Constitution. Congress regulates admiralty partially through the Commerce Clause. American admiralty law formerly applied only to American tidal waters. It now extends to any waters navigable within the United States for interstate or foreign commerce. In such waters admiralty jurisdiction includes maritime matters not involving interstate commerce, including recreational boating.

Admiralty law in the United States developed from the British admiralty courts present in most of the American colonies. These courts functioned separately from courts of law and equity. With the Judiciary Act, though, Congress placed admiralty under the jurisdiction of the federal district courts. Although admiralty shares much in common with the civil law, it is separate from it. Common law does not act as binding precedent on admiralty courts, but it and other law may be used when no law on point is available.

Parties subject to admiralty may not contract out of admiralty jurisdiction, and states may not infringe on admiralty jurisdiction either judicially or legislatively. Since admiralty courts, however, are courts of limited jurisdiction (which does not extend to nonmaritime matters), 28 USC 1333(1), the "Savings to Suitors Clause", does provide for concurrent state jurisdiction so that non-admiralty remedies will not be foreclosed. Moreover, state courts may have jurisdiction where the matter is primarily local.

Under admiralty, the ship's flag determines the source of law. For example, a ship flying the American flag in the Persian Gulf would be subject to American admiralty law; and a ship flying a Norwegian flag in American waters will be subject to Norwegian admiralty law. This also applies to criminal law governing the ship's crew. But the ship must be flying the flag legitimately; that is, there must be more than insubstantial contact between the ship and its flag, in order for the law of the flag to apply. American courts may refuse jurisdiction where it would involve applying the law of another country, although in general international law does seek uniformity in admiralty law.

Just as the Federal Rules of Civil Procedure placed law and equity under the same jurisdiction in 1938, the 1966 rules subsumed admiralty. Nonetheless, the Supplemental Admiralty Rules take precedence over the Federal Rules of Civil Procedure in the event of conflict between the two.

Breaking Down "Maritime Law"

In most developed nations, maritime law is governed by a separate code and is a separate jurisdiction from national laws. The United Nations, through the International Maritime Organization (IMO), has issued numerous conventions that can be enforced by the navies and coast guards of countries that have signed the treaty outlining these rules. Maritime law governs many of the insurance claims relating to ships and cargo, civil matters between shipowners, seamen and passengers, and piracy.

Additionally, maritime law regulates the registration, license, and inspection procedures for ships and shipping contracts, maritime insurance and the carriage of goods and passengers.

Breaking Down "York Antwerp Rules"

A set of maritime rules that outline the rights and obligations of ship and cargo owners when cargo must be jettisoned to save a ship. The York Antwerp Rules are a codification of the law of general average, the maritime principle that specifies that all parties involved in a sea venture must proportionately share any losses that result from sacrifices made to the cargo to save the remainder.

The York Antwerp Rules were established in 1890 and have been amended several times. The rules are generally included in bills of lading, contracts of affreightment and marine insurance policies. Under the rules, a danger must be imminent, there must be a voluntary jettison of a portion of the ships cargo in order to save the whole and the attempt to avoid the danger must be successful. If these are true, then all parties involved in the maritime adventure must share proportionately the financial burden of the losses incurred to the owner(s) of any cargo that was jettisoned to save the vessel.

Breaking Down "Admiralty Proceeding"

Any matter that comes before an admiralty court that involves shipping or a shipping vessel.

Selected Readings

Admiralty law (also known as maritime law) governs all private legal matters involving events happening in the seas or in bodies of water that have multiple national jurisdictions.

In the United States, admiralty proceedings are handled by the U.S. federal district courts, but there may be state court issues involved with admiralty matters occurring within U.S. boundaries. In other countries, such as the United Kingdom and Singapore, admiralty courts are a separate venue and jurisdiction from other courts. Much of admiralty law is grounded in English statutes and other conventions that have evolved over hundreds of years since the advent of shipping commerce. As an example, passengers of the Titanic bringing civil claims against the ship were heard in an admiralty proceeding.

Breaking Down "The Jones Act"

A federal law that regulates maritime commerce in the United States. The Jones Act requires goods shipped between U.S. ports to be transported on ships that are built, owned, and operated by United States citizens or permanent residents. Also known as The Merchant Marine Act of 1920.

The Jones Act was enacted by the United States Congress in order to stimulate the shipping industry in the wake of the First World War. It is considered a protectionist legislation. The law focuses on issues related to maritime commerce, including cabotage, which is the transport of people or goods between ports in the same country. It also provides sailors with additional rights, including the ability to seek damages from the crew, captain or ship owner in the case of injury.

Perhaps the most lasting effect of the Jones Act was its requirement that goods shipped between U.S. ports be transported on ships built, owned, and operated by United States citizens or permanent residents. This requirement benefited the constituents of Wesley Jones, the U.S. Senator who introduced the act and who represented the state of Washington. Since Washington State had a large shipping industry, the act was designed to give it a monopoly on shipping to Alaska. While the act benefited his constituents, it increased the shipping costs of other states and U.S. territories.

The Jones Act increases the cost of shipping to Hawaii, Alaska, Puerto Rico, and other non-continental U.S. lands that rely on imports by restricting the number of vessels that can legally deliver goods. The supply of American built, owned, and operated vessels is relatively small compared to the global supply of ships, while the demand for basic goods tends to remain constant or grow. This creates a scenario in which shipping companies can charge higher rates because of a lack of competition, with the increased costs pass on to consumers. This may lead to consumers taking on more debt in order to finance purchases, which can have a negative effect on government finances.

The Act has been criticized for restricting who can conduct trade with Puerto Rico, and has been cited as a factor leading to the island's economic and budgetary troubles. A study released by the New York Federal Reserve in 2012 found that the cost of transporting a shipping container to Puerto Rico from the mainland was twice as high as shipping the same container from a foreign port.

Opponents of the act want it repealed, hoping that this will result in decreased shipping costs, lower prices, and less strain on government budgets. Proponents of the act include states with owners of navy yards, defense firms, and shipping industries, as well as the longshoremen and other personnel who work in ports. Scrapping the law will likely reduce the number of U.S. maritime jobs, while reducing shipping costs.

On several occasions, the U.S. government has granted temporary waivers on Jones Act requirements. This is typically done in the wake of a natural disaster, such as a hurricane, in order to increase the number of ships that can legally supply goods to an affected area.

Breaking Down "Inchmaree Clause"

A clause found in maritime insurance policies which provides coverage for the ship's hull from loss or damage caused by machinery. The Inchmaree clause, also called the negligence clause, covers damage that is caused by negligence of ship personnel, such as engineers and captains, when navigating. It is a type of additional perils clause.

Shipping cargo across vast oceans can carry great risk. In addition to storms potentially sinking or flooding a ship, the actions of the ship's crew and other personnel responsible for maintaining a properly working vessel may result in damage to the ship's cargo. For example, a boiler that is not properly maintained may burst, causing a ship to lose power and run aground, or a shaft may break loose and strike items held in the cargo bay.

Until the Inchmaree clause was established, most cargo insurance policies only covered perils that occurred while on the open sea, such as bad weather. This changed in the late 19th century. The Inchmaree clause is named after a British court case, Hamilton v. James and Mersey Insurance. The case involved the Inchmaree, a British steamer that sunk in Liverpool harbor in 1884. The ship's cargo was damaged when an internal pump flooded the holding area, but the cargo owners' claims were denied by the insurer because the damage was not caused by the "perils of the sea". The maritime insurance industry was pressured to provide additional coverage for accidents that were not caused by the sea, and instead caused by other factors such as negligence.

The clause typically provides additional coverage for damage or loss caused by broken drive shafts, burst boilers, hull defects and other problems associated with a ship and the ship's equipment. Additionally, policies will cover negligence from a ship's officers, engineers and crew, including errors in navigation.

IMO Conventions

The IMO was created in 1958 and is responsible for ensuring that existing international maritime conventions are kept up to date as well as develop new conventions as and when the need arises. Today, there are dozens of conventions regulating all aspects of maritime commerce and transport.

The IMO identifies three of these as its key conventions. They are:

The International Convention for the Safety of Life at Sea

The International Convention for the Prevention of Pollution from Ships

The International Convention on Standards of Training, Certification and Watch-keeping for Seafarers

Conventions are regularly amended to keep up with new business practices and technologies. On its website, the IMO has a complete list of existing conventions, their historical amendments and explanatory notes.

Enforcement

The governments of the of IMO's 171 member states are responsible for the enforcement of IMO conventions for ships of their nationality. Local governments enforce the provisions of IMO conventions as far as their own ships are concerned and set the penalties for infringements. In some cases, ships must carry certificates on board the ship to show that they have been inspected and have met the required standards.

Nationality of Ships

A ship's nationality is determined by the country where it is registered. Most ships are registered in the national registry of the country where their owners reside or operate their business. However, often for reasons of tax planning or to take advantage of more lenient local rules, some owners will register ships in countries that allow foreign ships to be registered. These registries are called "flags of convenience". Two common examples of flags of convenience are Panama and Bermuda.

Compensation for Injured Passengers and Seamen

Personal injury cases governed by maritime law raise unique issues requiring an attorney who specializes in such matters. For example, the legal rights of passengers hurt by the negligence of a cruise line will be curtailed by the terms of their ticket. In most cases this means the time limit for filing suit will be one year instead of three, and notice may be required in as little as six months.

For sailors hurt on the job, recovering compensation under maritime law can be even more complex. Federal legislation known as the Jones Act, found at 46 USC 883, sets forth the rights of injury victims who qualify as "seamen". A seaman is a male or female crew member whose service meets certain requirements under the act. This determination alone will often require consultation with legal counsel.

If the Jones Act applies, the injured crew member will be entitled to a jury trial and other protections similar to those afforded to injured railroad workers. The purpose of the legislation is to provide a fair process for sailors to file a negligence claim and receive compensation from their employer. Should the negligent act of an employer or coworker result in death, surviving family members are permitted to file suit.

Employees who do not qualify as seamen under the Jones Act have other means available for collecting injury compensation. The Doctrine of Unseaworthiness imposes a duty on ship owners to maintain and equip their vessels properly. If they do not, they will be liable for any resulting injuries to crew members. Similarly, the law of "maintenance and cure" requires employers to pay the expenses of injured crew members following an accident.

Federal maritime law combines modern legislation, centuries-old doctrines, international treaties, private contracts, and more into a single set of interdependent legal rules. Even in coastal cities, most personal injury lawyers are not proficient in admiralty law, and will not accept these cases. Those with legal rights or interests that may be affected by this area of the law are strongly encouraged to retain a specialist.

3. Intellectual Property

Some types of property involve images, ideas, concepts, or arrangements of words. Collectively, these are referred to as intellectual property (IP). For example, someone who designs a better mouse trap and then receives a patent for her idea possesses IP. This property may be sold or licensed to others, but the patent holder may sue if another party uses her patent without permission. Other types of IP include copyrights (such as artwork, photographs, and published books) and trademarks, which are used to identify a brand (the Nike swoosh, for example).

Copyrights

A copyright is a federal protection provided to the creators of original works, such as books, movies, recordings, music notation, photographs, software, etc. Copyright protections do not extend beyond the actual work being protected, though. For example, J.R.R. Tolkien's Harry Potter books are protected by copyright, but this doesn't stop other writers from publishing books about young wizards.

Copyright owners have the exclusive right to reproduce their works, produce "derivative" works, sell or distribute the work, lease the copyright to others, publicly perform the work, or display the work publicly.

You run a diversified multinational mass media and entertainment conglomerate whose mascot is a well-known mouse. The movie studio portion of your business decides to produce and distribute a wildly popular 3-D animation film about a fearless princess who sets off on a journey along with her cheerful sidekick snowman. The movie grosses over $400 million in the United States alone, with more profits to come. As you are counting your box office receipts, another filmmaker files a copyright infringement lawsuit against your company, claiming that a trailer for the animated blockbuster infringed on her short film about a snowman that has an uncanny resemblance to the one in your movie. She says the snowman from your film is "substantially similar to the depiction of the snowman character", and demands damages.

Sound familiar? This is exactly what happened in a 2014 intellectual property case involving a 2-D animator and Walt Disney Studios over the movie Frozen. While that case ended up settling out of court, it is a good example of basic copyright issues.

Copyright 101

First, we will take a brief look at where copyright law originates. Your creative works are your own. Going back to the Founding Fathers, the U.S. Constitution sets forth that Congress shall pass laws to secure for authors exclusive rights to their writings for limited times.

The Congress shall have Power To... promote the Progress of Science and useful Arts, by securing for limited Times to Authors and Inventors the exclusive Right to their respective Writings and Discoveries

Later, U.S. lawmakers passed federal statutes to help provide automatic legal protections to the authors of "original works of authorship", including literary, dramatic, musical, and artistic works. Since then, the protections have been extended to movies, sound recordings, and computer software — to name a few.

Certain types of works have been excluded from copyright protections over the years, including works in the public domain, processes and systems such as the Dewy Decimal system, and federal government works such as the U.S. tax code.

Getting Copyrights

Copyright protection is available for certain types of original works. It allows authors, artists, and other creators of original works to create works without fear of someone else copying and profiting from their work. FindLaw's section on Copyrights provides information and resources on getting copyright protection for your own work, licensing copyrights, using someone else's copyrighted material, and much more.

What Can Be Copyrighted?

Copyright is a type of intellectual property protection that protects the "form of material expression". This means that facts, ideas, concepts, or techniques of a particular work are not protected. For this reason, copyright protection is only available for works that are fixed in a tangible form. Examples of fixed in tangible form are a story written on paper or a painting on canvas. The categories of works that are protected under copyright law include software, paintings, literary works, photographs, movies, sound recording, musical works, and television broadcasts.

Rights of a Copyright Owner

A copyright owner is afforded certain exclusive rights over the work. The copyright owner has the exclusive right to reproduce the work, sell the work, and perform or display the work publicly. The copyright owner also has the exclusive right to create derivative works, which are new works based on the original copyrighted work. If the copyright owner would like to give these rights to another person, he or she has the option to transfer ownership or give a person a license to use the work. If the copyright owner transfers his or her rights, he or she ceases to be the copyright owner. If, on the other hand, the copyright owner gives someone a license, then he or she is still the owner of the copyright, he or she simply gives certain rights to use the work.

Requirements for Copyright Protection

The main requirements to receive copyright protection are that it is an original work and fixed in a tangible form. While registration with the U.S. Copyright Office is not a requirement for receiving copyright protection, there are benefits to registering a copyright. For example, registration of a copyright provides a public record of the copyright claim in the work. Registration is also required before you can file a copyright infringement lawsuit.

Original works created after March 1989 are not required to include a copyright notice to have copyright protection; however, there are benefits to having a copyright notice on your work. The notice of copyright alerts the public to the fact that work is under copyright protection and identifies the year the work was first published and the copyright owner. In addition, including a copyright notice doesn't require any formal steps — you simply need to include the notice in your work.

Copyright Ownership

Most people think that whoever actually makes a creative work owns the copyright in that work, but that often isn't the case. Artists, authors, and musicians can transfer copyright ownership or license certain rights of copyright ownership to other parties. Sometimes multiple people can also simultaneously have ownership of the copyright in a creative work.

When Creators Don't Own Copyrights

Here are some examples of when the creator of a work doesn't own the copyright in the work:

- Work Made for an Employer

When the creator of a work is an employee of a business, the business owns the copyright as long as the employee created the wok within the scope of their employment.

- Work for Hire

Companies sometimes hire independent contractors, and the copyrights in the work that those independent contractors produce rests with the hiring company.

The Copyright Act governs what qualifies as a work for hire:

A work specially ordered or commissioned for use as a contribution to a collective work, as a part of a motion picture or other audiovisual work, as a translation, as a supplementary work, as a compilation, as an instructional text, as a test, as answer material for a test, or as an atlas, if the parties expressly agree in a written instrument signed by them that the work shall be considered a work made for hire.

- Work Sold to Another

It's possible for the creator of a work to sell the entire copyright to someone else. At that point, the creator assigns all their rights in the work to the other person.

- Joint Copyright Ownership

If a work has two creators and their contributions are inseparable and part of a single creation, the work is considered a "joint work", and both authors have ownership of the copyright. Unless the creators agree to a different arrangement, each can take advantage of one of the rights included in the copyright (see below) as long as both creators share the income equally.

Methods of Transferring Copyrights

Most of the time, a creator will need to transfer some or all of the rights to the work in order to market it. If the creator transfers all ownership rights with no limitations, it is known as an "assignment"; if the creator transfers only some of the rights or places a time limit on the transfer, it is known as a "license".

There are many ways that copyrights can change hands. Besides an assignment or a transfer, copyrights can act as a security for an obligation or can transfer upon an owner's death. A court can also order the transfer of a copyright in certain situations, such as a divorce.

Fair Use or Public Domain?

The legal standards and rules for determining fair use or public domain content may seem confusing. These charts should help give you a better idea of the likelihood of whether your use of someone's work will run afoul of copyright law.

Does Your Use of the Work Constitute Fair Use?

The closer your answer is Yes to the following questions, the more likely your use is fair use. The right column illustrates examples of factors that make a finding of fair use more likely vs. copyright infringement.

Selected Readings

Factors	Examples
Are you creating something new?	Including excerpts in a commentary piece about the book vs. copying a book word-for-word
Is the copyrighted work factual?	Biography vs. work of fiction
Is the portion of the work used small in amount and significance in relation to the entire work?	Two sentences from a novel vs. a chapter of the book that goes to the heart of the story
Does your use have little or no market impact on the copyrighted work?	Excerpting from a travel book on Rome for a book review vs. copying an entire section for a new travel book on Rome

Is the Work in the Public Domain?

Publication Date	Public Domain?
Works published in the U.S. before 1923	Yes.
Works published in the U.S. in 1923 through 1963	Yes, if the copyright was not renewed during the 28th year after the work was first published.
Works published in the U.S. in 1964 through 1977	No. Automatic copyright renewal protects the work for 95 years.
Works published in 1978 or later	No. Work is protected by copyright for the life of the author plus 70 years. (a longer copyright term may apply)
Works published by the U.S. Federal Government	Yes, regardless of publication date.

Public Domain: Additional Factors and Copyright Renewal

Although the above chart provides helpful guidance in determining whether a work is in the public domain, there are a few additional steps that will help you in this analysis for published works.

- **Works Published in the U.S. from 1923 through 1963:** Likely in the public domain. Even though authors could extend protection of their works by filing a copyright renewal during the 28th year after the work was first published, many authors failed to file the renewal on time. Always check the U.S. Copyright Office database to make sure that there is no renewal on file for the 28th year of the published work. For those works published during this time and renewed on time, copyright protection endures for an additional term of 47 years, following the 28-year initial term. A 1998 law changed the additional term from 47 to 67 years; however, works that were already in the public domain in 1998 (e.g.

331

work published in 1932 or earlier, with copyright renewal) remain in the public domain.

- **Works Published in the U.S. from 1964 through 1977:** Copyright renewal is automatic and is protected for 95 years from the date of publication. Since the new law making copyright renewals automatic was changed in 1992, any works that were already in the public domain before 1992 remain in the public domain.
- **Works Published in the U.S. after 1977:** Enjoy copyright protection for the life of the author plus 70 years after the date of his or her death. In the case of "work made for hire" and anonymous and pseudonymous works have protection for 95 years from the publication date or 120 years from creation, whichever expires first.

Unpublished Works

The protection of life of the author plus 70 years also applies to unpublished works. You should note, however, that if an unpublished work is created before 1978, and subsequently published between 1978 and 2003, the copyright lasts through 2047, no matter when the author died.

International Copyright

There is no such thing as an "international copyright" that will automatically protect an author's writings throughout the world. Protection against unauthorized use in a particular country basically depends on the national laws of that country. However, most countries offer protection to foreign works under certain conditions which have been greatly simplified by international copyright treaties and conventions. There are two principal international copyright conventions:

- Berne Union for the Protection of Literary and Artistic Property (Berne Convention), and
- Universal Copyright Convention (UCC).

The Berne Convention and UCC

The United States became a member of the Berne Convention on March 1, 1989. It has been a member of the UCC since September 16, 1955. Generally, the works of an author who is a national or domiciliary of a country that is a member of these treaties or works first published in a member country or published within 30 days of first publication in a Berne Union country may claim protection under them.

Formal Requirements

There are no formal requirements in the Berne Convention. Under the UCC, any formality in a national law may be satisfied by the use of a notice of copyright in the form and position specified in the UCC. A UCC notice should consist of the symbol © (C in a circle) accompanied by the year of first publication and the name of the copyright proprietor (example: © 1995 John Doe). This notice must be placed in such manner and location as to give reasonable notice of the claim to copyright.

Since the Berne Convention prohibits formal requirements that affect the "exercise and enjoyment" of the copyright, the U.S. changed its law on March 1, 1989 to make the use of a copyright notice optional. U.S. law however, still provides certain advantages for use of a copyright notice; for example, the use of a copyright notice can defeat a defense of "innocent infringement."

Bilateral Agreements

Even if the work cannot be brought under an international convention, protection may be available in other countries by virtue of a bilateral agreement between the U.S. and other countries or under specific provision of a country's national laws.

Filing a Copyright Infringement Suit and Possible Damages

So what do you do if you believe your creative genius has been infringed? You sue in federal court under federal copyright statutes. But first, you'll want to speak with a knowledgeable attorney who has successfully handled these cases in the past. Why? There are a number of requirements to starting a copyright infringement lawsuit. First, you must have registered your work with the U.S. Copyright Office. These types of lawsuits are highly fact-intensive and often require a long court battle in order to come to a resolution. If you are able to prove infringement, you may be entitled to a number of important remedies, including an injunction to stop the defendant from continuing to illegally use your copyright.

You may also be able to receive monetary damages including actual damages.

Trademarks

A trademark is used to identify and promote goods or services, distinguishing them from the goods or services of others. They may take the form of words, symbols, or devices. For example, the green mermaid design used by Starbucks Coffee is a trademark used to identify its products. If another company tried to use this or a similar image, then Starbucks could probably sue for trademark infringement.

While corporations typically register their trademarks, it is not always necessary as long as the claimant (the company claiming trademark rights) can prove a legitimate business use of the mark. The key issue is whether another company's use of a mark will create confusion among consumers.

Trademark Registration

Registering a trademark with the USPTO is not a requirement to receive trademark protection. Instead, trademark protection is established through the legitimate use of the mark (in a commercial setting). Registration does provide certain advantages to the trademark owner. For example, registering a trademark with the USPTO provides a legal presumption that the registrant is in fact the owner of the trademark. Registration is also a prerequisite in order for the trademark registrant/owner to file a lawsuit related to the trademark in federal court.

If a person does decide to register his or her trademark, he or she must follow a specific set of standards and procedures. The application for a trademark must include: the name of the applicant, a name and address for communications between the applicant and the USPTO, a depiction of the mark, the list of goods and/or services the mark will be used for, and the filing fee. A specimen of use, which is a real world example of how the mark is used, may also be required of certain applicants. A few examples of a specimen of use is a brochure, website, tag, label, or a listing from the yellow pages. If an application is incomplete or doesn't conform to the standards set forth by the USPTO, the application and filing fee will be returned to the applicant.

Designating Trademark Protection

Speaking technically, a mark that is used in association with services is called a service mark, while a mark used to identify goods is called a trademark. But, trademark can generally be used to refer to both service marks and trademarks. A person who claims trademark protection in a particular slogan, symbol, short phrase, or name has that right to use "SM" for a service mark and "TM" for a trademark. There is no formal registration or other process required to use either of these letters. If a person decides to register a trademark with the USPTO, he or she also has the option to use the symbol "®". This symbol specifically indicates federal registration and can only be used in association with the goods and/or services that were specifically listed in trademark application.

Types of Trademarks

As a business, you want your products or services to not only stand out from the crowd but also identifiable through a distinctive brand. These slogans, symbols, and designs are collectively known as a "mark", either a trademark (for products), a service mark (for service-based businesses), or a trade dress (distinctive packaging, for example). The rules for each of these types vary slightly, but generally adhere to a few basic principles. And regardless of whether it is a trademark, service mark, or trade dress, they all are defined under trademark law as administered through the U.S. Patent and

Trademark Office (USPTO).

The Difference Between Trademarks and Service Marks

A trademark is a word, phrase, symbol or design, or a combination of words, phrases, symbols or designs, that identifies and distinguishes the source of the goods of one party from those of others. Common examples of well known trademarks would include Xerox, Exxon and Starbucks.

A service mark is the same as a trademark, except that it identifies and distinguishes the source of a service rather than a product. For example, a company such as Google may brand certain products with a trademark, but use a service mark on the internet searching service that it provides.

Trademarks legally conflict with each other if the use of one trademark causes confusion as to the product or service being offered, or as to the source of the products or services being offered. Generally, whoever used the trademark first owns it, and any subsequent users who cause confusion as to the products or their source will be forced to stop using the mark and may have to pay the trademark owner damages.

Trade Dress

Some brands don't just use a word, phrase or symbol to market their product, they also use distinctive packaging. A good example of this is a company such as Tiffany & Co., which uses a distinctive color and type of box to sell its jewelry. This use of distinctive packaging is what is known as "trade dress". Trade dress isn't simply limited to boxes, but can include distinctive use of color, shapes and even décor. Also, it may be possible in some instances to get legal protection for the unique look and feel of your website.

The goal of trade dress overlaps significantly with the goals of trademark law — to identify goods or products through distinctive features and reduce customer confusion. Accordingly, trade dress can often be registered as another types of trade — or service mark and receive protected under federal trademark laws.

Enforcing Trademark Rights

You are the owner of a famous brand of shoes and athletic clothing. You have made millions off of your product with the well-known, three-stripe trademark on the side of your track jackets and running shoes. Yet this last season you've noticed a trendy clothing designer has been using a confusingly similar four-striped mark on their garments and footwear. What can you do?

If you follow what athletic giant Adidas America did, you can bring a lawsuit alleging that the defendant "intentionally adopted and used counterfeit and/or confusingly similar imitations of the

Three-Stripe Mark knowing that they would mislead and deceive consumers into believing that the apparel was produced, authorized, or licensed by Adidas, or that the apparel originated from Adidas." In other words, you can go about enforcing your trademark rights through litigation.

Below you will find key information about how to bring about a trademark enforcement action.

Trademark Case Basics

If you believe your trademark has been infringed by another person or business entity, there are a number of things you will need to prove to a jury. As the plaintiff, you must prove:

1. You are the owner of a valid trademark;

2. You have priority of rights; and

3. Defendant's mark is likely to cause confusion in the minds of consumers about the source or sponsorship of the goods or services offered under the parties' marks.

Going back to the Adidas example, the plaintiff would have to prove ownership of the Three-Stripe trademark, that Adidas has priority to use the Three-Stripe mark, and that when clothing is sold with a four-strip mark or similar, there is likely going to be confusion by consumers as to who is manufacturing the product.

Registering Your Trademark

A good rule of thumb is to always register your trademark. Owning a federal trademark registration on the Principal Register will give the plaintiff a legal presumption of the first two requirements from above. What does that mean? It means that all Adidas has to do to meet the first two criteria in a trademark lawsuit is to provide documentation of being on the Principal Register. For Adidas, that is the proof that gives them the exclusive right to use the mark nationwide on or in connection with the goods or services listed in the registration. Also recall that a person or business is not technically required to register their trademark in order to have some rights in its use, but registration has many advantages.

Possible Remedies

There are a number of possible remedies a court has at their disposal, should you prove successful in a trademark infringement case. First, a court can order damages such as the cost of litigation, attorney's fees, and any profits the defendant made from illegally using the trademark. Second, a court could order the defendant to cease using the mark indefinitely. This is called an "injunction", and is likely to be a part of the court's order in many cases. Finally, a court can order the destruction of all infringing items. There may be more remedies depending on the court, but these are the most common.

Patents

A patent is a right granted to an inventor by the federal government that permits the inventor to exclude others from making, selling or using the invention for a period of time. The patent system is designed to encourage inventions that are unique and useful to society. Congress was given the power to grant patents in the Constitution, and federal statutes and rules govern patents.

The U.S. Patent and Trademark Office (USPTO) grants patents for inventions that meet statutory criteria. The following provides a general overview of what a patent is.

Patent Categories

There are three different kinds of patents: utility patents, design patents and plant patents.

1. Utility Patents: The most common type of patent, these are granted to new machines, chemicals, and processes.

2. Design Patents: Granted to protect the unique appearance or design of manufactured objects, such as the surface ornamentation or overall design of the object.

3. Plant Patents: Granted for the invention and asexual reproduction of new and distinct plant varieties, including hybrids (asexual reproduction means the plant is reproduced by means other than from seeds, such as by grafting or rooting of cuttings).

Determining What is Patentable

For an invention to qualify for a patent, it must be both "novel" and "non-obvious". An invention is novel if it is different from other similar inventions in one or more of its parts. It also must not have been publicly used, sold, or patented by another inventor within a year of the date the patent application was filed. This rule reflects the public policy favoring quick disclosure of technological progress. An invention is non-obvious if someone who is skilled in the field of the invention would consider the invention an unexpected or surprising development.

Naturally occurring substances and laws of nature, even if they are newly discovered, cannot be patented. Abstract principles, fundamental truths, calculation methods, and mathematical formulas also are not patentable. A process that uses such a formula or method can be patented, however. For example, a patent has been granted for an industrial process for molding rubber articles that depends upon a mathematical equation and involves the use of a computer program.

A patent cannot be obtained for a mere idea or suggestion. The inventor must have figured out the concrete means of implementing his or her ideas in order to get a patent. A patent also will not be granted for an invention with no legal purpose or for an unsafe drug.

Usefulness

An inventor applying for a utility patent must prove that the invention is useful. The invention must have some beneficial use and must be operable. A machine that will not operate to perform its intended purpose would not be called useful, and therefore would not be granted a patent. A useful invention may qualify for a utility patent only if it falls into one of five categories: a process, a machine, a manufacture, a composition of matter, or an improvement of one of these.

A process is a method of treating material to produce a specific physical change in the character or quality of the material, generally an industrial or technical process. A machine is a device that uses energy to get work done. The term manufacture refers to a process in which an article is made by the art or industry of people. A composition of matter may include a mixture of ingredients or a new chemical compound. An improvement is any addition to or alteration of a known process, machine, manufacture, or composition.

Examples of Patentable Items

These categories include practically everything made by humans and the processes for making the products. Examples of things that are patentable include:

- Computer software and hardware;
- Chemical formulas and processes;
- Genetically engineered bacteria, plants, and animals;
- Drugs;
- Medical devices;
- Furniture design;
- Jewelry;
- Fabrics and fabric design; and
- Musical instruments.

Applying for Patent Protection

Unlike a copyright, a patent does not arise automatically; an inventor must apply for a patent. The inventor must apply within one year of publicly disclosing the invention, such as by publishing a description of the invention or offering it for sale. An inventor, or his or her attorney, generally makes a preliminary patent search before applying for a patent to determine if it is feasible to proceed with the application. The application and a fee are submitted to the U.S. Patent and Trademark Office, where it is reviewed by a patent examiner.

If a patent is granted, the inventor must pay another fee, and the government publishes a description of the invention and its use. Only a patent attorney or patent agent may prosecute patents before the PTO. Before a person may be licensed as a patent attorney or patent agent, she must have a degree in certain technical or scientific fields.

Utility and plant patents last for 20 years from the application date; design patents last for fourteen years. If the owner of a utility patent does not pay maintenance fees, the patent will expire earlier. After a patent expires, the invention becomes public property and can be used or sold by anyone. For example, after the patent on Tylenol expired, other pharmaceutical companies began producing a generic version of the drug.

Enforcing Patent Rights

Let's say you own a small, innovative technology company that mainly produces data storage and access systems technologies for Smartphones. You own all the patents for your products, licensing them to bigger technology companies at a lucrative price. Now let's say a very well-known computer company decides to use your patented inventions in their music storage software without paying proper licensing fees. What do you have? You might have a case of patent infringement, as SmartFlash LLC did against Apple in 2015. While the jury verdict in favor of Smartflash, originally $533 million, was thrown out by a federal appeals court, the case still demonstrates how a person or business goes about enforcing their patent rights.

If you are the owner of a patent, and you believe it has been infringed, you will have to pursue your claim through civil litigation. These cases often involve lengthy fact-gathering and pre-trial preparation. They can also be quite expensive and complex. Below you will find key information on how to enforce your patent rights if you believe someone is infringing upon your rights, the court in which you will file your lawsuit, and where to go to find an experienced patent attorney in your area.

Federal Civil Court

If you believe you have a valid case against an alleged "infringer", your first step is to bring a patent infringement case. Patent infringement is not a crime; therefore you will need to bring your case in a federal civil court. Nor will your case be brought to the U.S. Patent and Trademark Office

(USTPO), which issues patents but does not deal in any enforcement actions.

Patent Litigator vs. Patent Agent

Patent infringement cases are civil lawsuits played out in a federal court. The person or business filing the lawsuit is the "plaintiff" and the party that is being charged with patent infringement is the "defendant". As a plaintiff in a patent case, you will hire a patent litigator to represent you. You may have heard the term "patent agent". To be clear, a patent agent is not an attorney and cannot represent you in court — that's the job of a patent attorney. You may use a patent agent to help you secure a patent on your invention, also called "prosecuting a patent".

Sound confusing? It is a little, but the key takeaway is that if you are attempting to begin a patent infringement case, you'll want to hire a seasoned patent litigator to help you in and out of court not a patent agent.

Patent Infringement Lawsuit Basics

Patent infringement cases can be lengthy and expensive, as we mentioned above. That's the downside. The upside is that if you are an inventor, you have a direct avenue to protect your hard work. A patent lawsuit allows the patent owner to sue any person or business who makes, sells, uses, or imports the invention into the U.S. (patent infringements). There are two primary ways in which an infringement can happen: literal infringement or similar invention under the doctrine of equivalents, i.e. "Does the accused product or process contain elements identical or equivalent to each claimed element of the patented invention?" Keep in mind, the party accused of patent infringement may have a number of defenses available to them including that the patent itself is invalid and should have never been issued.

Filing for a Patent Overseas

When an inventor files for a patent with the United States Patent and Trademark Office (USPTO), his or her invention is only protected in the United States. If a person wants to receive patent protection for his or her invention overseas, they will need to apply for a patent in each country. Nearly every country around the world has its own laws governing patents and an inventor must comply with the requirements of each country when filing a foreign patent application.

Under the Patent Cooperation Treaty (PCT) an inventor also has the option of filing an international patent application, which provides simultaneous patent protection in countries that are a party to the treaty. Any country that was a party to the 1883 Paris Convention for the Protection of Industrial Property is eligible to join the PCT. This type of application can be filed with the

International Bureau of WIPO in Geneva or in the national patent office of the inventor's country of residence or citizenship.

Foreign Patent Laws

The patent laws of foreign countries are different from U.S. patent laws in various ways. For example, most foreign countries bar the right to a patent if the invention is published before the date of the application; and if patent rights are granted, many countries require maintenance fees. Many countries also require that the patented invention be manufactured in their country after a certain period of time; and if this doesn't happen, the patent will become void. In most countries, a patent may also be subject to the grant of compulsory licenses.

The Patent Cooperation Treaty (PCT)

The Patent Cooperation Treaty (PCT) centralizes filing procedures and standardizes the application format, thus making it easier to apply for patent protection in multiple countries. As long as an applicant files the international application in a timely manner, he or she receives the same filing date in each country designated in the international application. If an applicant files for patent protection under the PCT within one year of the U.S. filing, he or she has up to 30 months (from the U.S. filing date) to file in any of the other countries that are parties to the treaty.

If you're interested in filing for a patent overseas, and the countries you would like patent protection in are part of the PCT, filing under the PCT procedures has many advantages. For example, an applicant has more time to decide if he or she would like to pursue patent protection in a foreign country, and has more time to take the steps that are necessary to acquire foreign patent protection. In addition, if an applicant uses the patent application that is set forth by the PCT, a designated Office can't reject the application on formal grounds during the phase of national processing.

U.S. Requirements for Filing a Patent Overseas

When an invention is made in the United States, the law requires that a person obtain a license from the Director of the USPTO before applying for a patent in another country. This license is required in two situations:

- If the foreign patent application will be filed before filing one in the U.S., or
- If the foreign patent application is filed less than six months after filing the U.S. application.

Six months after filing for a patent in the U.S., a license is only required if the invention has been ordered to be kept a secret, in which case, the person must obtain consent from the Director

before filing for a patent overseas.

Avoiding Infringement Problems

When another individual or entity (often a business) uses or diminishes the value of another's intellectual property in some way, it's referred to as "infringement". The following provides a general overview of how to avoid infringement of another's patent, trademark, or copyright.

Patents

Utility patents cover how products are made, work, or are used. Their owners can stop the unauthorized practice of their inventions for up to twenty years from filing. Design patents last fourteen years from when they were issued, and protect the appearance of products.

Precisely copying a patent is not the only way that a business can infringe on a patent. Knowingly or unknowingly incorporating a patented invention or practicing or incorporating an invention sufficiently similar to a patented invention can also constitute infringement. A patent owner can enjoin your business from practicing the patent, and can sue for damages. In some situations, an injunction can be equally or more costly than potential damages, since it may mean legal fees, retooling costs, and inventory loss.

The only way to discover potentially blocking patents is to search the U.S. Patent and Trademark Office (PTO) database. Just because nothing like your business's product is on the market doesn't mean that it, or something too similar to it, isn't already patented. Although searching back twenty years is all that is needed to ensure that your business isn't infringing on a patent, it may be worth searching farther back. If an older patent exists covering all or part of the subject matter of your company's product, it is a good indicator that the component is safe to manufacture. If your company's product is truly novel, you may wish to consider applying for a patent.

Trademarks

Trademarks show the source of a product, indicating a brand. They can be words, slogans, logos, sounds, three-dimensional symbols, or even scents. They need not be registered for common-law rights to protect their holders, but federal statutory protections only apply to federally registered trademarks. Trademarks do not expire. An unregistered mark or a mark registered with a state are indicated by a "TM" or "SM" (service mark). Federally registered marks bear the registered trademark symbol, ®.

Nothing closely resembling another business's trademark should ever be used. An exact copy is unnecessary to infringe a trademark, only a mark that is similar enough to likely cause consumer confusion.

Trademarks can be harder to track down than patents. A quick trademark search should first be done on the Internet, using a search engine to find businesses using the name or slogan. Marks that survive this type of search should also be checked against state and federal registers. As with patents, federally registered trademarks can be researched on the PTO database.

One of the frustrating things about trademark searches is that infringement can be fairly remote.

For example, a business may want to trademark "Thumper" as a name for a bass speaker. Assuming no other Thumper speakers are located, what other products named Thumper might the speakers be confused with? It is unlikely that the speakers would be confused with a baseball bat named Thumper, but that is not true with respect to a Thumper car stereo. What about a character name — would Disney protest because a character in the movie *Bambi* was named Thumper? How about if the only other user of the name is a strictly local business, Thumper Speaker Shack in Podunk, Montana? A thorough search will help your business understand all the possible risks, and will help its attorney advise it on whether it should look for another name.

Copyrights

Copyright infringement is almost never unintentional. Information, ideas, and technology (other than computer program source code) are generally not protected by copyright, only their precise embodiment. The old saw that if enough monkeys were put in a roomful of typewriters, one would eventually produce *Hamlet* is appropriate; the likelihood of infringing a copyright without conscious duplication is extremely remote.

4. Introduction to International Law
By Robert Beckman and Dagmar Butte

A. Purpose of This Document

This document is intended to provide students an overview of international law and the structure of the international legal system. In many cases it oversimplifies the law by summarizing key principles in less than one page in order to provide the student with an overview that will enhance further study of the topic.

B. Definition of International Law

International Law consists of the rules and principles of general application dealing with the conduct of States and of international organizations in their international relations with one another and with private individuals, minority groups and transnational companies.

C. International Legal Personality

International legal personality refers to the entities or legal persons that can have rights and obligations under international law.

1. States

A *State* has the following characteristics: (1) a permanent population; (2) a defined territory; (3) a government; and (4) the capacity to enter into relations with other States. Some writers also argue that a State must be fully independent and be recognized as a State by other States. The international legal system is a horizontal system dominated by States which are, in principle, considered sovereign and equal. International law is predominately made and implemented by States. Only States can have sovereignty over territory. Only States can become members of the United Nations and other international organizations. Only States have access to the International Court of Justice.

2. International Organizations

International Organizations are established by States through international agreements and their powers are limited to those conferred on them in their constituent document. International organizations have a limited degree of international personality, especially vis-à-vis member States. They can enter into international agreements and their representatives have certain privileges and immunities. The constituent document may also provide that member States area legally bound to comply with decisions on particular matters.

The powers of the United Nations are set out in the United Nations Charter of 1945. The main political organ is the General Assembly and its authority on most matters (such as human rights and economic and social issues) is limited to discussing issues and making recommendations. The Security Council has the authority to make decisions that are binding on all member States when it is performing its primary responsibility of maintaining international peace and security. The main UN judicial organ is International Court of Justice (ICJ), which has the power to make binding decisions on questions of international law that have been referred to it by States or give advisory opinions to the U.N.

3. Nationality of Individuals, Companies, etc.

Individuals are generally not regarded as legal persons under international law. Their link to State is through the concept of *nationality*, which may or may not require *citizenship*. *Nationality* is the status of being treated as a national of a State for particular purposes. Each State has wide discretion to determine who is a *national*. The most common methods of acquiring nationality at birth are through one or both parents and/or by the place of birth. Nationality can also be acquired by adoption and naturalization.

Companies, ships, aircraft and space craft are usually considered as having the nationality of the State in whose territory they are registered. This is important because in many circumstances States may have international obligations to regulate the conduct of their nationals, especially if they are carrying out act activities outside their territory.

Under the principle of *nationality of claims*, if a national of State A is injured by State B through internationally unlawful conduct, State A may make a claim against State B on behalf of its injured national. This is known as the doctrine of *diplomatic protection*.

D. Sovereignty of States Over Territiory

Sovereignty is the exclusive right to exercise supreme political authority over a defined territory (land, airspace and certain maritime areas such as the territorial sea) and the people within that territory. No other State can have formal political authority within that State. Therefore, sovereignty is closely associated with the concept of political *independence*.

Classical international law developed doctrines by which States could make a valid claim of sovereignty over territory. The doctrines included *discovery* and *occupation* and *prescription*. During the period of Western colonial expansion new territories and islands were subject to claims of sovereignty by discovery and occupation. Sovereignty could also be transferred to another State by *conquest* (use of force) or by *cession* where the sovereignty over the territory would be ceded by treaty from one State to another.

Since a State has sovereignty over its territory, the entry into its territory by the armed forces of another State without consent is a *prima facie* breach of international law. Among the attributes of sovereignty is the right to exclude foreigners from entering the territory, which is traditionally referred to as the right to exclude aliens.

Since a State has sovereignty within its territorial sea (with some exceptions such as the *right of innocent passage*), it has the exclusive authority to exercise police power within its territory sea. For example, if foreign ships are attacked by "pirates" in the territorial sea of a State, the only State that can exercise police power and arrest the pirates in the territorial sea is the coastal State.

E. International Obligations (Sources of Law)

It is generally accepted that the sources of international law are listed in the Article 38(1) of the Statute of the International Court of Justice, which provides that the Court shall apply:

a) international conventions, whether general or particular, establishing rules expressly recognized by the contesting states;

b) international custom, as evidence of a general practice accepted as law;

c) the general principles of law recognized by civilized nations;

d) subject to the provisions of Article 59, judicial decisions and the teachings of the most highly qualified publicists of the various nations, *as subsidiary means* for the determination of rules of law.

1. Treaties

International conventions are generally referred to as *treaties*. *Treaties* are written agreements between States that are governed by international law. Treaties are referred to by different names, including agreements, conventions, covenants, protocols and exchanges of notes. If States want to enter into a written agreement that is not intended to be a *treaty*, they often refer to it as a *Memorandum of Understanding* and provide that it is not governed by international law. Treaties can be bilateral, multilateral, regional and global.

The law of treaties is now set out in the 1969 Vienna Convention on the Law of Treaties which contains the basic principles of treaty law, the procedures for how treaties becoming binding and enter into force, the consequences of a breach of treaty, and principles for interpreting treaties. The basic principle underlying the law of treaties is *pacta sunt servanda* which means every treaty in force is binding upon the parties to it and must be performed by them in *good faith*. The other important principle is that treaties are binding only on States parties. They are not binding on third States without their consent. However, it may be possible for some or even most of the provisions of a multilateral, regional or global treaty to become binding on all States as rules of customary international law.

There are now global conventions covering most major topics of international law. They are usually *adopted* at an international conference and opened for *signature*. Treaties are sometimes referred to by the place and year of adoption, e.g. the 1969 Vienna Convention. If a State becomes a *signatory* to such a treaty, it is not bound by the treaty, but it undertakes an obligation to refrain from acts which would defeat the object and purpose of the treaty.

A State expresses its *consent to be bound* by the provisions of a treaty when it deposits an instrument of *accession* or *ratification* to the *official depository* of the treaty. If a State is a signatory to an international convention it sends an *instrument of ratification*. If a State is not a signatory to an international convention but decides to become a party, it sends an *instrument of accession*. The legal effect of the two documents is the same. A treaty usually *enters into force* after a certain number of States have expressed their consent to be bound through accession or ratification. Once a State has expressed its consent to be bound and the treaty is in force, it is referred to as a *party* to the treaty.

The general rule is that a treaty shall be interpreted in good faith in accordance with the ordinary meaning to be given to the terms of the treaty in their context and in light of its object and purpose. The preparatory work of the treaty and the circumstances of its conclusion, often called the *travaux preparatoires, are a* supplementary means of interpretation in the event of ambiguity.

2. Custom

International custom — or customary law — is evidence of a general practice accepted as law through a constant and virtually uniform usage among States over a period of time. Rules of customary international law bind all States. The State alleging the existence of a rule of customary law has the burden of proving its existence by showing a consistent and virtually uniform practice among States, including those States specially affected by the rule or having the greatest interest in the matter. For example, to examine the practice of States on military uses of outer space, one would look in particular at the practice of States that have activities in space.

Most ICJ cases also require that the States who engage in the alleged customary practice do so out of a sense of legal obligation or *opinio juris* rather than out of comity or for political reasons. In theory, *opinio juris* is a serious obstacle to establishing a rule as custom because it is extremely difficult to find evidence of the reason why a State followed a particular practice. In practice, however, if a particular practice or usage is widespread, and there is no contrary State practice proven by the other side, the Court often finds the existence of a rule of customary law. It sometimes seems to assume that *opinio juris* was satisfied, and it sometimes fails to mention it.

Therefore, it would appear that finding consistent State practice, especially among the States with the most interest in the issue, with minimal or no State practice to the contrary, is most important.

Undisputed examples of rules of customary law are (1) giving foreign diplomats criminal immunity; (2) treating foreign diplomatic premises as inviolable; (3) recognizing the right of innocent passage of foreign ships in the territorial sea; (4) recognizing the exclusive jurisdiction of the flag State on the high seas; (5) ordering military authorities to respect the territorial boundaries of neighboring States; and (6) protecting non-combatants such as civilians and sick or wounded soldiers during international armed conflict.

3. General Principles of Law

General principles of law recognized by civilized nations are often cited as a third source of law. These are general principles that apply in all major legal systems. An example is the principle that persons who intentionally harm others should have to pay compensation or make reparation. General principles of law are usually used when no treaty provision or clear rule of customary law exists.

4. Subsidiary Means for the Determination of Rules of Law

Subsidiary means are not sources of law, instead they are subsidiary means or evidence that can be used to prove the existence of a rule of custom or a general principle of law. Article 38 lists only two subsidiary means — the teaching (writings) of the most highly qualified publicists (international law scholars) and judicial decisions of both international and national tribunals if they are ruling on issues of international law. Writings of highly qualified publicists do not include law student articles or notes or doctoral theses.

Resolutions of the UN General Assembly or resolutions adopted at major international conferences are only recommendations and are not legally binding. However, in some cases, although not specifically listed in article 38, they may be subsidiary means for determining custom. If the resolution purports to declare a set of legal principles governing a particular area, if it is worded in norm creating language, and if is adopted without any negative votes, it can be evidence of rules of custom, especially if States have in practice acted in compliance with its terms. Examples of UN General Assembly Resolutions which have been treated as strong evidence of rules of customary international law include the following:

- GAR 217A Universal Declaration of Human Rights (1948)
- GAR 2131 Declaration on the Inadmissibility of Intervention in the Domestic Affairs of States and the Protection of their Sovereignty (1965) [Declaration on Non-Intervention]
- GAR 2625 Declaration on Principles of International Law Concerning Friendly Relations and Cooperation among States in Accordance with the Charter of the United Nations (1970) [Declaration on Friendly Relations]
- GAR 3314 Resolution on the Definition of Aggression

Some of these resolutions have also been treated as subsequent agreement or practice of States on how the principles and provisions of the UN Charter should be interpreted.

In addition, Article 38 fails to take into account the norm-creating effect of modern global conventions. Once the international community has spent several years drafting a major international convention, States often begin in practice to refer to that convention when a problem arises which is governed by the convention — in effect treating the rules in the Convention as customary. Furthermore, if the Convention becomes universally accepted the provisions in the Convention may become very strong evidence of the rules of custom, especially if States which are not parties have also acted in conformity with the Convention. Examples of such conventions would be the 1959 Vienna Convention on Diplomatic Relations and the 1969 Vienna Convention on the Law of Treaties.

5. Hierarchy of Norms

In theory there is no hierarchy among the three sources of law listed in Article 38 of the ICJ Statute. In practice, however, international lawyers usually look first to any applicable treaty rules, then to custom, and last to general principles.

There are two types of norms or rules — not previously discussed — which do have a higher status. First, *peremptory norms* or principles of *jus cogens* are norms that have been accepted and recognized by the international community of States as so fundamental and so important that no derogation is permitted from them. Examples of *jus cogens* principles are the prohibitions against wars of aggression and genocide. A war of aggression is the use of armed force to take over another State or part of its territory. Genocide is the killing or other acts intended to destroy, in whole or in part, of a national, ethnical, racial or religious group.

Second, members of the United Nations are bound by the Article 103 of the United Nations Charter, which provides that in the event of a conflict between the obligations of members under the Charter — including obligations created by binding decisions of the Security Council — the Charter obligations prevail over conflicting obligations in all other international agreements.

6. Role of the International Law Commission (ILC)

The ILC was established by the UN in 1948. The 34 members of the ILC are elected by the General Assembly after being nominated by member States. They possess recognized competence and qualifications in both doctrinal and practical aspects of international law and the ILC reflects a broad spectrum of expertise and practical experience.

The mandate of the ILC is the progressive development and codification of international law. The ILC usually spends many years studying areas of international law before presenting draft articles to the General Assembly for adoption as a draft convention. The primary written products of the ILC aside from the draft articles themselves are the detailed periodic reports prepared by the Special Rapporteurs on each subject and the official commentary for each draft article. Sometimes the official commentary to an ILC draft article or the Rapporteur's report will indicate whether that draft article is intended to codify a rule of customary law or is intended to progressively develop the law on that point. When the ILC Draft Articles are approved, they are approved together with the official commentaries.

The official commentaries to ILC draft articles and the reports of the ILC and its rapporteurs can be considered for two purposes. First, they are part of the *travaux préparatoires* when interpreting a treaty related to the subject of the draft article. Second, they are the writings of 34 highly qualified publicists speaking in unanimity and therefore serve as a subsidiary means for determining rules of customary law.

Selected Readings

F. Jurisdiction of Stares

1. Principles of Jurisdiction

The concept of *jurisdiction* refers to the power of a State to prescribe and enforce criminal and regulatory laws and is ordinarily based on the *territorial principle*, under which a State has jurisdiction over activities within its territory. Some states also claim jurisdiction over activities outside their territory which affect their territory.

States can also claim jurisdiction based upon the *nationality principle* by extending jurisdiction over their nationals even when they are outside the territory. For example, civil law countries extend their criminal law to cover their nationals while abroad while common law countries usually only do so in exceptional cases.

There is also a very narrow category of crimes — including genocide and war crimes — over which States may assert jurisdiction based upon the *universality principle, which gives* all States have jurisdiction irrespective of nationality or location of the offence.

Almost all States claim jurisdiction under the *protective principle*, under which a State asserts jurisdiction over acts committed outside their territory that are prejudicial to its security, such as treason, espionage, and certain economic and immigration offences. The most controversial basis for jurisdiction — followed by very few States — is the *passive personality principle*, which establishes jurisdiction based on the nationality of the victim. In recent years States have asserted jurisdiction over terrorist acts outside their territory directed against their nationals, thereby basing jurisdiction on a combination of the protective and passive personality principles.

Modern counter-terrorism treaties establish jurisdiction among State Parties based on the *presence of the offender* within their territory. If a persons who are alleged to have committed the offence established in the treaty (e.g, hijacking of an aircraft) is present in their territory, a State Party to the treaty is under an obligation to take the persons into custody, and to either prosecute them or extradite them to another State Party that has jurisdiction over the offence.

If two or more States have jurisdiction over a particular offence, they are said to have *concurrent jurisdiction*. In such cases the State which is most likely to prosecute the offender is the State which has custody over him. No State may exercise jurisdiction within the territorial sovereignty of another State. The police of State A cannot enter the territory of State B to arrest a person who has committed a crime in State A. Also, if a crime takes place in the territorial sea of a coastal State, no State other than the coastal State my intercept and arrest the ship carrying the offenders.

States enter into bilateral treaties to provide for the *extradition* of alleged offenders. Sending an alleged criminal to another State for investigation or prosecution in the absence of an extradition treaty is referred to as *rendition*.

The high seas and outer space are outside the territorial jurisdiction of any State. The general principle of jurisdiction in these common areas is that ships, aircraft and spacecraft are subject to the jurisdiction of the "flag State", or State of registration. The general principle is that ships on the high seas are subject to the exclusive jurisdiction of the flag State, and cannot be boarded without its express consent. The most notable exception is piracy. All States have a right to board pirate ships on the high seas without the consent of the flag State.

2. Immunities from Jurisdiction

The principle of *sovereign equality of States* requires that the official representatives of one State should not be subject to the jurisdiction of another State. For example, the law of the sea provides that warships are subject only to the jurisdiction of the flag State. Even if warships commit acts contrary to the right of innocent passage or the laws and regulations of the coastal State, the coastal State's only remedy is to escort the offending warship out of the territorial sea.

The principle of *State immunity or sovereign immunity* provides that foreign sovereigns enjoy immunity from the jurisdiction of other States. The principle of *diplomatic immunity* provides that the diplomatic agents of the sending State have complete immunity from the criminal jurisdiction of the receiving State. Since this immunity belongs to the sending State and not to the diplomat, it can be waived by the sending State. Also, the receiving State has the right to expel any diplomatic agent from its country by declaring them *persona non grata*. The premises of an embassy or diplomatic mission as well as its records and archives are also inviolable. The authorities of the receiving State cannot enter a foreign embassy without the express permission of the head of mission, even in the case of an emergency.

G. Status of the Seas, Outer Space and Antarctica

1. High Seas

The high seas are governed by several fundamental principles. First, no State may purport to assert sovereignty over any part of the high seas. Second, all States have the right to exercise the freedoms of the seas, including freedoms of navigation, freedom of overflight, freedom to lay submarine cables and pipelines, and freedom to conduct marine scientific research. Freedom of fishing was a traditional high seas freedom but fishing on the high seas is subject to restrictions as set out in the 1982 United Nations Convention on the Law of the Sea. It is generally agreed that freedom of the seas also includes the right of all States to use the high seas for military purposes, including weapons testing and naval exercises.

2. Exclusive Economic Zone

Coastal States are permitted to claim an exclusive economic zone (EEZ) of up to 200 nautical miles from the baselines from which the territorial sea is measured wherein they have the sovereign right to explore and exploit the natural resources of the sea and of the seabed and subsoil. The EEZ is neither under the sovereignty of the coastal State nor part of the high seas. It is a specific legal regime in which coastal States have the rights and jurisdiction set out in UNCLOS, and other States have the rights and freedoms set out in UNCLOS. Other States have the right to exercise high seas freedoms in the EEZ of any State. With respect to jurisdiction over matters outside of economic activities, the principles of jurisdiction governing the high seas apply in the EEZ.

3. Deep Seabed Beyond the Limits of National Jurisdiction

The natural resources of the deep sea bed beyond the limits of national jurisdiction are vested in mankind as a whole under the principle of the *common heritage of mankind*. No State may claim or exercise sovereignty or sovereign rights over any part of this area or its resources and it is governed by the International Sea Bed Authority (ISBA) No State or natural or juridical person may appropriate any part of the area or its resources except under the authority of the ISBA.

4. Outer Space

The principles governing the use of outer space are similar to those that the high seas. First, no State may purport to assert sovereignty over any part of outer space. Second, all States have the freedom to use outer space for peaceful purposes. Third, States on whose registry a space object is launched shall retain jurisdiction and control over the space object and over any persons on board the space object.

5. Antarctica

Official claims to sectors of the ice-covered continent of Antarctica were made by seven States — Argentina, Australia, Chile, France, New Zealand, Norway and the United Kingdom. A sector was also claimed by Admiral Byrd on behalf of the United States, but the United States never officially adopted Byrd's claim, and refused to recognize the claims of the six claimant States. In

1959 the seven claimant States, together with 5 other States whose scientists had been conducting research in Antarctica (Belgium, Japan, South Africa, the United States and the USSR) entered into the Antarctic Treaty. The Antarctic Treaty "froze" the claims of the seven claimant States, and stated that no new claims to sovereignty would be made. It also stated that Antarctica should be used only for peaceful purposes. The Antarctic Treaty permits States parties to conduct scientific research in Antarctica and its provisions are generally respected by non-party States as customary law.

H. Principles Governing Relations Between States

The general principles governing friendly relations between States are set out in UN General Assembly Resolution 2625. It states that the progressive development and codification of the seven principles below would secure their more effective application within the international community and would promote the realization of the purposes of the United Nations. Therefore, the resolution sets out the consensus in the international community on the content of the following seven principles:

(1) States shall refrain in their international relations from the threat or use of force against the territorial integrity or political independence of any State, or in any other manner inconsistent with the purpose of the United Nations

(2) Pacific settlement of disputes

(3) Non-intervention in matters within the domestic jurisdiction of any State, in accordance with the Charter

(4) Co-operation with one another in accordance with the Charter

(5) Equal rights and self-determination of peoples

(6) Sovereign equality of States

(7) States shall fulfil in good faith the obligations assumed by them in accordance with the Charter

I. Responsibility of States for Wrongful Acts

The 2001 ILC Articles on the Responsibility of States for Internationally Wrongful Acts set out the principles in this important field of international law. The ILC Articles are a combination of codification and progressive development. Even though the ILC Articles have not been adopted as an international convention, some of the provisions have been referred to by international courts and tribunals as reflective of customary international law.

States are responsible to other States for their *internationally wrongful acts*. A State commits *internationally wrongful act* when conduct consisting of an act or omission (a) is attributable to the State under international law; and (b) constitutes a breach of an international obligation owed by that State to the injured State or the international community. Therefore, if a dispute arises between two States, the first question is whether the offending State owed an international obligation to the injured State under either a treaty or under customary law. The second question is whether that obligation was breached by conduct consisting of either an act or an omission that is attributable to the offending State.

The rules on attribution are based on common sense. The conduct of an organ of the State is attributable to the State because a State acts through its official representatives, such as its Head of State, Minister of Foreign Affairs, Ambassadors and government ministries and departments. The official acts of these persons and organs are attributable to the State. The conduct of private persons or private entities is generally not attributable to the State unless the State knew of the conduct and failed to act in relation to that conduct when it had an international obligation to act. However, the conduct of a person or entity empowered by the law of the State to exercise elements of government authority is attributable to the State and a State may also ratify and adopt the conduct of private persons or control their conduct in such a manner that it can be attributed to the State.

A State is in breach of an international obligation when conduct attributable to it is not in conformity with what is required by the obligation. A State may not rely on provisions of its internal or domestic law as justification for failure to comply with an international obligation. The responsible State is under an obligation to *cease the wrongful act* if it is continuing. It is also under an obligation to offer appropriate *assurance and guarantees of non-repetition*, if circumstances so require. In addition, the responsible State is under an obligation to make full *reparation* for the injury — both material and moral — caused to the other State by the internationally wrongful act.

The *forms of reparation* under international law are *restitution, compensation and satisfaction*. The preferred form of reparation is *restitution*, which requires the State to re-establish the situation which existed before the wrongful was committed. Insofar as the damage is not made good by restitution, the State much pay *compensation* to cover the financially assessable damage, including loss of profits insofar as it is established. If the injury cannot be made good by either restitution or compensation, the State must provide *satisfaction*, which may consist of acknowledgement of the

breach, an expression of regret, a formal apology or another appropriate remedy.

There are defenses available to the responsible State which preclude the wrongfulness of an act, including valid consent by the injured State, self-defence, force majeure, distress, necessity and valid countermeasures. The ILC Articles set out the requirements which must be met before these defenses can be invoked. Some of the provisions of the ILC Articles on these "defences" can be classified as "progressive development" rather than a codification of customary international law.

J. THE ROLE OF THE ICJ

The ICJ is the chief judicial organ of the United Nations. All members of the UN are automatically parties to the Statute of the International Court of Justice. The jurisdiction of the ICJ in "contentious disputes" between States is subject to the principle of consent. It can obtain jurisdiction in three ways. First, the States parties to a dispute may enter into an *ad hoc* agreement to refer a particular legal dispute to the court. Second, States can submit an "optional clause declaration" to the UN Secretary-General declaring that they accept the jurisdiction of the ICJ over certain categories of disputes with other States which have also filed an optional clause declaration. This category of disputes is quite rare, as many States are not willing to accept the jurisdiction of the ICJ in advance for wide categories of disputes. Third, many international conventions contain dispute settlement clauses called "compromissory clauses" allowing disputes between States parties to the convention to refer disputes concerning the interpretation or application of provisions of that convention to the ICJ by one of the parties to the dispute. Some conventions allow States to "opt out" of such compromissory clauses.

If a dispute between two States is decided by the ICJ, the decision is final and binding as between the parties to the case. It is not binding on other States. However, to the extent that the ICJ pronounces on issues of customary law or treaty law, its judgment will be treated as an authoritative interpretation of international law by many States.

The ICJ also has advisory jurisdiction. The UN Security Council and the UN General Assembly may request advisory opinions on any legal question. The UN General may also authorize other UN organs or specialized agencies to request advisory opinions on legal questions arising within the scope of their activities.

Glossary of 101 Key Legal Terms

We have carefully selected 101 terms that we think you need to know BEFORE you start your LEC studies. The goal is not to provide a comprehensive list of all the legal terms that will be on the LEC exams, but to review words that most JDs know prior to entering a bar review program. LEC review questions can frequently hinge on the specific definitions of key terms. Therefore, your knowledge of these terms can be essential to answering a question correctly.

For some of you who have worked with the U.S. legal system, many of these words will be commonplace. For others, you may be unfamiliar with some of these words. Wherever you fit on this spectrum, please review the following list and make sure you are familiar with these words and their meanings.

While we have presented these terms in order of subject, it is important to note that many of the terms could show up in any area on the LEC — questions on criminal law will frequently involve terms from trial procedure, constitutional law and evidence. We have broken these terms up into these subject areas solely to give you some context as to where they fit in the overall system of U.S. jurisprudence.

GENERAL TERMS

common law: A body of law based on past decisions of judges where litigation of cases is done by referring to past interpretations of law. Although in practice, many of these laws have been codified as civil and criminal code, common law principles are still applied on the MBE and in almost all jurisdictions.

CIVIL/TRIAL PROCEDURE

PEOPLE

litigant: An individual in a legal action; one who is in the process of litigation.

plaintiff: The party who brings a civil action (that is, who sues) in court.

defendant: The party accused of committing a violation of law in a criminal case (being prosecuted); or the party defending an action in a civil case (being sued).

respondent: The person who officially answers the allegations set forth in a petition that has been filed with a court. In a civil action, the respondent could also be referred to as the defendant.

adversary: The opposing party. The plaintiff is the defendant's adversary and vice versa. A court system is designed to be "adversarial" in nature.

appellant/appellee: The party who appeals a court decision to a higher court / the party against whom an appeal is taken.

PROCESS — BRINGING/TRYING THE CASE

action: A civil proceeding whereby one party alleges being wronged by another party and seeks redress for that wrong.

proceeding: The process by which judicial action occurs pursuant to civil or criminal procedure.

process: Legal means, such as a summons or writ, used to subject a defendant in a lawsuit to the court's jurisdiction.

appearance: Presence; the participation in the proceeding by a party summoned in an action. Appearance can be made either in person or through the party's attorney.

summons: A form used to commence a civil action and acquire jurisdiction over a party.

PROCESS — ACTIONS BY COURT

writ: A written order issued by a court, either requiring the performance of a specified act or giving authority and commission to have the act performed.

service: The exhibition or delivery of a writ, notice, etc., officially notifying a person of some action or proceeding in which that person is concerned.

Glossary of 101 Key Legal Terms

PROCESS — COURT'S AUTHORITY

venue: The physical place where a legal matter occurs or may be determined; or the geographical area within which a court has jurisdiction. Venue relates only to a place or territory within which either party may require a case to be tired.

jurisdiction: The geographical, subject matter, and monetary limitations of a court. A court must have both personal jurisdiction — meaning the ability to hear a case concerning a specific person to impose a personal liability on him — and subject matter jurisdiction — meaning the court can hear a case concerning a topic of consideration, thing in dispute, or right claimed by on party against another.

domicile: The place where a person has a true and permanent home — a person may have several residences, but only one domicile.

PROCESS — FINDING FACT & LIMITING ACTIONS

discovery: A process whereby parties to an action may be informed as to facts known by other parties or witnesses.

statute of limitations: A statute that declares that no actions of a specified kind can be commenced after a specified period of time (generally beginning after the cause of action arose).

DOCUMENTS

docket: A judicial log containing the complete history of each case in the form of brief chronological entries summarizing the court proceedings. The docket also lists all cases before a court at a particular time.

complaint: The initial pleading in an action formally setting forth the facts and reasons for which the demand for relief is based; the complaint must name parties to be charged, specific factual allegation, and damages sought.

petition: A formal request made to a court, initiating a proceeding or requesting an action by a court.

motion: An oral or written request for a ruling or order made by a party to the court.

answer: A paper submitted by a defendant in which he/she responds to, and admits or denies, each of the plaintiff's allegations.

OUTCOMES

disposition: The result of a judicial proceeding by withdrawal, settlement, order, judgment, or sentence; final determination of the parties' dispute.

adjudicate: To hear or try and judicially determine a case or factual issue.

judgment: A determination of the rights of the parties in an action or special proceeding.

order: An oral or written direction of a court or judge; a pronouncement.

consolidate: The joining of two or more actions or cases to be tried together.

vacate: To set aside a previous action or ruling.

dismissal: Termination of a proceeding for a procedurally prescribed reason.

remand: To send back a case from an appellate court to the lower court from which it came for further proceedings on an issue.

appeal: A subsequent proceeding to have a case examined by an appropriate higher court to see if a lower court's decision was made correctly according to law.

CONSTITUTIONAL LAW

constitutional law: This law focuses on how to interpret and apply the law of the United States Constitution (the highest law of the land).

checks and balances: The principle used in the Constitution that allows the three branches of government (executive, legislative, judicial) to share some responsibilities, and allows each branch some authority over the activities of the other branches. Some examples of checks are: the President's veto power, which is a check on Congress; Congress' power to override a veto, which is a check on the President's power; and the Supreme Court's right of judicial review, which is a check on Congress. Checks and balances provide a multi-headed system of government rather than a monarchy.

Congress: The two houses that make up the legislative branch of government. Congress is made up of the House of Representatives and the Senate. Congress is responsible for making all federal laws. Article I, Section 8, of the U.S. Constitution gives the Congress a number of powers, including: collecting taxes, regulating commerce, and providing funding for the military.

bicameral: Means "two rooms". This term refers to a legislative body, such as the U.S. Congress or the British Parliament that is divided into two separate houses.

Glossary of 101 Key Legal Terms

Cabinet: A board of advisors to the President composed of the heads of the executive Cabinet departments and any other officials whom the President chooses. The Cabinet includes: the Secretary of State, the Secretary of the Treasury, the Secretary of Defense; the Attorney General, among others.

Bill of Rights: The first ten Amendments to the U.S. Constitution. These ten Amendments protect the fundamental freedoms of Americans from any infringement by the government.

due process: The Constitutional guarantee that a defendant will receive a fair and impartial trial. In civil law, due process refers the legal rights of someone who confronts an adverse action threatening liberty or property.

civil liberties: Individual freedoms (e.g., life, liberty, property), most of which are protected by the Bill of Rights, from government interference.

certiorari: An appellate proceeding for re-examination of the actions of a lower court; most commonly applied to actions before the U.S. Supreme Court.

moot: Generally used to mean not necessary to be decided and/or undecided. Moot can also mean no longer ripe or relevant.

CONTRACTS

GENERALLY

contract: A legally enforceable agreement between two or more parties consisting an offer, an acceptance, and consideration.

consideration: Bargained-for exchange. Usually this is the price paid by one side and the goods supplied by the other. However, consideration can be anything of value to the other party; and it can be negative, such as refraining from doing something that someone had a legal right to do.

condition: A fact or circumstance that must occur before a part is under a duty to perform.

liquidation: The formal braking up of a company or partnership by realizing (i. e. , selling or transferring to pay a debt) the assets of the business. Liquidation usually happens when the business is insolvent or bankrupt.

repudiation: Where a party refuses to comply with a contract, which refusal amounts to a breach of contract.

void: A contract is void if it cannot be performed or completed. A void contract is void from the beginning; and the normal remedy, if possible, is to put the parties back in their initial positions. Contracts are void where one party lacks the capacity to perform the contracted task, or the contract is based on a mistake or illegality.

CONTRACTUAL RELATIONSHIPS

fiduciary: A person or institution that remains in a special relationship to another with regard to the management of money or property; the person or institution must exercise a standard of care in such management activity imposed by law or contract.

surely: One who is legally liable for the debt, default, or failure to carry out a duty of another.

CONTRACTUAL OBLIGATIONS & ACTIONS

replevin: An action brought for the owner of items to recover possession of those items when those items were wrongfully taken or are being wrongfully kept.

estoppel: A rule of law that prevents a person from alleging or denying a fact in court, because of his/her own previous act.

due diligence: The formal process of investigating the background of a business, either before buying it or as another party in a major contract.

warranties: Promises made in a contract. Breach of a warranty results in liability to pay but will not be a breach of contract.

TORTS

GENERALLY

tort: A civil action alleging an injury or wrong committed — either with or without force, and either intentionally or negligently — to the person or property of another.

cause of action: Grounds on which a legal action may be brought (e.g., property damage, personal injury, goods sold and delivered, work labor and services.)

liability: An obligation to do or refrain from doing something; one's responsibility for his/her conduct; or one's responsibility for causing an injury.

damages: Relief sought for a wrong or injury. Damages can be in the form of monetary compensation or an injunction to refrain from certain conduct. Three main types of civil damages are: 1. Compensatory damages (i.e., reimbursement for actual loss or injury); 2. Injunctive relief (i.e., the stopping of conduct that is offensive to one party's rights); 3. Punitive damages (i.e., monetary compensation awarded in excess of ordinary damages, as punishment for an excessive wrong-doing).

compensatory damages: Reimbursement for actual loss or injury, as distinguished from exemplary or punitive damages.

OBLIGATIONS/ORDERS

injunction: Relief sought from a court to order a party to do or stop doing a specific act.

remedy: A form of relief designed to redress a plaintiff's harm; can be monetary or injunctive.

indemnity: Security against loss or damages; exemption from penalty or liability.

joint and several liability: Where parties act together and the injury sustained by the aggrieved party is incapable of apportionment. In addition to all the parties being responsible together (i.e., jointly), each party is also liable individually (i.e., severally) for the entire amount of the plaintiff's damages. Therefore, a plaintiff could recover the entire amount of damages from any one responsible party individually, leaving that party to recover the shares from the rest of the responsible parties.

PROPERTY

real property: A body of law dealing with rights in land, separate and distinct from intellectual property and personal property.

easement: A right in land owned by another that gives the holder of the easement the right to use the land for a specific purpose.

eminent domain: The process by which the government takes private property for public use by condemnation (i.e., the legal process by which real estate owned by a private party is taken for public use without the owner's consent, but upon the award and payment of just compensation).

condemnation: The process by which private property is taken for public purposes; requires government action.

equitable action: A civil action seeking non-monetary damages. An action that may be brought or the purpose of restraining the threatened infliction of wrongs or injuries, and the prevention o threatened illegal action.

lien: A claim upon the real or personal property of another as security for an outstanding debt.

intestate: The circumstance where a person dies without a will.

parcel: A piece of land, usually under a single ownership.

lease: An agreement that gives rise to a relationship of landlord and tenant (also called lessor and lessee); a lease can also deal with personal property.

lessor/lessee: Respectively, the owner of the real property who leases it to another (also called a landlord) and the person who is leasing the real property from another (also called the tenant).

Title: Ownership of or rights in a specific property.

abandonment: Voluntary relinquishment of a property right or an interest in a property, where there is no intention of either resuming possession of the property or maintaining rights in it.

assignment: The transfer of a party's interest in a lease from one party (assignor) to another party (assignee). While generally the tenant's interest is assigned, the landlord may assign its interest in the lease, as well (i.e., through the sale of the property). Once an assignor/tenant's interest has been assigned, the assignee becomes responsible to the landlord for payment of rent and fulfillment of other lease obligations; however, in the event of default by the assignee, the landlord can still hold the assignor responsible unless the landlord has previously agreed to release it from liability.

covenant: A promise to either do something or refrain from doing something on or concerning a piece of real property.

CRIMINAL LAW

bail: A sum, usually monetary, given (technically "posted") as security against the future appearance of a defendant.

citation: A reference to other cases of authority in support of an argument or statement; A summons to appear before a court.

Glossary of 101 Key Legal Terms

acquit: The act of freeing a person from the charge of an offense by means of a decision to discharge; to find the defendant no guilty; government presents insufficient evidence.

habeas corpus: "You have the body." A writ that serves to require the presence of a person before a court or judge — often directed to the person detaining another, commanding him/her to produce the body of a person detained for a determination of whether the person has been denied his/her liberty without due process of law.

expunge: To wipe away; the authorized act of physically clearing information in files, computers, or other depositories; this is often done with criminal records.

warrant: A written order issued by an authority (e.g., a court) directing the arrest of a person.

verdict: The determination of a jury on the facts — based on the Latin words "ver" and "dicta", meaning "to speak the truth".

subpoena: Legal process, paperwork, that commands a witness to appear and testify.

grand jury: A group of citizens who are called to listen to evidence of criminal allegations that is presented by the prosecution. The group must then determine whether there is probable cause to believe an individual committed an offense.

EVIDENCE

evidence: A form of proof or probative matter legally presented at the trial of an issue by the acts of the parties and through witnesses, records, documents, concrete objects, etc., for the purpose of inducing belief in the minds of the court or the jury.

corroborate: To strengthen; to add weight by additional evidence.

cross-examination: Questioning by a party or his/her attorney of either an adverse party or a witness called by and adverse party.

jury: A prescribed number of people selected according to law and sworn to make findings of fact and determine the outcome of cases, either civil or criminal.

mistrial: A trial that has been terminated and declared void before a verdict is reached due to an extraordinary circumstance, serious prejudicial misconduct, or hung jury; a mistrial does not result in a judgment for any party but merely indicates a failure of trial.

oath: A swearing to the truth of a statement.

perjury: The art of lying or giving false testimony under oath.

examination: An inspection or investigation. As pertains to court action, the term is used to describe a preliminary hearing before the district court to determine whether there is sufficient cause to hold a person to answer a felony charge before the circuit court.

incompetency: Lack of legal qualification or fitness, usually mental or physical, to discharge a legally required duty or to handle one's own affairs; also relates to matters not admissible in evidence.

hearing: A preliminary examination where evidence is taken for the purpose of determining an issue of fact.

exhibit: A paper, document, or other article produced to a court during a trial or proceeding and, on being accepted, is marked for identification or admitted into evidence.

interrogatories: Written questions of one party that are served on an adversary, who must then provide written answers thereto under oath.

deposition: A sworn oral testimony of a witness, under oath.

affidavit: A sworn statement made in writing and signed.